NOTES OF DISSENT

NOTES *of* DISSENT

Essays on Indian History

KESAVAN VELUTHAT

PRIMUS BOOKS

PRIMUS BOOKS
An imprint of Ratna Sagar P. Ltd.
Virat Bhavan
Mukherjee Nagar Commercial Complex
Delhi 110 009

Offices at

CHENNAI LUCKNOW
AGRA AHMEDABAD BANGALORE COIMBATORE
DEHRADUN GUWAHATI HYDERABAD JAIPUR JALANDHAR
KANPUR KOCHI KOLKATA MADURAI MUMBAI
PATNA RANCHI VARANASI

First published 2018

ISBN: 978-93-86552-70-9 (hardback)
ISBN: 978-93-86552-71-6 (POD)

Published by Primus Books

Laser typeset in Times New Roman
by Guru Typograph Technology
Crossings Republic, Ghaziabad 201 009

Printed and bound in India by Replika Press Pvt. Ltd.

for

ROMILA THAPAR

Contents

Preface

THE ESSAYS BROUGHT together in this volume were written on different occasions and under different provocations on different topics. My apology for bringing them together is given in the Introduction; I do not intend to say anything more here.

I should like to place on record my sense of gratitude to a few individuals who have placed me under debt in the process of writing these essays and bringing them together. M.G.S. Narayanan, my teacher, has always been a friend, philosopher and guide. He read all the essays and offered constructive criticism. B. Surendra Rao helped me in sharpening my tools and lent his time and other resources in improving these most generously. B.P. Sahu and the late Basudev Chatterji, likewise, offered their insightful criticism and suggestions. Manu V. Devadevan was of immense help in innumerable ways. I thank all of them wholeheartedly, assuring them that the shortcomings in the essays are in spite of them!

Members of my family put up with my failures and absences and helped me in numerous ways in my research. I thank them.

How do I thank Romila Thapar adequately? She taught me not only how to study history but also the importance of dissent, both in history and historiography. She also permitted me to inscribe this book in her honour. Thank you ma'am, most of all for being there.

KESAVAN VELUTHAT

Acknowledgements

The author and the publisher wish to acknowledge that the essays included in this volume were published/presented earlier as follows:

'From Dissent to Norm to Tradition: The Dialectics of Early Indian Religious History', presented at the Symposium on 'Dissent and Tradition in Religion in India', Indian History Congress, Gaur Banga University, Malda, 30 December 2015.

'The Mauryan Presence in South India', published in *Kaveri: Studies in Epigraphy, Archaeology and History* (*Professor Y. Subbarayalu felicitation volume*), ed. S. Rajagopal, Chennai: Panpattu Veliyiittakam, 2001, pp. 217–28.

'Making the Best of a Bad Bargain: The Brighter Side of Kaliyuga', published in *Indian Historical Review*, vol. 41, no. 2, 2014, pp. 173–84.

'Laughter in the Time of Misery: Political Criticism in an Early Modern Sanskrit Poem', adapted from the author's 'Introduction' to *Mahiṣaśatakam* of Vāñcheśvara Dīkṣita, edited and translated into English by Kesavan Veluthat, Kottayam: Mahatma Gandhi University, 2011.

'Regional History in the Making of Regions', General President's Address to the Andhra Pradesh History Congress, Avanigadda, 5 January 2013.

'Of Ubiquitous Heroines and Elusive Heroes: The Cultural Milieu of Medieval *Maṇipravāḷa Kāvyas* from Kerala', Foundation Day Lecture, Indian Council of Historical Research, New Delhi, 18 March 2013.

'*Kāṇa-Janma-Maryādā*: Origin and Development of Land Relations in Medieval Kerala', presented at the Symposium on 'Economic Change in Indian History' held by Aligarh Historians' Society at the University of Delhi, 16–17 May 2010.

'Congealing of Castes: The Case of Medieval Kerala', presented at the Seminar on 'The Caste Question and the Historian's Craft', Centre for the Study of Developing Societies, Delhi, 26–8 February 2014.

'Use of "Hindu" Idioms in Christian Worship and Propaganda in Kerala', published in *Studies in History*, vol. 25, no. 2, n.s., 2009, pp. 253–66.

Introduction

How do I justify this collection? The essays included here, written on occasions so varied from, and under provocations that have no comparison with, one another, have very little in common. They relate to different regions of India, ranging from the Indo-Gangetic divide to the extreme south-west of the peninsula, and to divergent periods ranging from the first millennium BC to the latter half of eighteenth century AD. The subject matter, too, is as divergent. How does one claim, even tenuously, that there is anything in common among, let alone a single theme running through, such dissimilar subjects as religious ideology, cultural transactions, social crisis, political criticism, regional historiography, cultural milieu of literature, land relations, formation of castes, Christian worship and propaganda and so on? But I do feel that there is one thing that binds all the essays together. I may be permitted to say a word or two in an attempt to offer an apology for these essays and bringing them together between two covers.

I should like to claim that there is one common strand running through the essays included here, in spite of their apparent divergences and variations in theme and spatio-temporal frame. They can be described, somewhat audaciously, as notes of dissent in one way or another. 'Audaciously', because I am convinced that dissent is crucial to the furtherance of knowledge in any field. When one generation concurs with, or conforms to, the knowledge that it inherits from earlier generations, knowledge may get authenticated but will tend to stay where it is. Knowledge gets reaffirmed when questions are answered; but it advances when those very answers—whether final and sacrosanct or provisional and irreverent—are questioned. Those who have so questioned the answers handed down as received wisdom have often been looked upon as so many heretics; and they have been administered hemlock or burnt at stake. Some, clever enough to recant, escaped but still maintained that 'yet it moves'. Later generations, however, realized that such 'heresy' actually represented better, more advanced knowledge and accepted it in the place of the wisdom they were questioning. And these, in turn, were questioned and rejected by still later generations. Thus, knowledge went on growing through this dialectical process. Dissent, thus, is central to the advance of knowledge, which in any case is not a product at any point in time. There is no finality about it.

This is true in the case of the discipline of history to a greater extent than many other disciplines. Notwithstanding claims to origins dating from classical antiquity or even earlier, it is only in the modern period that history acquired the status of critical knowledge, produced by interrogating evidence teased out of sources from the past. No sooner had it established itself as a critical discipline in the West than it arrived in India under the new political masters. Whether or not Indian civilization had a sense of the past or tradition of historical writing, the way in which India tried to come to grips with the past underwent a total change with the work of the Orientalists and Indologists in the eighteenth and nineteenth centuries, whatever our criticism today about their aim and agency. True, the details presented by them were handy for the apologists of the empire; it was equally useful to the nationalists as well. Idealization and mystification were certainly part of the fare that was served; but a rich database, founded on the critical appreciation of sources from the past, was made available for later generations to work on. Independence rendered much of the myths produced on its basis irrelevant—the Empire was no longer there for anybody to defend or attack! That, however, did not cheat historians out of employment. There was the need to understand the present—a present characterized by an economy that had been bled white by two centuries of colonial rule and a society that lay prostrate for various reasons. The only way to come to grips with the present was by acquiring a scientific knowledge of the past. Along with the projects of reconstruction in post-Independence India, history-writing too became an intensely political activity. When D.D. Kosambi wrote his seminal books in the 50s and 60s, he was violently shaking the fabric of historiography in India. Those who considered themselves guardians of the 'glorious Indian tradition' felt threatened and were up in arms against the writings of Kosambi and those who followed him. However, when the dissent that Kosambi articulated was carried forward by others such as R.S. Sharma, Romila Thapar, Irfan Habib and company—by no means are these of the same ideological preoccupation—the dissent was gradually becoming the norm. School textbooks, which are the slowest to accept any change in knowledge, incorporated the views of these scholars. However, things did not move in unilinear progression. Surprisingly, research which is more than half a century old remains dissent and heresy, and continues to be looked upon as 'anti-national' in the current rhetoric of 'nationalism'. It is not even recognized, let alone respected, that dissent has been a hallmark of the intellectual tradition of Indian civilization. This, in one sense, is not surprising. Forces that are not exactly progressive will be opposed to this kind of historiography which privileges evidence and its critical questioning over blind faith and obscurantist myths used for furthering political interests. Historical writing that follows rational, transparent methods of enquiry will shake the very foundations of these myths masquerading as historical facts. That will undermine the bases of the ideology and programme of such reactionary politics. Yes, the kind of politics that we have been witnessing in recent years hates historian's history, a history that uses evidence teased out from a critical analysis of sources following the canons and methods of that discipline. It is here that dissent becomes all the more crucial.

The essays brought together here are rather modest in their claims. They do not pretend to offer any shift in the paradigm of historical studies; nor do they boast that new ground is broken in any particular field of historical study. What they presume, however, is that they differ—with varying degrees of mildness or violence—from what has been handed down as accepted knowledge in the area with which they are concerned. It all began with a joint study of the Bhakti Movement in south India that I was privileged to undertake with M.G.S. Narayanan. It was a larger project on 'Dissent, Protest and Reform in Indian Civilization' that the Indian Institute of Advanced Study, Shimla, had lunched. Narayanan took me, a greenhorn who had just completed his Masters, as a research assistant in the project. My job was to collect inscriptions and literary texts, both primary and secondary, pertaining to the Tamil Bhakti Movement. We would spend hours and hours at his place discussing different ways of looking at the documents I had collected. We discussed, debated and quarrelled during the process of writing as well. Finally, when I was asked to proofread the typescript, I saw my name there as a co-author! In the course of our writing it, we had realized that rather than looking at the phenomenon as a mere literary movement or, as some had already realized, a movement with a heavy anti-caste content, there were factors which supported the establishment, the strong institution of the brāhmaṇical temple and the new monarchy. The element of dissent in that literature, which many had not noticed, was against Vedic orthodoxy and in favour of the Purāṇic Hindu institution of the temple, which was the institutional expression of the new formation that had come into existence. The paper, which is included here as an appendix for technical reasons, received immediate acceptance in the world of scholarship, with top authorities in Indian history hailing it as a 'landmark'.

It was the confidence that I had gathered by this encouragement from peers and elders that emboldened me to accept the invitation to speak in the symposium on 'Dissent and Tradition in Indian Religion' held by the Indian History Congress at Malda, about four decades since the earlier project. The first essay here is substantially the text of my presentation in that symposium. I argue that religious traditions have been evolving and that dissent to accepted norms has always played a major role in this process of evolution. The pattern I seek to elucidate is one in which a given set of religious ideologies and practices is dissented to from within, these notes of dissent becoming gradually part of the accepted norm and then getting sanctified as *the* tradition in the days to come. It is to these that further dissent is articulated. I specifically take up situations in the mid-first millennium BC and mid-first millennium AD in north India and towards the last quarter of the millennium in south India, each of these conjunctures representing veritable watersheds in the history of these regions. The second essay on the Mauryan presence in south India examines the widely held notion that the Mauryan Empire included the whole of the Indian subcontinent. I seek to show, with the help of evidence from south India, that much of this is hyperbolae produced within a colonial/nationalist discourse of historiography. Archaeological evidence shows unequivocally that the so-called Mauryan presence is very meagre but for epigraphic suggestions of a fleeting administrative intervention; and the way in which early Tamil literature is asked to testify to this presence is flawed. What do we really have? I do not find anything more than a post-Mauryan narrative which seeks to bring south India under a unitary state supposed to have been presided over by the 'Imperial' Mauryas.

The next essay on *kaliyuga* is my response to one of the most important interventions in the study of early medieval Indian history. The world of historiography was taken by storm when R.S. Sharma published his justly famous article on the Kali Age. Celebrations, elaborations and repetitions, some bordering on the ridiculous, followed. Sharma had shown with the help of unimpeachable evidence and impeccable logic that the period of the early Purāṇas that contain references to Kali Age elaborately for the first time, i.e. the third and fourth centuries of the Common Era, represented a period of social crisis. He saw the pathological fears concerning features of the Kali Age as representing an imminent social crisis, which was among the causative factors behind the emergence of a feudal formation in India. When I read the evidence, going beyond what Sharma has quoted, I saw that the Kali Age is represented not only as the darkest and the most evil; it is also shown, in the same texts, as the brightest and the most benign! This contradiction demanded an explanation and what I have done in the third chapter is to offer one in my own way.

Mahiṣaśatakaṃ by Vāñcheśvara Dīkṣita is a hundred verses in praise of a buffalo. Humour at its best, it goes beyond humour and criticizes the political and social order of the period of its composition, Tañjāvūr in the eighteenth century. While scholars who had studied the poem earlier had made a literary appreciation of it, they had, strangely, missed the political criticism in it—arguably among the sharpest in Sanskrit poetry. What I do in the next essay is to introduce the poem, giving its historical background and showing why the poet should have been so angry as to come down on the system as heavily as he has done. I also show the way in which he criticizes the king, the court, the bureaucracy and the system as a whole.

The essay on regional history is substantially the text of the General President's address I had given at the Andhra Pradesh History Congress, 2013. I argue that regions are a matter of construction, made by particular sections of society in response to the demands of developments at particular spatio-temporal conjunctures. Illustrating my argument with the help of the region of Kerala, I show that 'Kerala' meant different things to different people at different points in time, an argument which may be uncomfortable for a few, especially those using or abusing history for political purposes. The timing of the session of Andhra Pradesh History Congress, in the context of the birth of Telangana, was particularly significant.

My essay on *Maṇipravāḷam*, originally given as the Foundation Day Lecture of the Indian Council of Historical Research, questions what generations of scholars on Malayalam literature and Kerala history had believed about a set of erotic poems in the mixed language called *Maṇipravāḷam* that had evolved in Kerala from the thirteenth century. While earlier scholars had looked upon this corpus as products of a lascivious feudal aristocracy—they described the period of its production as 'the age when the *nampūtiris* went into heat'—I read the historical context of their production as one characterized by trade and urbanism. Accordingly, I show that it is the urban sensibility and ambience, something very different from the picture drawn by writers in the past. I also show its heavy debt to the *kāvya* tradition in Sanskrit, as well as the comparability of the *milieux* that produced both.

The next two essays—the one on the origin and development of land relations in medieval Kerala and the other on the rise of what are known as the 'temple-dwelling' castes in Kerala—are by-products of my earlier researches on the brāhmaṇa settlements in Kerala. One of the oft-repeated statements in the narrative of Kerala history dominated by what Elamkulam P.N. Kunjan Pillai had written was a putative Hundred Years' War, supposed to have been fought between the Cēras and Cōḻas in the eleventh century. Pillai had taken it as the causative factor behind most features of the economy, society and polity of medieval Kerala—landlordism, matrilineal system, caste, political fragmentation and so on. Not only is the premise of a Hundred Years' War imagined, but the logic of explaining these economic and social phenomena as resulting from a war is fallacious. My own reading of the evidence points to the historical processes which led to the development of these phenomena. In the case of the former, I argue that the huge estates in land that the brāhmaṇical groups had acquired, both as the property of the temples they controlled and their own property, was exactly in the same pattern which obtained elsewhere in south India. When a class of non-cultivating, upper caste groups came to possess such vast estates of land, naturally, a graded hierarchy of intermediaries evolved with varying shades of rights over land. The process was uneven, slow and complex. So also, the way in which new castes emerged, i.e. how endogamous kinship groups became professional groups with hereditary title to land and occupation, is demonstrated by the experience of the temple-serving castes of medieval Kerala.

The piece on Revd Johann Ernst Hanxledon, S.J., fondly known to Malayalis as *Arnos Padre*, shows how the Catholic Church was not unwilling to use idioms and symbols of other religions in worship and propaganda, in spite of the somewhat fundamentalist attitude that the Church had taken in the period following the Counter Reformation, especially the Synod of Diemper that was held in Kerala in 1599. It is amazing that such ideas as the cycle of births and rebirth, totally opposed to Christian doctrine, are used by the *padre* without any difficulty and that they found ready acceptance among the members of the community. What we today tend to look at as 'ours' and 'theirs' did not perhaps bother people of those days too much.

I do not make any claim that I have shaken the earth by these essays by presenting totally new ideas. I do claim, however, that I have tried to question many things that have been handed down to us as received wisdom. If that helps in prompting scholars to reconsider some of the cherished ideas, then I shall have reason to believe that these notes of dissent have had their purpose served.

CHAPTER 1

From Dissent to Norm to Tradition

The Dialectics of Early Indian Religious History

AMONG THE MALADIES that afflict our society today is the increasing use of religion for secular purposes, what in India is described as 'communalism'. In the Indian context, communalism is both an ideology and a programme. At the ideological level, it assumes that followers of a particular religion have common economic, social and political interests. Followers of each religion, thus, are thought to have their own interests, which are distinct from, even opposed to, those of other religionists. Distinctions and unities of other digits are thus blurred and identities are forged. Masses are indoctrinated in this manner and it becomes necessary to identify a monolith of a 'religion' under whose banner they can be rallied. Differences within such a putative 'religion', be they doctrinal, sectarian or what have you, are sought to be wished away and an impression is created that 'our religion' has been single, unified, and that it has been there from time immemorial. Not only is such a perception factually inaccurate but it is also socially dangerous. In the circumstances, it is the bounden duty of the historian to show that what is presented as Hindu religion today is not a seamless entity, fully mature and evolved at the time of its origin—or is it without an origin, *anādi*?—and then continuing immutably for all times to come. It has gone, and is going, through considerable tension and the resolution of the tension every time has resulted in a new synthesis. I propose to demonstrate this through a few examples from early India.

Taking the discussion forward from research I had conducted on religious traditions some time ago, I presume to make a few generalizations about the dialectical way in which religious processes developed in early India.[1] The pattern I seek to elucidate is one in which a given set of religious ideologies and practices is dissented to from within, these notes of dissent becoming gradually part of the accepted norm and then getting sanctified as *the* tradition in the days to come. It is to these that further dissent is articulated. I shall specifically take up situations in the mid-first millennium BC and mid-first millennium AD in north India and towards the last quarter of the millennium in south India, each of these conjunctures representing veritable watersheds in the history of these regions.

I

It is well-known that the middle of the first millennium BC was a period when society in north India went through a deep churning. Scholars have laid bare the importance of the so-called heretical sects such as Jainism and Buddhism which had their origin in this period; it is also well-known that these two were not alone, there having been many more such projects questioning what were accepted as norms. Among these, less noticed but not less important, were the questioning of the Vedic tradition from what is taken as 'within', contained in the Upaniṣads. One reason for the lack of attention paid to them as notes of dissent to the tradition is perhaps the fact that they were made to look to have functioned very much within the Vedic tradition—without questioning and rejecting the authority of Vedic texts and thus carrying the tradition forward. But if one goes deep into the ideology and philosophy of the Upaniṣads, expressions of disapproval of the Vedic rituals and the inadequacy of the knowledge contained in the *saṃhitās* is hard to miss.[2] In fact, most early Upaniṣads show a tendency to go beyond the ritual-ridden Vedic ideology, in a language that is not exactly polite. The leading ideas of the Upaniṣads, such as the sole reality being the *ātman*, etc., met with acceptance more in the kṣatriya circles than among the brāhmaṇas.[3] It was later on that they were adopted by brāhmaṇas and interwoven with the ritual.[4]

We can see this in many places. For instance, a narrative in *Chāndogya Upaniṣad* tells us that five learned brāhmaṇas requested Uddālaka Āruṇi to give them instruction concerning the *ātman* Vaiśvānara. Uddālaka is diffident, and all the six now go to King Aśvapati of Kekaya for the right kind of instruction.[5] *Bṛhadāraṇyaka Upaniṣad*, likewise, has a more telling story (which has its parallel in *Kauṣītakī Upaniṣad*). Gārgya Bālāki, the Vedic scholar of repute, volunteers to expound the *brahman* to Aśvapati Kaikēya, the king, and does it in twelve explanations which, however, were erroneous. The king corrects him, with the statement that 'It is a reversal of the rule that a brāhmaṇa should approach a kṣatriya asking "please tell me about *brahman*"'.[6] What this narrative, cherished by two different Vedic schools, emphasizes is that it is the king and not the brāhmaṇa, 'famed as a Vedic scholar', who possessed the knowledge of *brahman* and *ātman*, the central doctrine of the entire Vedānta philosophy.[7] The point is emphasized further in the story of the king Pravāhaṇa Jaivali contained in the *Chāndogya Upaniṣad*. The king instructs two brāhmaṇas concerning the *ākāśa* as the ultimate substratum of all things, which they were ignorant of.[8] There is an interesting conversation between Nārada, the learned brāhmaṇa, and Sanatkumāra, the god of war. When the former claims to have acquired adequate learning in subjects such as 'the four *Veda*s, *Itihāsa-purāṇa* (the fifth *Veda*), *devavidyā*, *brahamvidyā*, *kṣatravidyā*, *nakṣatravidyā*, *sarpa-deva-janavidyā*, etc.', the latter trashes it all and says that 'these are just names!'[9] Perhaps the crowning statement in the series is contained at the end of a detailed discourse where the king Pravahāṇa Jaivali of Pāñcāla gives instructions to Śvētaketu Āruṇi regarding *ātman* and its transmigration—the central doctrine of Vedānta: 'this knowledge has never reached the brāhmaṇas before you; hence the whole earth is ruled by kṣatriyas'.[10]

As important as the non-brāhmaṇa, kṣatriya character of the new knowledge is its content which is at variance with that of the Vedic *saṃhitās*. We have already seen Sanatkumāra's contempt for the knowledge contained in the Vedic *saṃhitās* and other conventional texts. This may represent the reservations that the exponents of the new knowledge had not only about the received wisdom of the Vedic world but also about their subject-matter, i.e. about what is called the *karma-kāṇḍa* of the Vedas. To be sure, there is less of open criticism and rejection of Vedic rituals in the Upaniṣads than obtaining in, say, the Buddhist thought. This may have been a function of various factors; but the Upaniṣadic voices registering disapproval of the rituals are neither too feeble nor without interest. The older Upaniṣads seem to have conceded to the Vedic sacrifices only a relative recognition. Hostile references to the sacrificial rites are explained away as allegory. Thus, Paul Deussen finds a note almost of mockery in *Bṛhadāraṇyaka Upaniṣad*, where it is said that:

> he who worships another divinity (than the Ātman), and says 'It is one and I am another,' is not wise, but he is like a house-dog of the gods. Therefore just as many house-dogs are useful to men, every individual man is useful to the gods. Now the theft of only one house-dog is displeasing, how much more of many? Therefore it is displeasing to them that men do not know this.[11]

In a similar fashion, the remark of Yājñavalkya, again in *Bṛhadāraṇyaka Upaniṣad*, sounds very contemptuous: 'What is the sacrifice? Brute beasts!'[12] Contempt for sacrifices is nowhere clearer than in another passage in the same Upaniṣad, where it is said that Yama (the god of the dead) dwells in sacrifice and sacrifice, in the fees![13] Similarly, Deussen takes what has been described as the 'Song of the Dog' in the *Chāndogya Upaniṣad* for a satire on the greed of the priests, to which was given an allegorical interpretation in later times.[14]

A comparison of the concerns of the *saṃhitās* and the Upaniṣads will be useful in explaining this change. Whereas the former had sacrifice (*yajña*) as the chief means of worshipping the many deities, there is more of metaphysical speculation around a single, supreme power as well as the individual self in the latter. These are known, respectively, as *brahman* and *ātman*. This is not the place for us to go into the details of the way in which the two are conceived and their interrelations defined.[15] With such changes in concerns and an increased emphasis on asceticism, there is a clear shift from the community to the individual. *Ātman*, or 'self' in a language shorn of all obscurantism, holds the key to it. In the shift from the many deities to *brahman*, perhaps via *prajāpati*, we see a similar shift. A consideration of the changes in the material milieu, as well as the kṣatriya initiative in the new knowledge and the questioning of the old Vedic, brāhmaṇical knowledge may explain this.

The age of the early Upaniṣads, i.e. roughly the first half of the first millennium BC, has been shown as one of considerable disquiet in the context of northern India, particularly the Gangetic Plains. Whether one puts it all down to the advent of iron or, alternatively, to multiple causal factors, it is now accepted on all hands that there was considerable change at the economic, social and economic planes in the region—something which deserves the description of an epochal transformation.[16] The locus of geographical activity of the Vedic people had shifted from the Indus Valley and the Indo-Gangetic Divide to the Upper and Middle Ganga Valleys. A predominantly pastoral economy had been replaced by a largely settled agrarian economy. Diversification of production and complexities in exchange patterns had brought in elements such as the traders and artisans. There was increased production in almost all fields. Production of surplus meant its unequal distribution and greater differentiation in society, introducing elements to reckon with in society. Centres of trade had emerged as urban centres, forming the bases of what historians have described as Second Urbanization. Life in general had witnessed a change at a qualitative level. State was making its appearance, in an incipient manner to begin with and then in a bold, authentic way, with 'the establishment of kingdoms, oligarchies and chiefdoms, and the emergence of towns'.[17] The emergence of a state system frequently coincides with unequal power relations and access to resources and considerable social disparity. Such changes would have sought support from various ideological justifications.

If we take the changes in the fields of economy, society and polity into account, changes in ideology and philosophy can be explained with greater confidence. The gradual demise of an economy based on cattle-keeping and gift-exchanges saw the increasing irrelevance of the *yajña*-type of communitarian rituals where not only were cattle sacrificed but also given away as gifts in the form of *dāna* and *dakṣiṇā*. Potlatch-like disposal of the surplus would no more be relevant in an economy where there is systematic production and distribution of surplus. A philosophical system which stresses on the individual and expresses concern over his relation with life in this world and the next becomes more appropriate than one which has the community as the central concern. Notions of the cycle of births and deaths are of individuals. These, such as contained in the *Kaṭha Upaniṣad*, or the notion of *saṃsāra* or transmigration of the soul, become relevant here, as also the thoughts about *mokṣa* or deliverance from these cycles. Renunciation becomes a major aspect of religious activity and the renouncer or *muni* becomes a parallel source of authority.[18] It is here that important questions of the *ātman* and *brahman* raise themselves. That the knowledge regarding these was unavailable in the Vedas or other conventional texts so far known is a point repeated over and over again in the Upaniṣads. This new knowledge was embodied in the Upaniṣads, in the secret knowledge imparted by the teacher to the disciple. In fact, the word *rahasyam*, 'secret', is repeatedly used as a synonym for Upaniṣad.[19] The fact that the custodians of this new, secret knowledge were not brāhmaṇas but kṣatriyas acquires importance in the context of the emergence of the kingdoms and chiefdoms in north India in this period. The statement in the *Chāndogya Upaniṣad* that 'the whole earth is ruled by kṣatriyas' (*sarveṣu lokeṣu kṣatriyasyaiva praśāsanam abhūd*) becomes extremely meaningful here. We may reverse the causality somewhat mischievously: 'the whole earth is ruled by kṣatriyas; hence this knowledge has never reached the brāhmaṇas before you' (*yatheyaṃ sarveṣu lokeṣu kṣatriyasyaiva praśāsanam abhūd tasmād u na prāk tvattaḥ purā vidyā brāhmaṇān gacchati iti*). This may hold the key to answering our question.

These notes of dissent, however, were contained and accommodated through a process of appropriation. The Upaniṣadic dissent lent itself more readily for appropriation than, for instance, the Jain or Buddhist dissent. Tensions are clear in the early layers of the Upaniṣads; but gradually they were made part of the ritual and doctrine of the Vedic creed. Insofar as the Upaniṣads did not openly reject the authority of the Vedas, *mīmāṃsā* philosophy was able to do the job of appropriation effectively. The Upaniṣads were promptly claimed as 'Vedānta', 'the end of the Veda'.[20] A whole new *vrata* called the *Aupaniṣada vrata* was invented and made part of the sacraments of a *brahmacārin* during which he is supposed to study the Upaniṣads.[21] The Upaniṣads or Vedānta was counted as part of the brāhmaṇa along with *vidhi* ('precepts or commandments') and *arthavāda* ('explanation of the meaning').[22] The whole of brāhmaṇa literature was then claimed as part of the Veda, which claim is summed up in the famous definition, 'Veda means *Mantra* and *Brāhmaṇa* (*mantrabrāhmaṇayorveda nāmadheyam*)'.[23] What was a note of dissent to begin with had become the norm; and a new tradition had been created.

II

Another major watershed in the history of northern India can be identified in the middle of the first millennium AD. Romila Thapar rightly describes these four centuries (AD 300–700) as representing 'threshold times'.[24] Among the more important features of this period was the development of 'Purāṇic Hinduism', a term used to distinguish it from Vedic Brāhmaṇism. Many of the Purāṇas got redacted in this period although their precise dating is problematic. It is a moot point whether the innumerable substratum cults and practices which existed in the regions that the Vedic people came across appropriated Vedic traditions or whether the Vedic traditions appropriated these to constitute this 'new' religion. In any case, it is seen that through a process of what has been described as 'acculturation', a large number of deities worshipped in different parts of the country were identified, sought to be ordered in a particular pattern and made part of a larger system. This was achieved in different ways: by taking these deities as *avatāras* or incarnations of one who was taken as the more important in a system, by looking upon the deities as kinsmen or attendants of a major deity. Alternatively, one of these 'major' deities was presented to have had many names, each representing the name of a local cult object or hero. For instance, names of trees such as *Nyagrodha*, *Udumbara*, *Aśvattha*, etc., which might have been totems of different groups, are taken as names of Viṣṇu in *Viṣṇusahasranāma*. The way in which Vaiṣṇavism developed, incorporating different substratum cults, can be taken as a good example of the process.[25]

Three important aspects that had their roots in the changes of this period led to a religious ethos different from that which was dominated either by Buddhism or Vedic Brahmanism. The image emerged as the focus of worship and this form of worship, centred on *pūjā*, superseded the Vedic sacrifice. Devotional worship—*bhakti*—became the most widespread form of worship this religion.[26] Apart from the performance of *pūjā*, repeating the names of the deities, observance of fasts and feasts, pilgrimage and hearing the sacred stories around these deities were part of the methods of worship. Needless to say, the process through which it all evolved was complex. It certainly must have involved tensions, although there is little that the sources show directly.

It is in this context that the descriptions of the *kaliyuga* acquire significance. It is with something approximating to a pathological fear that the horrors of an impending *kaliyuga* are prophesied in the Purāṇas, which were composed around this period. That the Purāṇas use future tense for times following the catastrophic Mahābhārata War is significant. Catastrophes are time markers, and a new era, in this case the *kaliyuga*, begins with it. The splendour of an earlier age had come to an end. The authors of the Purāṇas locate themselves in the splendorous age before the War; hence anything after that would belong to the future. Using the future tense for times past has other implications as well.[27] *Kaliyuga* will be an age of horror, everything turning topsy-turvy. Avarice and wrath will be common. There will be open animosity among humans. *Dharma* will suffer a setback. Murder with no justification will be the order of the day. Vices of all sorts will increase, and virtue will cease to flourish. People will take vows and break them soon after. People will become addicted to intoxicating drinks and drugs. Teachers will no longer be respected and students will attempt to injure them. Teachings will be insulted. Lust will wrest control of human mind. Brāhmaṇas will be neither learned nor honoured, kṣatriyas will not be brave, and vaiśyas will not be just in their dealings. All sorts of imaginable and unimaginable evils will be rampant.

R.S. Sharma has explained these descriptions as representing a crisis that society was going through.[28] The more important features of the Kali Age, for him, were the:

> mixing of *varṇas* or *varṇasaṃkara*, hostility between *śūdras* and *brāhmaṇas*, refusal of vaiśyas to pay and sacrifice [*sic*], oppression of people with taxes, widespread threat and robbery, insecurity of family and property, destruction of *yogakṣema*, growing importance of wealth over ritual status, and dominance of *mleccha* princes.[29]

Sharma looked at this social crisis as among the causative factors behind the emergence of a feudal formation in India.

Social crisis it certainly must have been. It is significant that the fears of this crisis are expressed in a language of religion. The prescriptions of things to be done and avoided in *kaliyuga* (*kalidharma* and *kalivarjya* respectively), and the ways for mitigating its evils, accompanied the expressions of the pathological fear about what is in store for the days of immanent evil. At the same time, the antidotes for the evils of *kaliyuga* were present in *kaliyuga* itself. I have shown elsewhere that in the same texts which present the *kaliyuga* as a dark age, there are descriptions which show its positive side as well, particularly in that any good deed would yield immediate result in *kaliyuga* unlike earlier ages.[30] The *Bhāgavatapurāṇa*, admittedly a later text, says:

> The discerning ones, who know the essence [of things], always prefer the age of *kali* when just by singing psalms all desired things can be earned, when ultimate peace is possible, and when the cycle of birth and death is destroyed. In [the age of] Kali will be born those who are engaged in [the worship of] Nārāyaṇa. . . .[31]

The earlier *Viṣṇupurāṇa* puts the following into the mouth of Vyāsa:

> What takes ten years in *kṛta*, ten *ayana*s (half-years) in *tretā*, ten months in *dvāpara*, it takes only ten days and nights in *kali*. What brāhmaṇas gain as the result of *tapas*, *brahmacarya*, *japa*, etc. [all] men gain in *kali*. . . . What [people] achieve by meditation in *kṛta*, performance of *yajña*s in *tretā*, and *arcanā* in *dvāpara*, they achieve by singing psalms in *kali*. Men achieve great heights of *dharma* in [the age of] of *kali* with the least effort and hence I am happy with *kali*. With a little effort, great heights of *dharma* can be gained in *kali*.[32]

Vyāsa hastens to add: 'This is the only good thing about *kali*, the most evil [of ages].' These sentiments are adumbrated in Purāṇas like the *Matsya* and *Brahmāṇḍa*.[33]

This apparent contradiction becomes starker and starker when we go forward in time. Earlier texts like *Matsyapurāṇa* and *Brahmāṇḍapurāṇa* have only suggestions to these positive aspects of the Kali Age. By the time we come to the *Viṣṇupurāṇa* and *Bhāgavatapurāṇa*, the statements are unequivocal. Even when it is recognized that *kaliyuga* is evil, that age is also represented as the best of all ages, even those born in earlier yugas like the *kṛta*, *treta* and *dvāpara* desiring birth in this age. It is this later representation that presents the starkest contrast. What is interesting is that many of these contradictory statements occur in quick succession in the same texts. The representation of *kaliyuga* as the darkest of all the four ages, on the one side and as the best on the other, in the same texts, is a matter of curiosity. How do we reconcile with, and explain, this dual representation of the same subject in diametrically opposite ways?

The answer seems to lie in the appeal to religion, particularly *bhakti*, that too of Viṣṇu, who seems to be the hero of the Kali Age. *Kaliyuga* is celebrated, in all these descriptions, on account of the fact that *bhakti* yields easier and more immediate results in that age. It is in *kaliyuga* that Viṣṇu can be worshipped by the easiest mode—such as singing psalms and repeating his names. The other items in the mode of worship prescribed for *kaliyuga* include observance of fast on *ekādaśī* and other days, smearing sandalwood paste and *gopī* on one's person, worshipping *sālagrāma*, chanting the names of Viṣṇu, reading and listening to the *Gītā* and the Purāṇas, etc.

To be sure, these statements in favour of *kaliyuga* are not unqualified. Nearly all the texts quoted here are convinced that Kali is an enemy of dharma, that Kali is merciless, and that Kali is terrible. *Kaliyuga* is, without doubt, the most evil of all ages. Thus, what is presented as good about it, in spite of its evils, is that *bhakti* and the modes of worship associated with it can yield immediate results in the age of *kali*. The best way to explain these statements is to see them as exhortations to make use of the possibilities offered by *bhakti*. They are the sole redeeming features in an otherwise miserable period, 'the sigh of the oppressed creature, the heart of a heartless world, and the soul of soulless conditions'. The favourable light in which śūdras and women are presented in the *Viṣnupurāṇa* is to be placed in this context.[34]

Bhakti helped in making the inequality and the consequent suffering palatable by creating an illusion of equality. One of the features that make the Kali Age superior to all other ages in the descriptions we saw is that it enables the devotee to realize god faster and by 'effortless' (*niryatna*) means. While rituals of all sorts were prescribed for earlier ages—*tapas* (penance) for *kṛta*, *yajña* (sacrifice) for *tretā* and *tantra* (worship of idols) for *dvāpara*—simply singing psalms would do the job in *kali*.[35] Other modes of worship prescribed for Kali Age, like observance of fast on specific days such as *ekādaśī*, smearing sandalwood paste and *gopī* on one's person, worshipping *sālagrāma*, chanting the names of Viṣṇu, reading the *Gītā*, and suchlike, too, are rather 'effortless'. This indicates two major aspects of the new mode of worship: (1) a reduced emphasis on ritual to the point of its repudiation and (2) increased emphasis on other, inexpensive and effortless means. Both are of importance. In fact, it would seem that the complex societal conditions emerging in this period demanded this new mode of worship.

In a condition characterized by 'mixing of *varṇas* or *varṇasaṃkara*, hostility between śūdras and brāhmaṇas, refusal of *vaiśya*s to pay and sacrifice [*sic*], oppression of people with taxes, widespread threat and robbery, insecurity of family and property, destruction of *yogakṣema*, growing importance of wealth over ritual status, and dominance of *mleccha* princes',[36] performance of rituals, Vedic or Tāntric, was next to impossible, a condition that had been lamented by the writers on the horrors of *kaliyuga*. What was possible in the circumstances was to gracefully find alternatives to the impracticable rituals. In the place of the complicated rituals which would take very long both to perform and yield results, simpler means like signing psalms (*saṅkīrtanas*) and chanting the names of Viṣṇu were found preferable, as they were relatively inexpensive and did not require the cooperation of those who are unwilling. They yielded quick results as well. Here it will be interesting to ask why they rejected ritual or at least emphasized on minimalist ritual, least effort and fast service. *Bhakti* had, in a manner of speaking, 'democratized religion'. Was this characteristic of a social churning perhaps much greater than has been recognized? Was it a note of dissent to the orthodox tradition, characterized by extensive ritual, requiring much effort and a long time period? In any case, later developments in Purāṇic Hinduism in general and Vaiṣṇavism in particular show that this dissent had gradually become the norm and was moving towards the making of a tradition.

III

South India was going through a major transition in the last quarter of the first millennium AD—a transition from the early historical to the early medieval, according to recent scholarship.[37] To be sure, it was slow, uneven and extremely complex. In the field of religion, it is a matter of common knowledge that there was a considerable presence of Jainism, Buddhism and the Ājīvika faith in the early historical period; so also, the presence of Vedic sacrifices, the cult of Purāṇic deities and a few related myths are documented in early Tamil texts.[38] At least two texts—the *Paripāṭal* and *Tirumurugāṟṟuppaṭai*—speak about temples of Viṣṇu and Murugan respectively, too. Thus, it will be wrong to think that what has been described as the Bhakti Movement of the *Āḻvārs* and *Nāyaṉārs* introduced an entirely new religious thought and practice to south India in the early medieval period and weaned that part of the country away from the cults of tribal, folk deities of the *tiṇais*.[39] However, a regional synthesis had taken place, through which the Tamil bucolic deity of the pastoral tract, Māyōn, had been identified as the dark hero of the Yadus, Kṛṣṇa. Māl or Tirumāl of *Paripāṭal* had likewise become Viṣṇu of the Purāṇas.

This development can be traced through various stages. The three early *Āḻvārs*, namely Pūtam, Pēy and Tirumaḻiśai, express a simple form of devotion and appear to be preoccupied more with the intellectual than the emotional aspects of *bhakti*.[40] The temple is the focus of their religion only in a generic sense at this stage, and references are to the ones in northern Tamilnadu, in the territory of the Pallavas, such as Vēṅkaṭam (Tirupati), Mallai (Mahābalipuram), and Tiruvaḷḷikkēṇi (Triplicane). The elaboration of *bhakti* with its elaborate Purāṇic mythology as well as the detailed *Āgamaic* iconography and forms of worship in the Tamil country can be seen as a development of the last quarter of the first millennium AD, coeval with the proliferation of the temple and its growth in both space and range of economic and social activities. Temples developed in south India as centres of brāhmaṇa settlements, which were also at the centre of newly emerging agrarian pockets coming up in the wake of the expansion of rice cultivation. In showing that the Bhakti Movement of the *Āḻvārs* and *Nāyaṉārs* was essentially temple-based and that the hymnists were singing about deities consecrated in particular temples and not God in the absolute, we have demonstrated an organic connection between this new phenomenon in the realm of ideology and the emerging social realities.[41]

Another important feature of the period in the history of south India was the arrival of the state. This began with the establishment of the Pallava and Pāṇḍya monarchies in the north and the south respectively by the end of the seventh century. The Cēras on the West Coast and the Cōḻas in the Kāvēri valley were to come a little later and in a more refined and elaborate manner. This was a new political experience in south India, and is clearly distinguished from the situation that obtained in the preceding early historical period. The new formation was characterized by unequal power relations and access to resources and some social disparity. Such changes would have, as mentioned earlier, sought support from various ideological justifications. It is against this background that we have to see the Bhakti Movement as also a reflection and legitimation of the emerging order. The role that the temple played in this is too well-known to bear one more repetition.[42] Being a movement with its institutional base in the temples, what it tried was to seek justification and legitimacy to that institution and all it represented, including the new social and political order that was being established.[43]

The Bhakti Movement has been represented as a movement of dissent, protest and reform, primarily against caste inequalities. This is based on the tradition that the *bhakti* 'saints' counted among themselves members of different castes, high and low. But, there are several gaps in such simplistic formulations, which are actually products of a milieu of the National Movement in the 1920s and 1930s in which social reform movements, particularly caste movements, had a major place. In reality, however, most hymnists of both the Vaiṣṇava and Śaiva persuasions can be seen as of the two upper castes, namely brāhmaṇa ritual specialists and members of 'kṣatriya' ruling houses. As Bharati Jagannathan says, it is very questionable if the *bhakti* movement invited fishermen and farmers, hunters and housewives to a devotional milieu shorn of hierarchy.[44] We see in the hymns, along with vituperations on Buddhism and Jainism, severe criticism of the sacrificial ritual and Vedic Brāhmaṇism. Toṇṭaraṭippoṭi Āḻvār, for instance, sings:

> You (Viṣṇu) are manifestly more fond of
> those servants, even if they may be born as outcastes,
> who express their love for your feet, than
> the Caturvedins who are strangers to your service[45]

This rejection of Vedas and Vedic sacrifices comes out even more strongly in the *Mukundamālā*, a Sanskrit poem composed by

Kulaśekhara Āḻvār, the author of Tamil *Perumāḷ Tirumoḻi*, when he says:

> Done without praising His lotus feet,
> Recitation of the Vedas is but a cry in the forest;
> Practicing hard austerities day in and day out can but get rid of obesity;
> Sacrifices are but pouring ghee into ash;
> And bathing in holy waters is but a bath of an elephant—
> Victory to the lord Narayana[46]

Again, Madurakavi's statement that the *Caturvedins*, the lords of the four Vedas, regarded him as vile and that he accepted only Nammāḻvār whose hymns represent a Tamil rendering of the Vedas, expresses the same sense of disapproval of Vedas and Vedic Brāhmaṇism. The acceptance of Nammāḻvār's *Tiruvāymoḻi* as the Tamil Veda was another way of registering this dissent, which can be seen in the Vaiṣṇava tradition ever since a community of devotees was consolidated. The devotee was the alter ego of the deity; to worship him was to worship the deity and to disparage him was to disparage the deity. Thus, Toṇṭaraṭippoṭi, the name of an *Āḻvār*, means 'Dust at the Feet of Devotees'.

It is this that consolidated itself as the Vaiṣṇava sect or *sampradāya*. The *Bhāgavatapurāṇa* is to be located in this context. The text shows a close knowledge of the *Āḻvār* tradition.[47] In fact, the Purāṇa has been shown as heavily influenced by the Tamil *bhakti* tradition, a south Indian contribution to the development of Vaiṣṇavism.[48] Thus the *bhakti* of the *Āḻvārs*, which had articulated this dissent, was gradually appropriated later by the time of the *ācāryas*, who showed greater rigidity and orthodoxy. The inclusiveness of the *Āḻvārs* had gone. While the earlier devotees of the Bhakti Movement used Tamil and took pride in it—*bhakti* poetry is thought to constitutes a considerable portion of the Tamil literary canon—Sanskrit started claiming a greater place as the language of religious discourse under the *Ācāryas*. Such Tamil as was used was heavily mixed with Sanskrit, so much so that it was looked upon as a new language: *Maṇipravāḷam*. The synthesis had been complete as the tradition reached other parts of India—notably Vṛndāvan and Bengal through the *Śrīvaiṣṇava* sect.

We have taken up a few episodes here, which show a pattern in the process of religious evolution in early India. The pattern of the emergence of dissent to established orthodoxy, the way in which it is sought to be appropriated by the orthodoxy and the changes within orthodoxy itself following such appropriation and finally the newly synthesized orthodoxy becoming the tradition is illustrated here. These pertain to historical conjunctures which witnessed what could be described as 'turning points' in the history of early India. There emerge serious questionings of established orthodoxy in the context of major disquiets in society, which emergences are not unrelated to the larger developments. While certain forms of dissent were contained, or appropriated, certain others remained as an alternative. True, there were also substratum cults and practices, which did not quite become part of the larger process. Similarly, there were expressions of stronger dissents which could not be contained. In any case, what the pattern demonstrates is the nature of religion more as a process then as a finished product. It will also hopefully show that there is no primacy for any one tradition, as there has always been plurality in the field.

NOTES

1. I take this discussion forward from research I had carried out about four decades ago: M.G.S. Narayanan and Kesavan Veluthat, 'The Bhakti Movement in South India', in *Indian Movements: Aspects of Dissent, Protest and Reform,* ed. S.C. Malik, Shimla: Indian Institute of Advanced Study, 1978, pp. 1–50, reproduced in the Appendix below.
2. Romila Thapar, 'Ideology and the Upanisads', in *Society and Ideology in India: Essays in Honour of Professor R.S. Sharma*, ed. D.N. Jha, Delhi: Munshiram Manoharlal, 1997, pp. 11–27.
3. I have used brāhmaṇa with lower case 'b' to indicate the caste of that name and with upper case 'B' to indicate the texts of that name.
4. Paul Deussen, *The Philosophy of the Upanishads*, Edinburgh, T. & T. Clark, 1906, p. 8.
5. *Chāndogya Upaniṣad*, 5, 11–24. All references are to the electronic version available at the website http://gretil.sub.uni-goettingen.de/gretil/1_sanskr/1_veda/4_upa/chupsb_u.htm (accessed 14 November 2016).
6. *Bṛhadāraṇyaka Upaniṣad*, 2, 1.15: *pratilomam caitat yad brāhmaṇaḥ kṣtriyam upeyād brahma me vakṣyatīti*. References are to the electronic version of the Upaniṣad available at http://gretil.sub.uni-goettingen.de/gretil/1_sanskr/1_veda/4_upa/brupsb_u.htm (accessed 14 November

2016). In E.B. Cowell ed. and tr., *Kauṣītakī Brāhmaṇa Upaniṣad*, Bibliotheca Indica Series, Calcutta, Baptist Mission Press, 1861, Chapter 4, pp. 103–6, it is Ajātaśatru who instructs Gārgya Bālāki.

7. Deussen, *The Philosophy of the Upanishads*, p. 18.
8. *Chāndogya Upaniṣad*, 1, 8–9. *Chāndogya Upaniṣad*, 1, 9.3 says that Atidhanvan had previously imparted this instruction to Udaraśāṇdilya. It appears from the names that the former was a kṣatriya and the latter, a brāhmaṇa.
9. *Chāndogya Upaniṣad*, 7, 1.4: *nāma vā ṛgvedo yajurvedaḥ sāmaveda ātharvaṇaścaturtha itihāsapurāṇaḥ pañcamo vedānām vedam pitryo rāśirdaivo nidhirvākovākyam ekāyanam devavidyā brhamavidyā bhūtavidyā kṣtravidyā nakṣatravidyā sarpadevajanavidhyā || nāmevaitad ||*
10. *Chāndogya Upaniṣad*, 5, 3.7: *yatheyaṃ na prāk tvattaḥ purā vidyā brāhmaṇān gacchati tasmād u sarveṣu lokeṣu kṣatriyasyaiva praśāsanam abhūd iti*. For the detailed discourse, see *Chāndogya Upaniṣad*, 5, 3.1ff.
11. Deussen, *The Philosophy of the Upanishads*, p. 62. The expression in *Bṛhadāraṇyaka Upaniṣad*, 1, 4. 10, however, is *paśavaḥ*, 'domesticated animals'. Śaṅkara's lengthy gloss on this passage, desperately quoting from much later texts such as the *Bhagavad Gītā*, is at pains to defend the passage; but the picture that emerges in the end is what Deussen has delineated.
12. Deussen, *The Philosophy of the Upanishads*, p. 62. Even here the expression is *paśavaḥ*. *Bṛhadāraṇyaka Upaniṣad*, 3, 9.6.
13. *Bṛhadāraṇyaka Upaniṣad*, 3. 9.21: *yamaḥ kasmin pratiṣṭhita iti | yajña iti | kasmin nu yajñaḥ pratiṣṭhita iti | dakṣiṇāyāṃ iti |*
14. Deussen, *The Philosophy of the Upanishads*, p. 62. The passage in question is from *Chandogya Upaniṣad*, 1, 12. Śaṅkara tries to see in these dogs gods or *ṛṣis* (*devatarṣirvā*) in disguise!
15. For an elaborate treatment of the philosophy of the Upaniṣads, see Deussen, *The Philosophy of the Upanishads*.
16. Romila Thapar, *The Penguin History of Early India: From the Origins to AD 1300*, London: Penguin Books, 2001, p. 31.
17. Ibid., p. 137.
18. Romila Thapar, 'Renunciation: The Making of a Counter Culture', in *Ancient Indian Social History: Some Interpretations*, Hyderabad: Orient Longman, 1978.
19. Deussen, *The Philosophy of the Upanishads*, p. 10. The etymology of the word *upa-niṣad*, which literally means that which is taught to one who is 'seated nearby', indicates this secret character. In fact, the *Nṛsiṃhatāpanīya Upaniṣad* uses the expression *iti rahasyam* eight times in the same context where other early Upaniṣads would use the

expression *iti Upaniṣad*, suggesting that the two are synonyms. In older texts too, where mention is made of Upaniṣad texts, such expressions are used as *guhyā ādeśāḥ, paramam guhyam, vedaguhya-Upaniṣatsu gūḍham, guhyatamam*, etc., *Chāndogya Upaniṣad*, 3, 5.2; *Kaṭha Upaniṣad*, 3, 17; *Śvetāśvatara Upaniṣad*, 5, 6; etc.

20. Deussen, *The Philosophy of the Upanishads*, p. 3. The description of the Upaniṣads as 'Vedānta' occurs as early as the *Śvetāśvatara Upaniṣad*, 6, 22 and *Muṇḍaka Upaniṣad*, 3, 2.63. 2.6. The Upaniṣads have ever since bore the name 'Vedānta' and expressions such as *Śrutyanta* ('End of the *Śruti*, i.e. *Veda*') are used to describe the Upaniṣads in classical Sanskrit.
21. *Gautama Dharmasūtra*, 8, 15; *Sāṅkhāyana Dharmasūtra*, 2, 11–12.
22. Deussen, *The Philosophy of the Upanishads*, p. 1.
23. This statement of Sāyaṇa, occurring in the *bhūmikā* to his *bhāṣya* of *Ṛg Veda*, seems to base itself on Āpastamba's *Yajña Paribhāṣā*, and forms the basis of much of *mīmāṃsā* understanding of the Vedic corpus. I thank Professor Ramakrishna Bhat for this information. In fact, this attempt at claiming the entire body consisting of *mantra* and *brāhmaṇa* as forming part of a single corpus had begun from the time of Jaimini himself. *Mīmāṃsāsūtra*, 2, 1.31–3 is clear: *api vā prayogasāmarthyānmantro 'bhidhānavācī syāt. taccodakeṣu mantrākhyā. śeṣe brāhmaṇaśabdḥ.*
24. Thapar, *The Penguin History of Early India*, pp. 280–325. For a discussion of the social change in this period, R.S. Sharma, *Early Medieval Indian Society: A Study in Feudalisation*, Delhi: Orient Longman, 2001.
25. Suvira Jaiswal, *Origin and Development of Vaiṣṇavism: From 200 BC to AD 500*, second edition, Delhi: Munshiram Manoharlal, 1981. Minor variations notwithstanding, the larger course that Śaivism took, too, is comparable.
26. Thapar, *The Penguin History of Early India*, pp. 319–20.
27. Romila Thapar, *The Past Before Us: Historical Traditions of Early North India*, Ranikhet: Permanent Black, 2013, pp. 294–5.
28. R.S. Sharma, 'The Kali Age: A Period of Social Crisis', in *India: History and Thought (Essays in Honour of Professor A.L. Basham)*, ed. S. Mukherjee, Calcutta: Subarnarekha, 1982; reproduced in D.N. Jha, ed., *The Feudal Order: State, Society and Ideology in Early Medieval India*, Delhi: Manohar, 2000, pp. 61–78.
29. Sharma, 'The Kali Age', p. 63.
30. Kesavan Veluthat, 'Making the Best of a Bad Bargain: the Brighter Side of Kaliyuga', *Indian Historical Review*, vol. 41, no. 2, 2014, pp. 173–84.

31. *Bhāgavatapurāṇa*, Gita Press, Gorakhpur, *samvat* 2024 edition, *Skandha*, 11, *Adhyāya*, 5, vv. 19–42.
32. *Śrīviṣṇupurāṇa*, Gita Press, Gorakhpur, samvat 2045 edition, *aṃśa 6, adhyāya 2*, vv. 15–19.
33. *Matsyapurāṇa*, *Adhyāya* 106, vv. 57–8, http://gretil.sub.uni-goettingen.de/gret_utf.htm#MatsP (accessed 14 November 2016); *Brahmāṇḍapurāṇa*, Part 1, Chapter 31. vv. 71–3, http://gretil.sub.uni-goettingen.de/gretil/1_sanskr/3_purana/brndp1_u.htm (accessed 14 November 2016).
34. *Śrīviṣṇupurāṇa*, Gita Press, Gorakhpur, *samvat* 2045 edition, *aṃśa* 6, *adhyāya* 2 vv. 6–8, 35–6.
35. For details, Veluthat, 'Making the Best of a Bad Bargain'.
36. Sharma, 'The Kali Age', p. 63.
37. For a discussion of the literature available on this problem and a definitive statement, see Kesavan Veluthat, *The Early Medieval in South India*, New Delhi: Oxford University Press, 2009, pp. 19–60; Rajan Gurukkal, *Social Formations of Early South India*, New Delhi: Oxford University Press, 2012, pp. 205–23.
38. For a brief overview, K.A. Nilakanta Sastri, *Sangam Literature: Its Cults and Cultures*, Madras: Swathi Publications, 1972, chapter on 'Religion: Creeds and Beliefs', pp. 66–77.
39. Five different *tiṇais* or 'landscapes' are recognized in the Tamil country, each of which followed a distinct mode of subsistence and worshipped deities suited to the landscape and livelihood of each.There is considerable literature on the concept of the *tiṇai* in early historical Tamiḻakam. For a succinct presentation, see Gurukkal, *Social Formations of Early South India*.
40. K.A. Nilakanta Sastri, *Development of Religion in South India*, Madras: Orient Longman, 1963, p. 45; R. Champakalakshmi, 'From Devotion and Dissent to Dominance: The *Bhakti* of the Tamil *Āḻvār*s and *Nāyaṉār*s', in *Religion, Tradition and Ideology: Pre-colonial South India*, New Delhi: Oxford University Press, 2012, esp. p. 56.
41. Kesavan Veluthat, 'The Temple-base of the Bhakti Movement in South India', in *Proceedings of the Indian History Congress*, Waltair, 1979, reproduced in K.M. Shrimali, ed., *Essays on Indian Art, Religion and Society*, New Delhi: Munshiram Manoharlal, 1987.
42. Kesavan Veluthat, 'Religious Symbols in Political Legitimation: The Case of Early Medieval South India', paper presented at the seminar on 'Religion and Social Consciousness', Department of History, University of Hyderabad, September 1991. Reproduced in *Social Scientist*, January–February 1993; Veluthat, 'The Temple and the State: Religion and Politics in Early Medieval South India', in *State and Society in*

Pre-modern South India, ed. R. Champakalakshmi, Kesavan Veluthat and T.R. Venugopalan, Thrissur: Cosmobooks, 2002, pp. 96–110.

43. Narayanan and Veluthat, 'The Bhakti Movement in South India'.
44. Bharati Jagannathan, *Approaching the Divine: The Integration of Āḻvār Bhakti in Śrīvaiṣṇavism*, Delhi: Primus Books, 2015, p. 6. We had shown earlier that hagiographical accounts of the presence of men of the lower castes, such as Nantan (a Paṟaiyan—agrestic slave), Tiruppāṇa (a Pāṇan—wandering mistrel), Kaṇṇappa (a Vēṭan—hunter), etc., actually were exceptions which proverbially proved the rule. Narayanan and Veluthat, 'The Bhakti Movement in South India'.
45. *Tirumālai*, 42, quoted in Champakalakshmi, 'From Devotion and Dissent to Dominance, p. 60. This is reflected in the following verse of the *Bhāgavatapurāṇa*: 'I take a śvapaca (dog-eater), whose mind and words are dedicated to Him, as superior to a brāhmaṇa, who has all the twelve qualities but who has turned away from the lotus feet of Viṣṇu, for the former cleanses the entire earth [by his devotion]'.

    viprāddviṣaḍguṇayutādaravindanābha-
    pādāravindavimukhād śvapacam variṣṭham
    manye tadarpitamanovacane hitārtha-
    prāṇam punāti sa kulam na tu bhūrimānaḥ.
    Bhāgavatapurāṇa, Skandha 7, *Adhyāya* 9, v. 10.

46. *Mukundamālā*, 13.
    āmnāyābhysanānyaraṇyaruditam kṛchravratānyanvaham
    medśchedapadāni pūrtavidhayaḥ sarve hutam bhasmani
    tīrthānāmavagāhanāni ca gajasnānam vinā ytpada
    dvandāmbhoruhasṃstutim vijayate devaḥ sa nārāyaṇaḥ.
47. *Bhāgavatapurāṇa, Skandha* 11, *Adhyāya*, 05. vv. 38–4.
    kalau khalu bhaviṣyanti nārāyaṇaparāyaṇāḥ
    kvacit kvacin mahārāja draviḍeṣu ca bhūriśaḥ
    tāmraparṇī nadī yatra kṛtamālā payasvinī
    kāverī ca mahāpuṇyā pratīcī ca mahānadī

48. Friedhelm Hardy, *Viraha-Bhakti: The Early History of Kṛṣṇa Devotion in South India*, New York: Oxford University Press, 1983; J.A.B. van Buitenen, 'On the Archaism of the *Bhāgavatapurāṇa*', in *Krishna: Myths, Rites and Attitudes*, ed. Milton Singer, Honolulu: East-West Centre Press, 1966, pp. 23–40 (also in J.A.B. van Buitenen, *Studies in Indian Philosophy and Literature*, Delhi: Motilal Banarsidass, 1981, pp. 223–42; Edwin Bryant, *Krishna: The Beautiful Legend of God* (Śrīmad *Bhāgavatapurāṇa* Book X), New York: Oxford University Press, 2003. I thank Bharati Jagannathan for inviting my attention to this.

CHAPTER 2

The Mauryan Presence in South India

PROFESSOR Y. SUBBARAYALU is one of those few historians of south India who combines a thorough mastery of the sources with a wider perspective and a concern with the larger context of study. He does not lose himself in the mass of details to believe that *that* constitutes history. Nor does he allow himself to be carried away by seemingly attractive theories and sweeping generalizations. In fact, in his Presidential Address to Section V of the Burdwan session of the Indian History Congress (1983),[1] he had advocated the importance of an all-India perspective in writing the history of south. The reference there to one of my articles was a great morale booster for the young researcher in me. Taking my cue from that point, I venture, in this chapter, to pay my homage to Professor Subbarayalu by trying to show how clarity in the understanding of regional history can enable better understanding of issues in sub-continental history. I hope to do this by looking at the evidence of Mauryan presence in south India.

Historians have taken the 'Mauryan Problem' in south Indian history as capable of providing a sheet anchor for the chronology of historical developments in this part of the country.[2] They take it also as something of an 'appendix' to the history of the Mauryan Empire itself, where centrality indeed goes to the empire. Some of them even believe that 'Mauryan contacts played an important part in the transformation of a semi-tribal society in Tamiḻakam into a caste-class society of the classical Indian type.'[3] The purpose of this chapter is to reconsider evidence relating to the contacts that existed between the south and the north in the fourth to third centuries BC and later, and to estimate the extent of Mauryan presence in the south. To what extent did this really help in the transformation of south India is a question that need not detain us very much.

One of the most accepted 'facts' about the history of early south India is related to the contacts that it is thought to have had with the Mauryan Empire. Different kinds of evidence are summoned to testify to this. Among them are the large number of Aśokan edicts distributed in the peninsula, the statements in the *Arthaśāstra* about trade contacts with south India and the merchandise coming from there, early Tamil songs referring to the Mauryas, their mighty armies and the raids they undertook to south India and various suggestions in that literature about the otherwise intimate knowledge that south India had about the Magadhan region.[4] In this chapter, we present a preliminary report of an attempt to read the evidence afresh, along with archaeological data from south India, aimed at ascertaining the extent of that presence and assessing its fall-out. The search also extends itself to documents of a later period indicating a Mauryan touch, with a view to looking at the possibility of the Mauryan influence coming as a post-Mauryan phenomenon, the result of a continuing and moving tradition. If one succeeds in answering these questions properly, not only could there be greater clarity in the understanding of the beginnings of south Indian history but problems related to the nature of Mauryan society and state can also be addressed with greater confidence.

The occurrence of Aśokan inscriptions in several places in Karnataka is taken as unimpeachable evidence attesting to the Mauryan presence in south India.[5] In fact, the thickest cluster of Aśokan inscriptions is in that state. They belong generally to the category of Minor Rock Edicts. One group of them makes a reference to 'officers of the state' stationed in Suvarnagiri, an unidentified centre thought of as a 'provincial capital' of the Mauryan Empire.[6] Another record shows that a scribe who may have been keen on showing off his proficiency in Kharoshthi as well engraved the inscriptions in Brahmi while neither of these scripts nor the language of the records itself would have made any sense to the local population.[7] In fact, one record states in so many words that the Rajukas should be asked to communicate the contents of the inscriptions to the people, showing clearly that the local people would not have been able to read them all by themselves.[8] The Karnataka versions of the Minor Rock Edicts are more elaborate in their contents than their counterparts found elsewhere in the subcontinent, prompting an acknowledged authority on Mauryan history to suggest that such explicit statements were necessary in areas that were less comprehensively integrated with the Mauryan Empire.[9] In the circumstances, is it likely that the Minor Rock Edicts from Karnataka are hardly evidence of any significant political control of the Mauryas in that part of the country? Of course, they do suggest a presence of the Mauryan state going beyond just one or more predatory raids.

In this context, the recently discovered fragmentary inscription from Sannathi acquires importance.[10] It was discovered on the pedestal of an idol consecrated in a temple in the Yadgir district in Karnataka. There are a few interesting facts about this inscription. Though it is very fragmentary and highly damaged containing only parts of the XII and XIV Major Rock Edicts, it is striking that the Major Rock Edict XIII is *omitted* and that what are called the Separate Rock Edicts, so far found only in the Kalingan sites, are included there. Similarly, there are interesting peculiarities in points of the linguistics of this record as well. On the basis of these features, I have suggested elsewhere that the region around Sannathi constituted a separate conquest or raid of Aśoka and that he did not want to remind the people so conquered of something which was not exactly pleasant.[11] In other words, what Sannathi indicates are a relatively recent interest and a recent presence of the Mauryas in that region.

Against this background, Aśoka's statement that the chiefdoms of south India, such as the Cōḻa, Pāṇḍya, Cēra and Atiyamān, were his neighbours acquires importance.[12] Interestingly, this statement does not figure in any of the inscriptions from Karnataka, for the Major Rock Edicts in which it appears do not obtain there. Even in Sannathi, where fragments of a few Major Rock Edicts do survive, the possibility is ruled out by the fact that the XIII Rock Edict is omitted. This is not to suggest that Aśoka made a false claim about the extent of his 'empire'. However, one has some reason to subject the sweeping generalizations drawn by historians so far to re-examination.

One way of examining the extent of Karnataka's integration into the Mauryan system is by looking at the archaeological context of the sites of Aśokan inscriptions from Karnataka. Unfortunately, many sites have not been studied from an archaeological point of view. Such sites as have been studied, however, offer interesting results. Foremost among them is Brahmagiri, in the Molakalmuru Taluk in Chitradurga district, about 72 km. to the north-east of Chitradurga and some 50 km. to the south of Bellari. In fact, Brahmagiri forms, together with Siddapura and Jatinga-Rameshwara, part of a single complex, each of these places from where the Minor Rock Edicts of Aśoka have turned up being within the vicinity of one another. M.H. Krishna of the Department of Archaeology of the erstwhile Mysore State carried out excavations in Brahmagiri in 1940.[13] Again, Mortimer Wheeler excavated there in 1947 in a more systematic way.[14]

Interestingly, the granite outcrop on which the inscriptions occur is locally known as *Akṣaraguṇḍu*, literally, the 'Hillock of Letters'. It is believed that the rock with writings on them has magical, healing powers. Men and cattle, afflicted with certain ailments, are administered water used to wash the rock. The archaeological findings of Krishna are not published as thoroughly as they ought to have been. He seems to have been working under a rather obsessive assumption that Brahmagiri was indeed the Isila mentioned in the inscriptions from Siddapura. Wheeler is highly critical of Krishna's findings and rejects his chronology and cultural sequence. Wheeler concentrated his work on the foot of the hillock and identified a sequence of three cultures. The earliest of these, beginning about early first millennium BC, is called the Brahmagiri Stone Axe Culture. This is a crude chalcolithic culture divided into two sub-periods—IA and IB—and draws to about the second century BC. The typical Iron Age-Megalithic culture going on to first century AD follows this culture. After this Period II is that of the Andhra culture, evidence of which is available from first to third centuries AD. What is striking about Brahmagiri is that there is no cultural transition of any violent kind. The cultures overlap smoothly, one interlocking with the other as it were. This shows that the site witnessed a continuous occupation throughout the period from which we have evidence.

Of these three periods, it is obvious that what corresponds chronologically with the Mauryan period is the Brahmagiri Stone Axe Culture. It is characterized by the presence of microliths of ribbon-flake blades, crescents, side-scrappers and blunted-back types and axes of common pointed butt type. The typical mesolithic types such as lunates, burins, triangles and even real crescents are, however, absent from here. An occasional copper object or two also have turned up towards the last phase, making it technically 'chalcolithic'. Even the pottery from this level is interesting. Both sub-periods IA and IB are characterized by handmade pottery. The more prominent one is of a coarse grey fabric, sometimes with a thin slip of the same clay. The dominant type in both sub-periods is of round-bottomed vessel. The larger portion of the shreds indicates crude ceramic techniques, but there is some evidence of polishing the pots, particularly at the upper levels. One also comes across painted and incised pottery, which is characteristic of the Brahmagiri Stone Axe Culture. Post-holes show features of houses or huts.

Another site that has been studied somewhat meticulously is Maski in the Lingasagur Taluk, Raichur district.[15] The ancient site covers a sprawling area of about 50 acres on the Maski *nullah*, a tributary of the Tungabhadra. The site, surrounded by gneissic outcrops on three sides, is ideal for settlement. The one known as the *Durgada Guḍḍa*, literally the 'Hillock of the Fort', on the western side of which is the Aśokan Edict, is the biggest. B.K. Thapar and his team from the Archaeological Survey of India carried out excavations in different trenches in Maski in 1954. The cultural sequence in Maski is not as clear as it is in Brahmagiri. Four cuttings—MSK9, MSK10, MSK11 and MSK12—were made, of which only MSK10 provides a complete sequence and affords evidence of three successive cultures.[16] The lowest level is represented by chalcolithic culture, where there is a break towards the end. The date of this layer, as far as it could be judged from the extant material, is from the early first millennium to fourth century BC. The next phase, represented by the Iron Age-Megalithic culture, covers a period from the second century BC and goes to first century AD. Above this level is what is described as early historical culture, reaching third century AD. Curiously, MSK12 has a deposit of about four and a half feet from natural surface to the present ground level, which represents what the excavator has called the medieval period, i.e. AD 1000 to 1600.

As in the case of Brahmagiri, the period of the Aśokan inscriptions falls either in the chalcolithic or in the interface between the chalcolithic and megalithic horizons in Maski. The equipment consists largely of microliths made of chert, agate, carnelian and opal apart from meagre copper implements. The largest numbers of tools are asymmetrical flakes and parallel-sided blades. Other types such as serrated blades, lunates, trapezes, discoid scrapers worked points and burins (?) are available, though limited in number. The pottery from Maski presents an interesting parallel to Brahmagiri as well except that wheel-thrown pottery too is available in Maski. Two varieties of plain pottery, a dull grey ware and a pinkish buff ware, are known from the earliest layer. Besides, examples of unslipped ware with a mat surface and dull colour are also present. Houses are few, but the post-holes show a pattern similar to Brahmagiri.

Unfortunately, other sites associated with Aśokan inscriptions have not been systematically excavated and studied. Koppal, in whose vicinity are the Gavimatha and Palkigundu inscriptions, has thrown up evidence of ancient habitation sites.[17] So also there are several of the so-called 'ash-mounds', which have been identified as indicating the presence of neolithic cattle-keepers.[18] A few hand axes have been picked up at the site of Nittur, which lies close to Tekkalakotta, the famous Neolithic site.[19] Udegolem, too, falls within the same broad culture complex. There is no information about the other sites except Sannathi where there are Buddhist associations dating from the first century BC.[20]

It thus becomes clear that the general picture of the archaeology of Aśokan sites is largely that of a Neolithic-Chalcolithic horizon, on its way to the Iron Age-Megalithic. In fact, dolmens characteristic of the megalithic culture are described in some parts of Karnataka as *Morera aṅgaḍi*, literally, 'the Mauryas' Shop', although there is no way in which the megaliths and the Mauryas can be connected. It is crucial that no item of the material culture thought to bear the Mauryan signature, as it were, such as the Northern Black Polished Ware, the punch-marked coins and suchlike, has shown itself up in these or other megalithic sites. Does it mean that the Mauryan presence in these areas did not go beyond the inscriptions written in a language and a script which did not make too much sense to the local population? Does it mean that beyond what may have been a temporary, passing presence of a few functionaries of the state, there was nothing that points to a more enduring impact of the Mauryas in these areas, particularly on economy, society and politics? It is important to look at other types of contact and influences from north India during this period before taking up these questions.

One of them that stands out is what is related to trade. In this connection, the privileged position that the *Arthaśāstra* gives to the *Dakṣiṇāpatha*—the 'Route to the South'—is crucial.[21] Kautilya speaks of articles of trade such as pearls, diamonds, conch-shells and plenty of gold.[22] It is curious that Kautilya does not include Karnataka in his list of the sources of gold. Speaking about the varieties of gold and the relative merits of each, Kautilya speaks about gold from places like the Jambū River, Śatakumbha mountain, Hāṭaka, Veṇu, etc.[23] However, evidence of gold from Karnataka from Mauryan times and even earlier is copious. As many as thirteen gold-working sites have been identified near Maski.[24] The rich gold mine of Hatti, where evidence of gold working is available from the eighth century BC, is in the neighbouring Raichur district, although it is not clear whether Hāṭaka has anything to do with the Hatti mines.[25] In any case, as a young researcher has stated, the name of the place, 'Suvarnagiri', literally the 'Mound of Gold', mentioned in the Siddapura and Brahmagiri edicts and thought of as the 'provincial capital' of the Mauryan state in south India, was 'both a fact and a metaphor'.[26] These sites are about 80 km. away from centres of mining copper and silver such as Chandravalli,[27] Kurubarmardikere,[28] Ingaldhal[29] and Malchite.[30] Perhaps the route via the river Vegavati and its tributary Chinna Hagari may have been taken, although these are not navigable to any great extent. Even to this day, in any case, the Chitradurga Copper Company extracts copper from Ingaldhal. Apart from these centres, evidence of ancient gold working comes from Honnemardi, Kotemardi and Bodimardi in Chitradurga district, not far from these sites of Aśokan edicts.[31] Koppal, the newly formed district in which are found the Gavimatha and Palkigundu inscriptions, is rich in ash- and cinder-mounds.[32] There is evidence of copper working in these sites from the first millennium BC.[33] Bellari district, from which the Nittur and Udegolem inscriptions have been discovered, too is rich in ancient copper working sites. Old copper mines are known in Thinthini in the Gulbarga district, not far from the site of the Maski inscriptions.[34] However, it is interesting that there is no evidence in this period of gold working in Kolar, the richest of Karnataka's gold mines; nor has any Aśokan inscription turned up anywhere near that place.

This discussion reveals that the contacts that northern India had with the south was less part of a political, imperial project than related to trade and commerce. That will raise an interesting question about what are taken as references to 'Mauryan-Dravidian political-military clashes'[35] figuring in early Tamil literature. In a song included in the collection of poems concerned with love, Mamulanar makes the following statement:

> along the hills adorned with waterfalls and roads cut for the smooth passage of the wheels of the decorated chariots of the masters of cavalry, the Vampa Moriyar, possessing the victorious banner and chariots of cyclonic speed, engaged in destroying enemies and sounding war-drums at Potiyil where ancient banyan trees spread out their branches, moved against the chieftains of Mokur for having refused to bow to the Kośar.[36]

Most of the points made in the interpretation of this passage are equivocal. They include questions of the identity of the Vampa Moriyar, Kośar and Potiyil, the date of the poem, the factuality or otherwise of the statement, and, above all, the implications of the statement itself. If several possibilities can be taken to constitute a certainty, this can indeed be taken as evidence of a Mauryan 'conquest' of the Tamil country, which, for M.G.S. Narayanan, is an 'emotion-packed experience near enough in space and time'.[37] The Kośar, who are taken by him as a people belonging to the Tulu region on the West Coast, are forced to Mokur in the south-east, in the High Ranges of the Western Ghats. The introduction of big chariots into the south is, for no valid reason, attributed to the 'Nandas and Mauryas', although the claim of the conquest itself is limited to the Mauryas. 'A Mauryan invasion of Mokur, not far from Maski, on the Mysore-Tamilnadu border, does not', to Narayanan, 'at all appear to be far-fetched';[38] but taking Maski in the Raichur district to the Karnataka-Tamilnadu border *is* far-fetched! What are taken to be references to the wealth of the Nandas of Pataliputra,[39] which in reality is a usual motif in the much later Puranic lore about the Nandas, are adduced as evidence of the 'thorough knowledge that the poets had with those North Indian situations and the nearness in space and time'. The name or title of the chief of Elimalai, Nannan, is taken as 'suggestive' of an 'association with Nandas of Pataliputra',[40] although contemporary sources and later traditions controvert this suggestion.[41] So also, the titles of the Cēra chiefs, namely, *Vānavarampan* and *Imayavarampan*, are taken as verbatim Tamil translations of the Aśokan title, *Devanampiya*. The derivation is not very safe since the alveolar *ṉ*, occurring in the middle of a word, does not get transformed into labial *m*. Thus, *vaṉpulam* does not become *vampulam*; *eṉpatu* does not become *empatu*. Therefore, *aṉpu* ('love') and *aṉpan* ('beloved') will not get transformed into *ampu* and *ampan* respectively.[42] Further, the argument that this was done by poets stated to be 'meticulous and fastidiously perfectionist in their use of words'[43] fails to inspire confidence. For, early Tamil literature is recognized as oral poetry employing all the techniques at the disposal of such composers, including the use of motifs, stock phrases, formulaic expressions, etc., where choice of words is not entirely in the hands of the poets.[44] Moreover, the argument that this is the only possible explanation as it is a title conferred on or used by the Cēras alone is self-defeating as it can cut both ways.

All this would show that the picture of Mauryan political presence in south India is overdrawn. It should be recognized that in terms of the level of political organization, there was no comparison between the two regions. Nothing is known about the level of political evolution that the regions of Karnataka had reached at his period. In the case of the Tamil-Malayalam regions, it is clear that the Cēra-Cōḻa-Pāṇḍya lineages mentioned in early Tamil literature bore no comparison with the refined imperial polity of the Mauryas. Nor did this part of the country see any material cultural penetration from the north.

However, there is no denying the fact that there was considerable influence of the culture of the Mauryan state in south India. This, as I suggested earlier, came in the wake of trade contacts and the spread of religious movements represented by Jain-Buddhist elements, about both of which there is considerable information. Jain-Buddhist influence is clearly identified in contemporary Tamil literature and the architecture of a later period. One of the most significant and lasting of these influences is, however, the Tamil Brahmi script, an improvisation of Brahmi, the script of Aśokan edicts. Brahmi, originally designed to write languages of the Indo-Aryan family, is adapted to represent Dravidian sounds such as *ḷa*, *ḻa*, *ṟa* and *ṉa*, which are alien to that family. This Tamil Brahmi was later to develop into the medieval scripts such as *Vaṭṭeḻuttu* and *Kōleḻuttu* and modern scripts such as Tamil and Malayalam, while Brahmi itself gave rise to Grantha. They are enduring monuments of the Mauryan cultural presence in the Deep South. This Tamil-Brahmi script bears the sobriquet, 'Cave Script'. They are found on rocks in caves, distributed on major trade routes in south India, and record the donation of the cave to the monks of Jain and Buddhist persuasions, made by chiefs or merchants. These records speak of associations of merchants, the *nigamas*, a word, and a thing, with clear north Indian origins in the pre-Mauryan period. Similarly, contemporary Tamil literature speaks about merchandise as *cāttu*, from Sansrit *sārtha*. The statements in the *Arthaśāstra* referred to earlier acquire significance in this context.

At another level and in a slightly later period, Kauṭilya makes his presence felt in the political ideas and institutions of south India from time to time and in various ways. Inscriptions from the seventh century onwards, giving evidence of Pallava rule in northern Tamilnadu and Pāṇḍyan rule in southern Tamilnadu, bear out the influence of the teacher in the organization of the newly evolved states in those regions. We see this Kauṭilyan influence taken to its logical extension when we come to the period of the Cēra kingdom on the West Coast. The details contained in the Syrian Christian copper plates, which grant land and certain privileges to the church of Tarsa at Kollam,[45] are almost as if they are copied from the *Arthaśāstra*. On the eastern side of the Ghats, we see Kauṭilya being explicitly invoked by the *sabha* of Uyyakoṇḍān Tirumalai. The *sabha* decides on a request of the masons to declare their caste status and does it by means of a *vyavasthā*, where the list of authorities quoted is headed by Kauṭilya.[46] The crowning instance of it all is perhaps a full-length translation of the *Arthaśāstra* into Malayalam in about the twelfth–thirteenth centuries.[47] This indicates the influence that the text had on state and society and the use to which it was put.

Our argument is that, notwithstanding the doubtful nature of the Mauryan political hegemony or even presence in south India, and the near-total absence of any penetration of Mauryan material culture, there is unimpeachable evidence of Mauryan influence in other aspects of south India. To be sure, the Mauryan dynasty had hardly any role in this. But the ideas and institutions, brought in the wake of trade and Jain-Buddhist religious expansion, did take deep roots in south India. This opening up also guided political together with social and religious ideas and institutions, if at a point in time later than that of the Mauryan Empire itself. This would mean, in a word, that what is perceived as the Mauryan influence in south Indian state and society will have to be looked at as post-Mauryan in date. This would also raise a larger question about the nature of the Mauryan state in general. In a historiographical tradition which was used to looking at the Mauryan state and society as a 'uniform structure' with 'complete control' over all that was within the 'territory', the kind of statements that we have seen in the writings of earlier scholars is natural. But when we look at them as a system trying to relate itself with different regions at different levels of development in different ways, then our submission will make better sense. The relationship itself was not uniform or static.

NOTES

1. Y. Subbarayalu, Presidential Address, Section V, in *Proceedings of the Indian History Congress*, Burdwan, 1983.
2. For example, K.A. Nilakanta Sastri, *A History of South India: From Prehistoric Times to the Fall of Vijayanagar*, 1966; repr., Bombay: Oxford University Press, 1971, pp. 88–9.
3. M.G.S. Narayanan, 'The Mauryan Problem in Sangam Works in Historical Perspective', in *Proceedings of the Indian History Congress*, Bhubaneswar, 1977, reproduced in Narayanan, *Foundations of South Indian Society and Culture*, New Delhi: Bharatiya Book Corp., 1994, p. 69.
4. For the epigraphical material, see inscriptions of Aśoka from Siddapura, Jatinga-Rameshwara, Brahmagiri, Palkigundu, Gavimatha, Maski, Nittur, Udegolem and Sannathi. For a recent study, C. Girisha, 'The Mauryan Presence in South India', unpublished M.Phil. Dissertation, Department of History, Mangalore University, 1998. For references in Tamil literature, Narayanan, 'The Mauryan Problem in Sangam Works in Historical Perspective'. For references in the *Arthaśāstra*, 7.12.22–5.
5. See n. 4 in this chapter. Any map of the distribution of Aśokan edicts would show that the thickest cluster of Aśokan edicts is in Karnataka.
6. B.L. Rice discovered the record. Rice, *Epigraphia Carnatica*, vol. II, Bangalore: Mysore Government Central Press, 1923, p. 2 ff.; E. Hultzsch, *Corpus Inscriptionum Indicarum*, vol. I, Oxford, Printed

for the Government of India by the Clarendon Press, 1925, pp. XXVI, 166 ff.

7. B.L. Rice, *Edicts of Aśoka in Mysore*, Bangalore: Mysore Government Central Press, 1892. The engraver Cipitaka has written the word *lipikarena* in Kharoshthi after giving his name at Brahmagiri and Siddapura. Is it a case of his being more at home in Kharoshthi, showing off his knowledge of other scripts, or simple confusion indicating scant knowledge of both?
8. Nittur, Boulder No. 2, l. 1, *Indian Archaeology: A Review, 1977–8*, ed. B.K. Thapar, New Delhi: Archaeological Survey of India, 1980, p. 63.
9. Romila Thapar, *Aśoka and the Decline of the Mauryas*, revd. edn. with an Afterword, Delhi: Oxford University Press, 1999, p. 276.
10. I.K. Sharma and J. Varaprasada Rao, *Early Brahmi Inscriptions from Sannathi*, Delhi: Harman Publishing House, 1993. I have used the version of K.V. Ramesh, 'The Aśokan Inscriptions at Sannathi', *Indian Historical Review*, vol. 14, nos. 1–2, 1987–8, pp. 36–42.
11. Kesavan Veluthat, 'The Sannathi Inscriptions and the Questions They Raise', in *Proceedings of the Indian History Congress*, Calicut, 1999, pp. 1081–7. Romila Thapar concurs with this view. She writes: 'The recent discovery of Ashokan edicts at Sannathi in Karnataka, similar to those found at Kalinga in Orissa and issued after the Kalinga campaign, raises the question of whether this region was conquered later by Ashoka.' Romila Thapar, *The Penguin History of Early India: From the Origins to AD 300*, London: Penguin Books, 2001, p. 178.
12. Major Rock Edict Nos. 2 and 13.
13. Mysore Archaeological Department, *Annual Report for the Year 1940*, Mysore, 1941; *Annual Report for the Year 1942*, Mysore, 1943.
14. The reports appear in *Ancient India*, no. 4, Delhi, 1947–8. See also the comments of V.D. Krishnaswami, 'Progress in Prehistory', *Ancient India*, no. 9, 1953.
15. *Ancient India*, no. 13, p. 35 ff.
16. For details, see ibid.
17. *Ancient India*, no. 4, p. 11; no. 13, p. 11.
18. Raymond Allchin, *Neolithic Cattle-keepers of South India: A Study of Deccan Ashmounds*, Cambridge: Cambridge University Press, 1963, passim.
19. *Indian Archaeology: A Review, 1963–64*, ed. A. Ghosh, Archaeological Survey of India, Government of India, 1967, p. 24.
20. *Indian Archaeology: A Review, 1966–67*, ed. M.N. Deshpande, Archaeological Survey of India, Government of India, 1975, p. 29.

21. *Arthaśāstra*, 7.12.22–5.
22. Ibid.
23. *Arthaśāstra*, 2.13, 3.
24. *Ancient India*, no. 13, p. 10.
25. Initial *ha* does not obtain in Kannada till about the twelfth century, when *pa* in the beginning of words starts getting replaced by *ha*. I thank Dr. Manu Devadevan for clarifying this.
26. Girisha, 'The Mauryan Presence in South India'. A place called 'Kanakagiri', which means the same as 'Suvarnagiri', in the vicinity of the find-spot of these inscriptions is presented as a likely candidate for identification as Suvarnagiri.
27. *Ancient India*, no. 4, p. 180 ff.
28. B.M. Pande and B.D. Chattopadhyaya, eds., *Archaeology and History*, vol. I, Delhi: Agam Kala Prakashan, 1987, p. 375.
29. R. Shankar, 'How Old are the Old Mine Workings of Ingaldhal (Karnataka)?', *The Journal of the Geological Society of India*, vol. 33, no. 1, 1989, pp. 64–70.
30. Pande and Chattopadhyaya, *Archaeology and History.*
31. Ibid.
32. *Ancient India*, no. 13, p. 11.
33. Pande and Chattopadhyaya, *Archaeology and History,* p. 397.
34. Shankar, 'Old Mine Workings of Ingaldhal (Karnataka)'.
35. Narayanan, 'The Mauryan Problem in Sangam Works in Historical Perspective', p. 70.
36. *Akananuru*, 251. See also translation by Narayanan, 'The Mauryan Problem in Sangam Works in Historical Perspective', p. 70, and his interesting comment in p. 79n2.
37. Narayanan, 'The Mauryan Problem in Sangam Works in Historical Perspective', p. 72.
38. Ibid.
39. Ibid., p. 76.
40. Ibid., p. 74.
41. Ibid., p. 81n23. The literature referred to here is enough to reject any Nannan-Nanda association.
42. I am grateful to Professor D. Murthy for discussing this point with me at great length.
43. Narayanan, 'The Mauryan Problem in Sangam Works in Historical Perspective', p. 76.
44. For early Tamil poetry as oral composition showing all these features, see K. Kailasapathy, *Tamil Heroic Poetry*, Oxford: Clarendon Press, 1968.

45. T.A. Gopinatha Rao, *Travancore Archaeological Series*, vol. II, nos. 9 (ii & iii), Trivandrum: Government Press, 1920, pp. 62–85.
46. J.D.M. Derrett, 'Two Inscriptions Concerning the Status of Kammalas and the Application of Dharmasastras', in *Professor K.A. Nilakantha Sastri 80th Birthday Felicitation Volume*, Madras, 1971; Kesavan Veluthat, 'The *Sabha* and *Parishad* in Early Medieval South India: Correlation of Epigraphic and Dharmasastraic Evidences', *Tamil Civilization*, vol. III, nos. 2&3, June and September 1985, pp. 75–82, takes up for discussion many other situations where Kautilya and other authorities are invoked.
47. K. Sambasiva Sastri and V.A. Ramaswami Sastri, eds., *Bhasa Kautaliyam*, 3 vols.; repr., Trivandrum, 1972–3.

CHAPTER 3

Making the Best of a Bad Bargain

The Brighter Side of *Kaliyuga*

ONE OF THE MAJOR contributions of Professor R.S. Sharma towards the understanding of the historical process in early India is the clarity he provided in relation to its early medieval period. He posited the notion of Indian feudalism with considerable empirical control and theoretical rigour, and went on sharpening his tools of analysis and refining the framework further and further. He showed a readiness to re-examine his earlier position by looking at the evidence afresh with newer and newer questions. A significant result of it was his interpretation of the descriptions of Kali Age in the early *Purāṇa*s and other texts.[1] He showed that the accounts of the four *yugas* and the progressive deterioration of *dharma* in each were evidence enough to show the changing nature of Indian society and its self-perception. In the course of elaborating this, he demonstrated—with the help of unimpeachable evidence and impeccable logic—that the period of the early Purāṇas that contain these references elaborately for the first time, i.e. the third and fourth centuries of the Common Era after the chronology of R.C. Hazra, represented a period of social crisis. He enumerated the features of the Kali Age as 'mixing of *varṇas* or *varṇasaṃkara*, hostility between śūdras and brāhmaṇas, refusal of vaiśyas to pay and sacrifice [*sic*], oppression of people with taxes, widespread threat and robbery, insecurity of family and property, destruction of *yogakṣema*, growing importance of wealth over ritual status, and dominance of *mleccha* princes'.[2] Sharma saw this as representing a social crisis, which was among the causative factors behind the emergence of a feudal formation in India. He also drew our attention to the strong coercive measures recommended in the prescriptive texts of the time in order to meet this crisis. Coercion, he noted, was also coupled with concessions.[3]

This was a major breakthrough in Indian historiography. Following him, scholars elaborated on this point and identified the social crisis as being at the root of the transition from the ancient to the medieval, or from 'antiquity to middle ages' in Indian history. B.N.S. Yadava, in an empirically rich essay, brought out further evidence of an almost pathological fear of the Kali Age in the Purāṇic and other texts.[4] He dated the maturing of the forces signifying this transition to the period between the sixth and the ninth centuries of the Common Era. Historians have ever since taken any mention of the term 'Kali' in an inscription or a text as representing a 'social crisis'. The rhetorical formulae in the courtly expressions to the effect that this king rescued the earth from the evils of the Kali Age or that that king was always ready to revive dharma which had suffered a setback on account of Kali were read in this manner.[5] Going a step further, a historian of south India even went to the extent of saying that since there is a description of a Kaḷabhra king as 'the Kali king' (*kaḷappiraṉennum kali araśan*) in an inscription, the Kaḷabhra Interregnum in south Indian history was a 'total crisis' which brought about a transition in the history of south India.[6] In reality, however, the whole thesis of a 'Kaḷabhra Interregnum' is based on slender evidence of doubtful validity, and to speak of certain 'ubiquitous enemies of civilization' who conquered the whole of Tamil-speaking south India and held the Pāṇḍyas, Cēras and Cōḻas under captivity will be against evidence.[7] There have been other, more sober assessments of the problem from the point of view of regions.[8] In any case, it must be said that Sharma's thesis on *kaliyuga* has been an extremely significant intervention in Indian historiography. It explained the morbid fears about an age to come, made in the future tense, as actually representing realities of the present in which the authors of these sections of the Purāṇas were located. What was taken as fears about the future was shown as anxieties about the present, when the social order was being seriously threatened by a number of factors. It is an indication of the importance of the theme that there has been some criticism of the thesis as well, as, for example, in the writings of B.D. Chattopadhyaya.[9]

The purpose of this chapter is to read the evidence further. It is not in a mood to pick holes in the formulations of the great master—perish the thought! On the contrary, I presume to follow his advice in approaching sources: *āge paḍho*—'read on'. I believe that by doing so I am paying a greater tribute to his memory than by repeating his own statements as a formula—which, to my mind, is more an insult than a tribute to any scholar.

There are statements in the texts including the Purāṇas that represent the *kaliyuga* in a colour entirely different from that which Sharma and Yadava have highlighted. In fact, one starts wondering whether the pathological descriptions of *kaliyuga* that our attention has been drawn to and the idyllic image that these statements present are about the same subject. For instance, *Jñānappāna* ('The Song of Wisdom'), a sixteenth-century Vaiṣṇava devotional poem in Malayalam by Pūntānam Nampūtiri, states unequivocally and cryptically that 'Of the four Yugas, this Kali is the best!' He has his reasons:

> How easy it is to win eternal rest!
> No great effort do you require, no pains
> Except only to say his holy names. . . .

The poet goes on to say that even those:

> Who live during the Yugas three
> They know they cannot possibly be free
> To Bhāratam during the Kali age
> They join their hands in salute, pay homage:
> 'To live there, even as a blade of grass
> 'We were not fortunate enough, alas!
> 'We lacked the worth to attain even this
> 'To come to birth by the high road to bliss,
> 'To all humans who dwell in Bhāratam
> 'And to Kali, we make salutation.[10]

His contemporary, Melputtūr Nārāyaṇa Bhaṭṭa, a legend of a scholar and poet from Kerala, is more elaborate in his devotional poem, the

Nārāyaṇīyam. In giving details of the form and complexion that Viṣṇu would take in different *yugas* and the ways in which he can be worshipped in each, he says that Viṣṇu takes a bluish hue in *kaliyuga* and that people worship him in that age by singing *saṅkīrtanas* ('psalms'). He goes on: 'Hail Kali Age, when people can please God by effortless means like singing psalms and suchlike. Even those who are born in Tretā, Kṛta, etc., desire birth in the Kali Age.' The poet also reports that King Parīkṣit had, long ago, drawn his sword to kill the merciless Kali, an enemy of dharma; but he did not kill him because he realized the truth (of Kali Age), as worshipping god yields immediate results in that age (i.e. *kaliyuga*).[11]

The paeans of *kaliyuga* are sung not by just two Nampūtiris from Kerala. The *Bhāgavatapurāṇa*, of which the *Nārāyaṇīyam* is an able paraphrase, is more elaborate. Queried about the form, complexion and mode of worship of Viṣṇu in different ages, Karabhājana, one of the nine yogins, says that Viṣṇu takes different names, forms and complexion in Kṛta, Tretā, *Dvāpara* and Kali, and is worshipped differently. After explaining these details in relation to the first three ages, he dwells upon *kaliyuga* at some length.

> In the age of Kali, O, listen, the intelligent ones worship the dark-hued, splendorous, Kṛṣṇa with all his entourage by means of *saṅkīrtanayajña*s. . . . Hari, the Lord of Welfare, is worshipped in each age appropriate to it. The discerning ones, who know the essence [of things], always prefer the age of Kali when just by singing psalms all desired things can be earned, when ultimate peace is possible, and when the cycle of birth and death is destroyed. In [the age of] Kali will be born those who are engaged in [the worship of] Nārāyaṇa here and there, more in the Draviḍa country.

In short, Viṣṇu will protect all such as would worship at his feet.[12]

In *Viṣṇupurāṇa*, considered to be earlier than the *Bhāgavata*, there is a similar section. After detailing the evils of the Kali Age to Maitreya, Parāśara told him that Vyāsa, however, had a different take on the subject. A few sages had gone up to Vyāsa to clear their doubts. They saw him bathing in the waters of Gaṅgā. They heard him chanting 'śūdras are good; Kali is good, women are good', as he was emerging from the water. When he was finished with his ablutions, the sages went up to him and asked: 'Sir, you were repeating over and over again that Kali is good, śūdras are good, women are good.

We desire to hear the secret of it all.' Smiling, Vyāsa said: 'Yes, I will tell you why I said "good, good".'

He told them that good deeds yield easier and more immediate results in *kaliyuga*.

> What takes ten years in Kṛta, ten *ayana*s (half-years) in Tretā, ten months in Dvāpara, it takes only ten days and nights in Kali. What brāhmaṇas gain as the result of *tapas*, *brahmacarya*, *japa*, etc. [all] men gain in Kali—hence I said Kali is good. What [people] achieve by meditation in Kṛta, performance of *yajña*s in Tretā, and *arcanā* in Dvāpara, they achieve by singing psalms in Kali. Men achieve great heights of *dharma* in [the age of] of Kali with the least effort and hence I am happy with Kali.

He concluded: 'with a little effort, *dharma*s can be gained in Kali'. It is, however, not as if his praise of Kali is unqualified: 'This is the only good thing about Kali, the most evil [of ages].'[13]

These sentiments are adumbrated in Purāṇas like the *Matsya* and *Brahmāṇḍa*. Speaking about the places considered holy in different ages, the *Matsyapurāṇa* says that Gaṅgā is especially holy in Kali [*yuga*] as Naimiṣa is in Kṛta, Puṣkara in Tretā, and Kurukṣetra in Dvāpara.[14] This is elaborated in *Nārayaṇīyam*, which prescribes effortless means of pleasing Him in the Kali Age.[15] The *Matsyapurāṇa* goes on to say: 'Worship Gaṅgā, particularly at Prayāga. There is no other medicine, O king, available in the terrible *kaliyuga*.' Similarly, the *Brahmāṇḍapurāṇa* says: 'Men achieve full realisation (*siddhi*) then [i.e. in *kaliyuga*]. . . . *Dharma* can be attained in a day in Kali, which takes a year in Tretā and a month in Dvāpara.'[16] There are similar statements in other texts as well.

This apparent contradiction becomes starker and starker when we go forward in time. Earlier texts like *Matsyapurāṇa* and *Brahmāṇḍapurāṇa* have only suggestions to these positive aspects of the Kali Age. By the time we come to the *Viṣṇupurāṇa* and *Bhāgavatapurāṇa*, the statements are unequivocal. Kali is represented as the best of ages, and even those who are born in other, supposedly better, *yugas* desire to be born in *kaliyuga*. It is this latter representation that presents the starkest contrast. What is interesting is that many of these contradictory statements follow one another in quick succession. The representation of *kaliyuga* as the darkest of all ages on the one side and the best of all the four ages on the other, in the same texts, is a matter of curiosity. How do we reconcile with, and explain, this dual representation of the same subject in diametrically opposite ways?

The answer seems to lie in the appeal to religion, particularly *bhakti*, that too of Viṣṇu, who is the hero of the Kali Age. *Kaliyuga* is celebrated, in all these descriptions, on account of the fact that *bhakti* yields easier and more immediate results in that age. The different forms and hues that Viṣṇu would take in the four *yugas* and the mode in which he can be worshipped in each are described in great detail. It is in *kaliyuga* that he can be worshipped by the easiest mode—such as singing psalms and repeating his names. There were other modes of worship as well, such as fasting on *ekādaśī* and other days, smearing sandalwood paste and *gopī* on one's person, worshipping *sālagrāma*, chanting the names of Viṣṇu, reading and listening to the *Gītā* and the Purāṇas, etc., apart from undertaking pilgrimages, bathing in the Gaṅgā, and so on. It is in *kaliyuga* that the more important of the *bhaktas* would take birth, particularly in the Draviḍa country. In fact, Melputtūr Nārāyaṇa Bhaṭṭa, in his *Nārāyaṇīyam*, goes a step further: 'O Lord, please count me as among them.'[17]

To be sure, these statements in favour of *kaliyuga* are not unqualified. Nearly all the texts quoted here are convinced that Kali is an enemy of dharma, that Kali is merciless, and that Kali is terrible. *Kaliyuga* is the most evil of all ages. Thus, what is presented as good about it is in spite of its evils, on account of the fact that it is in the age of Kali that *bhakti* and the modes of worship associated with it can yield immediate results. The best way to understand and explain these statements is to see them as exhortations to make use of the possibilities offered by *bhakti*, which are the sole redeeming features in an otherwise miserable period, as 'the sigh of the oppressed creature, the heart of a heartless world, and the soul of soulless conditions'.[18] The favourable light in which śūdras and women are presented in the *Viṣṇupurāṇa* is to be placed in this context.[19]

In a joint study of the Tamil Bhakti Movement that M.G.S. Narayanan and I had undertaken more than three and a half decades ago,[20] we had argued that the movement was, contrary to the general impression so far, seeking to reflect and legitimize the emerging social order. We had shown that rather than protesting against inequality, *bhakti* helped in making the inequality and the consequent suffering palatable by creating an illusion of equality. That study was in relation to a different spatio-temporal context; but many of the objective conditions obtaining in both situations seem to be comparable. One of the features that make the Kali Age superior to all other ages in the descriptions we saw is that it enables the devotee to realize god by 'effortless' (*niryatna*) means. While elaborate rituals were prescribed for earlier ages, simply singing psalms would do the job in Kali. The other modes of worship prescribed for Kali Age, too, are rather 'effortless'. This indicates two things in worship: (*a*) a reduced emphasis on ritual to the point of its repudiation, and (*b*) emphasis on other inexpensive and effortless means. Both are of importance. In this context, the knowledge that the *Bhāgavatapurāṇa* has of the *bhaktas* from the Draviḍa country is relevant. In fact, there have been arguments to the effect that the *Bhāgavatapurāṇa* is heavily influenced by the Tamil *bhakti* tradition.[21]

In a condition characterized by 'mixing of *varṇas* or *varṇasaṃkara*, hostility between śūdras and brāhmaṇas, refusal of vaiśyas to pay and sacrifice [*sic*], oppression of people with taxes, widespread threat and robbery, insecurity of family and property, destruction of *yogakṣema*, growing importance of wealth over ritual status, and dominance of *mleccha* princes', performance of rituals, Vedic or Tāntric, was next to impossible, a condition that had been lamented by the writers on the horrors of *kaliyuga*. What was possible in the circumstances was to gracefully find alternatives to the impracticable rituals. In the place of the complicated rituals which would take very long to both perform and yield results, simpler means like *saṅkīrtanas* and chanting the names of Viṣṇu were found acceptable, as they were relatively inexpensive without requiring the service of those who are unwilling to cooperate, and yielded quick results. Here it will be interesting to ask why they rejected ritual or at least emphasized on minimalist ritual, least effort and fast service. Was this characteristic of a social churning perhaps much greater than has been recognized? In any case, it goes totally against the orthodox tradition which was characterized by extensive ritual, much effort and a long time period.

It seems there was also an effort to justify the non-Vedic forms of worship and the merit of what has been described as 'Purāṇic Hinduism', even while it was insisted that the Vedas are the ultimate source of authority. Was this a response to the orthodoxy of Vedic Brāhmaṇism that did not approve of this kind of worship to begin with and then had to make concessions to, and finally accommodate, it? This seems probable. The *Bhāgavatapurāṇa* puts into the mouth of Āvirhotra, another of the nine yogins, that 'it is only by performing rituals prescribed by the Vedas—*vedoktameva kurvāṇaḥ*—that one achieves realization—*labhate siddhiṃ*'.[22] *Narayaṇīyam* is clearer: 'all rituals have been prescribed in the Vedas. Perform them alone, dedicated to god.'[23] But the concessions to the non-Vedic forms of worship of the Purāṇic Hindu variety are not far to seek. In a relatively lengthy discourse that follows quickly, the same Āvirhotra gives elaborate details of worshipping Hari through the medium of idols.[24] *Nārāyaṇīyam*, again, makes this clearer. 'Even other forms of rituals', it continues from the verse quoted here, 'are good enough to gain god's pleasure'.[25]

This had an added advantage. The form of worship invented for the changed situations was inclusive. It created an illusion of equality. With a large number of stories in the Purāṇas about people of all kinds of origins attaining great heights by singing psalms and chanting the names of god, the doors of religion were thrown open even to women and śūdras, who were always mentioned together and regarded as less than equal to the rest of society.[26] Thus, when *Viṣṇupurāṇa* says 'śūdras are good, women are good' along with '*kali* is good', this is what is meant: giving them the feeling that they are not any more despised. This also helped in accommodating newer sections of population into the fold of Purāṇic Hinduism, a new religion that was developing by this time. The śūdras, to be sure, remained śūdras and women remained women, with no change in their status whatsoever in the real world. It only worsened, if anything. In fact, śūdras are stated to be good because they would be 'keen to serve the twice-born'—*dvijaśuśrūṣātatparāḥ*. So also, women are good because they would 'serve their husbands with ease'—*anāyāsāt patiśuśrūṣayā*.[27] But the illusion of equality that was created by the ideology of *bhakti* propagated by these texts went a long way in helping them to make suffering sweet and acceptable. The theories of *karma* and *punarjanma* were always there for them to take solace in. At the very least, the upper sections of society told themselves and others that by creating such a picture, people accepted it that way.

In other words, these positive statements in the Purāṇas about the Kali Age, made almost in the same breath as the expression of fears of the age, are part of an ideological apparatus to meet the situation.

R.S. Sharma has drawn our attention to the strong coercive measures, coupled with some concessions, which were intended to meet the situation of crisis.[28] Another, not insignificant, means can be identified in *bhakti*, i.e. the ideological apparatus of religion. When the pied piper's pipe accompanied the slave driver's whip, the former seems to have worked better than the latter.

NOTES

1. R.S. Sharma, 'The Kali Age: A Period of Social Crisis', in *India: History and Thought* (*Essays in Honour of Professor A.L. Basham*), ed. S.N. Mukherjea, Calcutta: Subarnarekha, 1982, reproduced in D.N. Jha, *The Feudal Order: State, Society and Ideology in Early Medieval India*, Delhi: Manohar, 2000, pp. 61–78.
2. Ibid., p. 63.
3. Ibid., pp. 70–3.
4. B.N.S. Yadava, 'The Accounts of the Kali Age and the Social Transition from Antiquity to Middle Ages', *Indian Historical Review*, vol. V, nos. 1–2, July 1978–January 1979, reproduced in Jha, *The Feudal Order*, pp. 79–120.
5. D.N. Jha, 'Editor's Introduction', in Jha, *The Feudal Order*, pp. 8–10.
6. Rajan Gurukkal, 'Non-Brahmana Resistance to the Expansion of Brahmadeyas: The Early Pandyan Experience', in *Proceedings of the Indian History Congress*, Annamalainagar, 1984; Gurukkal, 'Early Social Formation of South India and its Transitional Processes', in *Essays on Indian History and Culture: Felicitation Volume to Professor B. Sheikh Ali*, ed. H.V. Sreenivasamurthy, B. Surendra Rao, Kesavan Veluthat and S.A. Bari, New Delhi: Mittal Publications, 1990; Gurukkal, *The Kerala Temple and Early Medieval Agrarian System*, Sukapuram: Vallathol Vidyapeetham, 1992, p. 27, etc., Gurukkal seems to have since modified his position slightly. See the following sentences which summarize his later reflections on the theme: '. . . an interregnum labeled after the Kalabhras. Actually the Kalabhra episode is based on weak evidence, but that is enough for the construct of an invasion. It hardly explains anything, for a predatory march would not be enough to usher in major socio-economic and political changes. An invasion thesis might do for explaining the disappearance of the chiefdoms. . . . There were a series of radical transformations at the fundamental level causing discontinuity.' Rajan Gurukkal, *Social Formations of Early South India*, New Delhi: Oxford University Press, 2012, p. 214.

7. I have rejected the idea of a 'Kaḷabhra Interregnum', and the thesis of a 'total crisis' based on it, in my Presidential Address to the Indian History Congress, reproduced in Kesavan Veluthat, *The Early Medieval in South India*, New Delhi: Oxford University Press, 2012.
8. B.P. Sahu, 'The Conception of the Kali Age in Early India: A Regional Perspective', reproduced in Sahu, *The Changing Gaze*, Delhi: Oxford University Press, 2013, pp. 46–60.
9. B.D. Chattopadhyaya, 'State and Society in North India: Fourth to Twelfth Century', in *Recent Perspectives of Early Indian History*, ed. Romila Thapar, Bombay: Popular Prakashan, 1995, pp. 330–1; Chattopadhyaya, *The Making of Early Medieval India*, New Delhi: Oxford University Press, 1993, pp. 13–14; Chattopadhyaya, 'Change through Continuity: Notes Towards an Understanding of the Transition to Early Medieval India', in *Society and Ideology in India: Essays in Honour of Professor R.S. Sharma*, ed. D.N. Jha, Delhi: Munshiram Manoharlal, 1997, pp. 135–61. Jha, 'Editor's Introduction', pp. 8–10, has taken up these points made by Chattopadhyaya.
10. Pūntānam, 'Jñānappāna', in *Puntanam and Melpattur: Two Measures of Bhakti*, tr. Vijay Nambisan, New Delhi: Penguin, 2009, pp. 58–9.
11. *Nārāyaṇīyam, daśaka* 92. vv. 5–6. http://gretil.sub.uni-goettingen.de/gretil/1_sanskr/5_poetry/2_kavya/narayniu.htm

    After stating that god can be realized by just singing psalms in the Kali Age, the poet says:

    so'yam kāleyakālo jayati muraripo yatra saṅkīrtanādyair-
    niryatnenaiva mārgairakhilada na cirāt tvatprasādam bhajante
    jātāstretākṛtādāviha kalisamaye sambhavam kāmayante . . . 6

    bhaktāstāvat kalau syur dramilabhuvi tato bhūriśastatra coccaiḥ
    kāverīm tāmraparṇīm anu kila kṛtamālaṃ ca puṇyām pratīcīm
    hā mām apyetadantarbhavamapi ca vibho kiñcidañcadrasam tvay-
    yāśāpāśairnibadhya bhramaya na bhagavan pūraya tvanniṣēvām. 7

    Moreover,

    dṛṣṭvā dharmadruham tam kalim apakaruṇam prāṅmahīkṣit parīkṣid-
    dhantum vyākṛṣṭakhaḍgo'pi na vinihatavān sāravedī guṇāmśāt
    tvatsevādyāśu siddhyēdasadiha na tathā tvatpare caiṣa bhīrur-
    yattu prāgeva rogādibhirapaharate tatra hā śikṣayainam. 8

12. *Bhāgavatapurāṇa*, Gita Press, Gorakhpur, *samvat* 2024 edn., *Skandha* 11, *Adhyāya* 5.

rāja uvāca:
kasmin kāle sa bhagavān kim varṇaḥ kīdṛśo nṛbhiḥ
nāmnā vā kena vidhinā pūjyate tadihocyatām. 19
Karabhājana uvāca:
kṛtam tretā dvāparam ca kalirityeṣu keśavaḥ
nānāvarṇābhidhākāro nānaiva vidhinejyate. 20
kṛtaśuklacaturbāhurjaṭilo valkalāmbaraḥ
kṛṣṇājinopavītākṣān bibhraddaṇḍakamaṇḍalū. 21
manuṣyāstu tadā śāntā nirvairāḥ suhṛdaḥ samāḥ
yajanti tapasā devam śamena ca damena ca. 22
hamsaḥ suparṇo vaikuṇṭho dharmo yogeśvaro 'malaḥ
īśvaraḥ puruṣo 'vyaktaḥ paramātmeti gīyate. 23
tretāyām raktavarṇo 'sau caturbāhustrimekhalaḥ
hiraṇyakeśastrayyātmā sruksruvādyupalakṣaṇaḥ. 24
tam tadā manujam devam sarvadevamayam harim
yajanti vidyayā trayyā dharmiṣṭhā brahmavādinaḥ. 25
viṣṇuryajñaḥ pṛśnigarbhaḥ sarvadeva urukramaḥ
vṛṣākapirjayantaśca urugāya itīryate. 26
dvāpare bhagavāñchyāmaḥ pītavāsā nijāyudhaḥ
śrīvatsādibhiraṅkaiśca lakṣaṇairupalakṣitaḥ. 27
tam tadā puruṣam martyā mahārājoplakṣaṇam
yajanti vedatantrābhyām param jijñāsavo nṛpa. 28.
namaste vāsudevāya namaḥ saṅkarṣaṇāya ca
pradyumnāyāniruddhāya tubhyam bhagavate namaḥ. 29
nārāyaṇāya ṛṣaye puruṣāya mahātmane
viśveśvarāya viśvāya sarvabhūtātmane namaḥ. 30
iti dvāpara urvīśa stuvanti jagadīśvaram
nānātantravidhānena kalāvapi yathā śṛṇu. 31
kṛṣnvarṇam tviṣā kṛṣṇam sāṅgopāṅgāstrapārṣadam
yajñaiḥ saṅkīrtanaprāyaiḥ yajanti hi sumedhasaḥ. 32
dhyeyam sadā paribhavaghnam abhīṣṭadoham
tīrthāspadam śivaviriñcinutam śaraṇyam
bhṛtyārtiham praṇatapālabhavābdhipotam
vande mahāpuruṣa te caraṇāravindam. 33
tyktvā sudustyajasurepsitarājyalakṣmīm
dharmiṣṭha āryavacasā yadagādaraṇyam
māyāmṛgam dayitayepsitamanvadhāvad-
vande mahāpuruṣa te caraṇāravindam. 34
evam yugānurūpābhyām bhagavān yugavartibhiḥ

manujairijyate rājan śreyasāmīśvaro hariḥ. 35
kalim sabhājayantyāryā guṇjñāḥ sārabhāginaḥ
yatra saṅkīrtanēnaiva sarvaḥ svārtho 'bhilabhyate. 36
nahyataḥ paramo lābho dehinām bhrāmyatāmiha
yato vindeta pramām śāntim naśyati samsṛtiḥ. 37
kṛtādiṣu prajā rājan kalāvicchanti sambhavam
kalau khalu bhaviṣyanti nārāyaṇaparāyaṇāḥ. 38
kvacit kvacinmahārāja draviḍeṣu ca bhūriśaḥ
tāmraparṇī nadī yatra kṛtamālā payasviṇī. 39
yē pibanti jalam tāsām manujā manujeśvara
prāyo bhaktā bhagavati vasudeve 'malāśayāḥ. 40
devarṣi-bhūtāpta-nṛṇāṃ pitṝṇāṃ na kiṅkaro nāyam ṛṇī ca rājan
sarvātmanā yaḥ śaraṇaṃ śaraṇyaṃ gato mukundaṃ parihṛtya kartam. 41
svapādamūlam bhajataḥ priyasya tyaktānyabhāvasya hariḥ pareśaḥ
vikarma yaccotpatitaṃ kathañciddhunoti sarvaṃ hṛdi sanniviṣṭaḥ. 42

13. `*Śrīviṣṇupurāṇa*, Gita Press, Gorakhpur, *samvat* 2045 edn., *aṃśa* 6, *adhyāya* 2.

Vyāsa uvāca:

. . . yatkṛte daśabhirvarṣaistretāyām hāyanena tat
dvāpare tacca māsena ahorātreṇa tatkalau. 15
tapaso brahmacaryasya japādeśca phalam dvijāḥ
prāpnoti puruṣastena kaliḥ sādhviti bhāṣitam. 16
dhyāyan kṛte yajan yajñaiḥ tretāyām dvāpare 'rcayan
yadāpnoti tadāpnoti kalau samkīrtya keśavam. 17
dharmotkarṣamatīvātra prāpnoti puruṣaḥ kalau
alpāyāsena dharmajñāstena tuṣṭosmyaham kalau. 18
vratacaryāparairgrāhyā vedāḥ pūrvam dvijātibhiḥ
tatassvadharmasamprāptyair yaṣṭavyam vidhivaddhanaiḥ. 19

14. *Matsyapurāṇa*, Adhyāya 106. http://gretil.sub.uni-goettingen.de/gret_utf.htm#MatsP, accessed 16 November 2016.

kṛte tu naimiṣaṃ kṣetraṃ tretāyāṃ puṣkaraṃ param
dvāpare tu kurukṣetraṃ kalau gaṅgā viśiṣyate. 57
gaṅgāmeva niṣeveta prayāgaṃ tu viśeṣataḥ
nānyatkaliyuge ghore bheṣajaṃ nṛpa vidyate. 58

15. *Nārāyaṇīyam*, daśaka 92, v. 9:

gaṅgā gītā ca gāyatryapi ca tulasikā gopikā candanam tat
sālagrāmābhipūjā parapuruṣa tathaikādaśī nāmavarṇā
etānyaṣṭāpyayatnānyapi kalisamaye tvatprasādapravruddhyā
kṣipram muktipradānītyabhidadhurṛṣayasteṣu mām sajjayethāḥ.

16. *Brahmāṇḍapurāṇa*, pt. 1, chapter 31, vv. 71–3. http://gretil.sub.uni-goettingen.de/gretil/1_sanskr/3_purana/brndp1_u.htm, accessed 16 November 2016.

    tadā cālpena kālena siddhiṃ gacchanti mānavāḥ
    dhanyā dharmaṃ cariṣyanti yugānte dvijasattamāḥ. 71
    śrutismṛtyuditaṃ dharmaṃ ye carantyanasūyakāḥ
    tretāyāmābdiko dharmo dvāpare māsikaḥ smṛtaḥ. 72
    yathāśakti caranprājñastadahnā prāpnuyātkalau
    eṣā kaliyugāvasthā saṃdhyāṃśaṃ tu nibodhata. 73

17. *Nārāyaṇīyam*, daśaka 92, v. 7.

    bhaktāstāvat kalau syuḥ dramilabhuvi tato bhūriśastatra coccaiḥ
    kāverīm tāmraparṇīmanu kila kṛtamālām ca puṇyām pratīcīm
    hā mām apyetadantarbhavam api ca vibho kiñcidañcadrasam tvay-
    yāśāpāśairnibadhya bhramaya na bhagavan pūraya tvanniṣevām.

18. Karl Marx, *Critique of Hegel's 'Philosophy Of Right'*, ed. Joseph O'Malley, Cambridge: Cambridge University Press, p. 131.
19. *Viṣṇupurāṇa, aṃśa* 6, *adhyāya* 2:

    śudraḥsādhuḥ kaliḥsādhurityevaṃ śṛṇvatāṃ vacaḥ
    teṣāṃ munīnāṃ bhūyaś ca mamajja sa nadījale. 6

    sādhusādhviti cotthāya śūdra dhanyosi cābravīt. 7
    nimagnaś ca samutthāya punaḥ prāha mahāmuniḥ
    yoṣitaḥ sādhu dhanyāstāstābhyo dhanyatarosti kaḥ. 8

    . . .

    śūdraiś ca dvijaśuśrūṣātatparair dvijasattamāḥ
    tathā strībhir anāyāsāt patiśuśrūṣayaiva hi. 35
    tatastritayamapyetanmama dhanyataraṃ matam
    dharmasaṃpādane kleśo dvijātīnāṃ kṛtādiṣu. 36

20. M.G.S. Narayanan and Kesavan Veluthat, 'The Bhakti Movement in South India', in *Indian Movements: Aspects of Dissent, Protest and Reform*, Shimla: Indian Institute of Advanced Study, 1978, reproduced in Jha, *The Feudal Order*, pp. 385–410.
21. Friedhelm Hardy, *Viraha-Bhakti: The Early History of Kṛṣna Devotion in South India*, New York: Oxford University Press, 1983. J.A.B. van Buitenen, 'On the Archaism of the Bhāgavata Purāṇa', in *Krishna: Myths, Rites and Attitudes*, ed. Milton Singer, Honolulu: East-West Centre Press, 1966 (also in van Buitenen, *Studies in Indian Philosophy and Literature,* pp. 223–42); Edwin Bryant, *Krishna: The Beautiful Legend of God* (Śrimad *Bhāgavatapurāṇa* Book X), New York: Oxford

University Press, 2003. I thank Bharati Jagannathan for inviting my attention to this.

22. *Bhāgavatapurāṇa*, 11, 3, 44–6.
23. *Nārāyaṇīyam*, daśaka 92, v. 1.

    vedaiḥ sarvāṇi karmāṇyaphalaparatayā varṇitānīti budhvā
    tāni tvayyarpitānyeva hi samanucaran yāni naiṣkarmyamīśa
    mā bhūd vedairniṣiddhae kuhacid api manaḥ karmavācām pravartir-
    durvarjyam ced avāptam tadapi khalu bhavatyarpaye citprakāśe.

24. *Bhāgavatapurāṇa*, 11, 3, 48–55

    labdhvānugraha ācāryāt tena sandarśitāgamaḥ
    mahā-puruṣam abhyarcen mūrtyābhimatayātmanaḥ. 48
    śuciḥ sammukham āsīnaḥ prāṇa-saṃyamanādibhiḥ
    piṇḍaṃ viśodhya sannyāsa- kṛta-rakṣo 'rcayed dharim. 49
    arcādau hṛdaye cāpi yathā-labdhopacārakaiḥ
    dravya-kṣity-ātma-liṅgāni niṣpādya prokṣya cāsanam. 50
    pādyādīn upakalpyātha sannidhāpya samāhitaḥ
    hṛd-ādibhiḥ kṛta-nyāso mūla-mantreṇa cārcayet. 51
    sāṅgopāṅgāṃ sa-pārṣadāṃ tāṃ tāṃ mūrtiṃ sva-mantrataḥ
    pādyārghyācamanīyādyaiḥ snāna-vāso-vibhūṣaṇaiḥ. 52
    gandha-mālyākṣata-sragbhir dhūpa-dīpopahārakaiḥ
    sāṅgam sampūjya vidhivat stavaiḥ stutvā named dharim. 53
    ātmānam tan-mayam dhyāyan mūrtiṃ sampūjayed dhareḥ
    śeṣām ādhāya śirasā sva-dhāmny udvāsya sat-kṛtam. 54
    evam agny-arka-toyādāv atithau hṛdaye ca yaḥ
    yajatīśvaram ātmānam acirān mucyate hi saḥ. 55

25. *Nārāyaṇīyam*, daśaka 92, v. 2.

    yastvanyaḥ karmayogas tava bhajnamayas tatra cābhīṣṭamurtim
    hṛdyām sattvaikarūpām dṛṣadi hṛdi mṛdi kvāpi vā bhāvayitvā
    puṣpair gandhair nivedyair api ca viracitaiḥ śaktito bhaktipūtair-
    nityam varyāṃ saparyāṃ vidadhad ayi vibho tvat prasādam bhajeyam

26. R.S. Sharma, 'Joint Notices of Women and Sūdras in Early Indian Literature', in *Light on Early Indian Society and Economy*, Bombay: Manaktalas, 1966, which reappears in Sharma, 'Co-References to Women and Sūdra in Ancient Indian Literature', in *Perspectives in Social and Economic History of Early India*, New Delhi: Munshiram Manoharlal, 1983.
27. See note no. 19 in this chapter.
28. Sharma, 'The Kali Age', pp. 70–3.

CHAPTER 4

Laughter in the Time of Misery

Political Criticism in an Early Modern Sanskrit Poem

IT IS OFTEN HELD that India had no tradition of political criticism taking the king and his actions to task. What it was used to were the innumerable panegyrics starting from hero-lauds such as the *gāthā-nārāśamsis* in Vedic literature and the *araśar-vāḻttus* of early Tamil songs and developing through the innumerable royal panegyrics or *praśastis* in the medieval period. This absence of any critical check, among other things, allowed kings to exercise unbridled power; nor was there any hereditary nobility that could offer any restraint on the despotic ways of the ruler. What Western political thinkers saw in pre-modern India was this kind of a polity and a social form suited to it and they called it Oriental Despotism. Criticism of any variety was impossible in such a political atmosphere. Here were a set of emasculated eminences who took all the atrocities of the state (read 'king') lying down without so much as opening their mouth against them. Although such an argument was handy for the British colonial masters, it is opposed to evidence. The *narmasaciva*, who was similar to the court jester, envisaged by the *dharmaśāstras*, the *vidūṣakas* ('jokers') in the plays and so on discharged this duty very effectively. Disguised criticisms of the *anyāpadeśa* ('allegory') type and even more explicit ones are available in Sanskrit and other Indian languages. It is too early for at least people of Kerala to forget how the *Cākyārs* almost terrorized rulers in their *kūttu* and *kūṭiyāṭṭam* performances. *Mahiṣaśatakaṃ*, a hundred verses in praise of a buffalo, which I presume to introduce here, has to be seen as an example of such political criticism.[1]

The author of this work, Vāñcheśvara Dīkṣita *alias* Kuṭṭikavi, lived in Tañjāvūr in the eighteenth century. The circumstances leading to the composition of this work are explained by the poet's namesake and great-grandson thus:

The banks of Kāveri shine with a large number of scholars, with temples of Śiva and Viṣṇu. The matchless city of Tañjāvūr is situated there, the capital from where kings of the Bhosale line ruled. Vāñcheśvara, of the line of their ministers and an intellectual who had seen the other side of Vedas and Vedāṅgas, used to lead the rulers along the path of justice from time to time. Once the boyish king got into the company of wicked friends and refused to listen to good counsel. In order to bring the king back from their company and lead him along the right path, he composed [verses] in praise of a buffalo and cleansed the intellect of the king of blemishes.[2]

However, the poet himself has a considerably different version in the text. He says that he retired to his village with these thoughts: 'Where are the kings of yore, verily life-saving elixir to the hosts of scholars who approached them, and where are these vulgar urchins who look upon knowledge as so much of poison? What shall I do? O mother Agriculture, protector of the worlds, I seek refuge in thee' (v. 3). Recognizing that 'he who protects you is your lord' (v. 9), he composed a hundred verses in praise of his lord, the buffalo. He makes it clear in the very beginning that it is not for the merit of the object, a lowly animal, that he takes up the project of composing a hundred verses in its praise; it is to denigrate those agents of the state who are intent on harassing him and punish them by the rod of speech (v. 10). What follows is merciless rebuke of the king and his officers. It is far from the story of reforming the king with a song, as it were, as the commentator will have us believe. A little digression on the historical background of the poet and the poem will be in place here, so that both can be placed in better perspective.

Tañjāvūr, formerly the capital city of the Cōḻas, was a major cultural centre of south India. That region came under the empire of Vijayanagara after the decline of the Cōḻas. Like other parts of the empire, lords known as Nāyakas had ruled over Tañjāvūr. When the Vijayanagara Empire declined in the seventeenth century, these Nāyakas became independent rulers of the respective regions. Thus Tañjāvūr, like Madurai or Bidnur or Gingee, became an independent kingdom. Although the political power that the Nāyakas wielded had no comparison with that of the Cōḻas, the cultural activities inaugurated by the Cōḻas continued in Tañjāvūr even under the Nāyakas. The ancestors of our poet were advisors of the Nāyakas of Tañjāvūr.

They came from Karnataka. The commentator describes his great-grandfather, the poet, as *Kannaṭijātãya,* 'of Kannada extraction'. This family seems to have been closely related to the Śaṅkarācāryas of Śṛṅgeri. The relations between that *maṭha* and Vijayanagara Empire are well-known. Govinda Dīkṣhita, a great scholar from this family, was a good friend of Cevvappa Nāyaka, an associate of Emperor Acyuta Rāya of Vijayanagara. When Cevvappa Nāyaka married the sister-in-law of Acyuta Rāya, he got the *nāyakattanam* ('nāyakadom') of Tañjāvūr region as dowry. Govinda Dīkṣita accompanied Cevvappa Nāyaka to Tañjāvūr. We have some information regarding the scholarly activities of members of this line of stalwarts.[3] A *mahākāvya* called *Harivamśāsāracarita* summarizing the *Mahābhārata*, a commentary of the *Sundarakāṇḍā* of the *Rāmāyaṇa* and a treatise on music called *Saṃgītasudhānidhi* are attributed to Govinda Dīkṣita. It is said that it was he who introduced the music of Vijayanagara to the court of Tañjāvūr, one reason that that music came to be known as 'Carnatic Music'. He also composed a treatise called *Ṣaḍdarśana* in the field of *mīmāmsā.* He is said to have organized a grand debate on the *advaita* of Śaṅkara, the *dvaita* of Madhva and the *viśiṣṭādvaita* of Rāmānuja in the court of Tañjāvūr, with none other than Appayya Dīkṣita, Vijayīndra Tīrtha and Tātācārya representing these schools respectively. Yajñanārāyaṇa Dīkṣita and Veṅkaṭa Makhin, both sons of Govinda Dīkṣita, were reputed for their scholarship and poetic abilities. The former was the poet laureate of the Nāyakas of Tañjāvūr. He composed a *mahākāvya* called *Raghunāthabhūpavijaya* and a play called *Raghunāthavilāsa*, both on his patron, Raghunātha Nāyaka of Tañjāvūr. In another work called *Alaṅkāraratnākara*, he exemplifies all major figures of speech in Sanskrit by means of verses in praise of his patron. A few verses about him, composed by the celebrated Nārāyaṇa Bhaṭṭa of Melputtūr from Kerala, have come to light.[4] In fact, the Bhaṭṭa was all praise for scholars from the Cōḻa country. Veṅkaṭeśvara Dīkṣita or Veṅkaṭa Makhin, the younger brother of Yajñanārāyaṇa Dīkṣita, was another great scholar and musicologist. He was the courtier of Raghunātha Nāyaka as well as Vīrarāghava Nāyaka, the last of the Tañjāvūr Nāyakas.

Ekoji, brother of the Maratta Chatrapati Śivaji, captured Tañjāvūr from the Nāyakas and established the rule of the Bhosales there. Although Venkaji had ruled for a short while following the death of Ekoji in 1683, Śahaji ascended the throne in 1687 after the death of the former. Veṅkaṭa Makhin seems to have joined the Maratta court. The Bhosales were not far behind the Nāyakas in the patronage of art and culture, including scholarship in Sanskrit. Śahaji, who ruled till 1710, was a scholar in his own right. He endowed brāhmaṇas with an *agrahāra* called Śaharājendrapura in Tiruviśanallūr near Kumbhakonam. Govinda Dīkṣita's successors seem to have got land in it. There is a beautiful couplet that our poet has composed about this *agrahāra*:

Śrīśaharājendrapure
Śrīśaharājendraviṣṭapaiḥ sadṛśe |

(In Śrīśaharājendrapura, comparable to the heaven of *Śrīśa* [Viṣṇu], Hara [Śiva], Aja [Brahmā] and Indra.)

For the deft use of the *double entendre*, our poet earned the title of *Śleṣacakravartin*, 'Emperor of Paronomasia'. He had shown his intelligence and poetic abilities even as a young boy. It is said that he accompanied king Śahaji to the Mīnākṣī Temple in Madurai, where the king composed the following couplet *ex tempore* on the goddess:

puri madhuram giri madhuram
garimadhurandharanitambabhārāḍhyam |
sthūlakucam nīlakacam
bālakalācandrāṅkitaṃ tejaḥ ||

When the king paused, young Vāñcheśvara mused:

hṛdi tarasā viditarasā
taditarasāhityavāṅ na me lagati |
kaviloke na viloke
bhuvi lokeśasya śāhajerupamā ||

Amazed, the king conferred on the poet the title 'Kuṭṭikavi', meaning 'Boy Poet', also suggesting affection.[5] He has written a couple of other *śatakas* or centuries such as *Dhāṭiśataka* and *Āśīrvādaśataka*, which I have not been able to lay my hands on. Like his predecessors, he too showed unswerving loyalty to royalty. Śahaji showed great respect for him in return.

However, things were not quite the same always. Śarabhoji and Tulalāji, who succeeded Śahaji, were weak rulers. Although Tulalāji did patronize literature and music to some extent, he was not very successful. He had five sons, two born outside marriage. Pratāpasiṃha, one of the latter, captured power. He is described as 'the wily Tanjorean' in contemporary English documents. The interest he showed in wine and women was notorious.[6] While the walls of the *sattras* (wayside inns) built by Śarabhoji and others are adorned with scenes from the *Mahābhārata*, similar structures sponsored by Pratāpasiṃha show scenes of *maithuna* (copulation)!

An undesirable ruler was not the only curse of Tañjāvūr in the latter half of the eighteenth century. A famine struck the area in 1730. The fertile valley of Kāvēri witnessed abject poverty. Contemporary British documents testify to the export of a large number of slaves from Nagapattinam. The British also led a military expedition against Pratāpasiṃha. The rivalries between the English and the French and the way in which the British threw in their lot in favour of the Nawab of Carnatic led to what are known as the Carnatic Wars, the details of which are too well-known to be recounted here. These wars had a bad effect on the economy of the Kāvēri valley in ways more than one. The depredations of Hyder Ali, destroying the embankments for irrigation and indulging in man-hunting in various ways, laid the countryside waste. As life became unbearable, all sorts of evils swallowed the land.

The conditions of that region are described vividly by Christian Frederic Schwartz (1726–98), a German Lutheran missionary who operated in Tañjāvūr in this period. The testimony of Schwartz is acceptable as his record is otherwise impeccable. He speaks about the miserable conditions of the region around Tañjāvūr in the wake of the terrible wars from the middle of the eighteenth century. Looting, arson, rape and other atrocities, which are essential items of any war, made life nearly impossible. The conversion of large numbers to swell the ranks of the 'disciple regiments' by the Mysorean conqueror and the destruction of irrigation canals and embankments are pointed out as other factors responsible for the terrible conditions of life. Schwartz writes:

When it is considered that Hyder Ali has carried off so many thousands of people, and that many thousands have died of war, it is not at all surprising to find not only empty houses, but desolate villages—a mournful spectacle indeed. . . . We have suffered exceedingly in this fortress from hunger and misery. When passing through the streets early in the morning, the dead were lying in heaps on dunghills . . . such distress I never before witnessed, and God grant I never may again.[7]

Schwartz has admitted that his congregation had indeed swollen, but with people who were not so much convinced of the superiority of the Gospel as driven by hunger! He says that it was difficult to teach the natives even the rudiments of a foreign faith with their mental powers diminished by famine.

Contagious diseases added to the problems. The Christian missionaries tell us about a terrible dysentery that visited the regions of Tranquebar. This and other forms of pestilence afflicted Tiruchchiṟāpaḷḷi, Tañjāvūr and the neighbouring regions in this period.[8] Misrule, war, diseases, British-French-Danish intrigues, the cruelties of the Nawab, attempts at Christian proselytization as well as persecution of Christians—it was when Tañjāvūr had been checkmated by all these forces that *Mahiṣaśatakam* had its origin. The context in which the poet took to agriculture is important: 'It is well-known that agriculture forestalls famine. And, Manu too has allowed agriculture and cattle-keeping for brāhmaṇas in times of distress. When kings are greedy and times are troubled by famine, let me take to agriculture for a living. What is wrong with that?' (v. 5). The way in which the expression *durbhikṣa* ('famine', 'distress') is repeated in the poem is significant. The poet shows how scared he is of war—*bibhemyāhavāt* (v. 6). In an advice that he gives scholars, he shows how fever and other diseases had affected the country of the Cōḻas:

Dear scholar, don't do anything foolhardy. Listen to me: I shall tell you what is best for you. My friend, don't leave Lord Buffalo, the true friend of men who grants wishes, and go to the town of Śrīraṅga ['the Theatre of

Prosperity'], the house of fever, where prosperity is distant; and what you have at hand is the sound of the bell round the neck of the buffalo whom the God of Death rides. (v. 8)

This poem shows how a concerned intellectual responded to the terrible times of distress in which he lived. Perhaps a comparison is in place. Tyāgarāja, the reputed musician, had lived in the same place almost during the same period. When life became nearly impossible on account of war, pestilence, famine and poverty, Tyāgarāja took it as the inevitable manifestation of the Kali Age, the darkest possible period. The only redemption that he saw was through the mercy of god. His songs are the expression of an innocent mind that sincerely believed that devotion—undiluted devotion—was the only panacea for this distress. William Jackson has shown that although it will not be possible to take up any one of his compositions and show that it can be read against the background of any particular event;[9] but one can clearly hear a reaction to the political and social decadence as well as economic misery of his times reverberating in them. When he was ordered to go and sing in the royal court, he politely refused saying that his songs were reserved for the divine. This was the courage that devotion gave him. In the situation of helplessness, he cried out to god. But our poet chose to laugh, and laugh aloud somewhat cruelly. The echo of this laughter reaches and shakes many quarters. An examination of its contents will show how, going beyond frivolous cynicism, there is serious political and social criticism, expressing protest against the establishment and the order of things.

The first part of the poem consists of sharp criticism of the king and his officers, after dilating on the meaninglessness of serving them in a world where scholars and scholarship have lost their relevance. Then there is a detailed section where the king and his officers are equated with the buffalo, and *vice versa*. In the third and final part is social protest, clothed in not-so-subtle sarcasm. In the poet's own words, what he does is to punish the king and the officers of the state with the rod of speech. While the kings and ministers of old had been verily the nectar of longevity for the scholars who depended on them, the present ones are vulgar urchins, for whom knowledge is but poison. It is surprising that people still desire to go through the hell of waiting at the outer doors of the royal palace even after seeing the advantages of agriculture, hailed by both theory and practice. From the description of the bad fate of two scholars, Śrīdhara and Ambu Dīkṣita, Pierre-Sylvain Filliozat thinks that the historicity of the work is likely. Be that as it may, the poet's own experience is enough to show the negative attitude of the times towards scholarship: the renowned Kuṭṭikavi is sleeping at the doorsteps of evil lords! It is not just the capital of one's own country: even towns like Śrīraṅgam are not any better.

The poet makes it clear that he is praising the buffalo just to pour scorn on the lords. He is putting his gifted tongue to good use just to disparage the lords who, not knowing his greatness, are engaged in harassing him. He is doing it by paying obeisance to his Royal Highness, the buffalo. He is running down the wicked officers who persecute him and punishing them with the rod of speech due to his anger towards them. If those kings become conscious of their drawbacks, he will be happy. The king is a fool; and his ministers are more so. Those who are around them are so many traitors who plunder everything. Even if you want to practise agriculture, O buffalo, don't do it in the Cōḻa country: I was able to save my loincloth; you do not have even that!

Filliozat seems to think that the denunciation and rebuke in this poem are directed more at the ministers, officers and other hangers-on of the king than to the king himself. He thinks that the story of the origin of the poem as given in the prologue of the commentary is probable.[10] Filliozat translates *rājā mugdhamatiḥ* in verse 12 as 'the king is innocent in spirit' (*le roi est innocent d'esprit*) and concedes only that a direct criticism of the courtiers is an indirect criticism of the king. Perhaps he is carried away by the statement in the *prastāvanā* (preface) of the Srirangam edition and the prologue of the commentary by the great-grandson of the poet himself. The glosses of the great-grandson on certain verses (vv. 1, 2, 11, 12, etc.) are keen to present the poet as very loyal to the king and such criticism as there are directed against the hangers on. See, for instance, the gloss on v. 11, which insists that 'by this [verse] it is suggested that despite the primacy of the king, the officers around him are scoundrels; so also, this work is not rebuking the king but only giving him good counsel'.[11] Further, taking the last two verses—which to my mind are interpolations—seriously too may have led Filliozat to this position.[12]

The subservience shown in these two verses does not gel with the strong criticism and severe sarcasm of the body of the text. It is likely that some pliant courtier interpolated these two verses at the end in order to please the king. Alternatively, even if the poet himself added them later on in order to escape punishment or so, they still have to be treated as interpolations—interpolation *is* interpolation, whether by the poet himself or by somebody else. Moreover, the 100th verse of the work,[13] where the poet sees himself as the gratified Rāma who has acquired Sītā (Rāma's wife in one register and furrow in the other), after crossing the ocean of distress with the help of the buffalo in whom the presence of all the major monkeys is attributed by a deft use of *śleṣa*-paronomasia, crowns the project. Anything after that is simply improper. Hence I take the last two verses as interpolations, with no major harm to the poem.

Be that as it may, the poet shows no mercy in ridiculing and criticizing the king. He wastes no time and begins the exercise in the third verse itself. After praising the kings of yesteryears such as Nānāji, Śahaji and their ministers such as Candrabhānu and Ānandarāya, those of the present are described as 'vulgar urchins' (*vṛṣaḷāsabhyāḥ*). To be waiting upon the kings at their outer gates is the worst of hells (v. 4). Kings are greedy (v. 5). Kings who cannot appreciate the poet's greatness are engaged in persecuting him (v. 6). The poet was composing the poem not so much for the greatness of the subject, a lowly animal, as for punishing the accursed officers and their lords who are engaged in harassing him (v. 10). He hopes that kings who can appreciate quality, hearing this essay on the buffalo, will learn about their own bad qualities from the suggestions in the speech of the poet. He wishes they start protecting their subjects according to law and earn the right to the power they wield (v. 11). The king is stupid (v. 12). The buffalo will be an illustrious member of the royal court; he does not have to worry that he does not have the necessary learning and expertise for it—those who are already there are even greater fools; and he would be verily *Vācaspati* ('Lord of Eloquence') among them (v. 22). The poet's words are sullied because he had earlier used them to praise the kings, mad with wealth and full of other vices (v. 26). Enough of these kings, who are totally lawless (v. 29). My ears are agitated by the cruel words, devoid of any compassion, of the evil kings who grow increasingly conceited every day; the buffalo's lowing is verily nectar to them (v. 31). The shabby kings are stupid and detestable; their face is fearsome for the heat generated by wealth. There is no use waiting at their courtyard (v. 32). It is hazardous to stay in the courtyard of the royal palace, dark with the smoke issuing from the long cigars in the hands of the conceited soldiers used to speaking only foul language and stinking of their spittle; the buffalo protects you from that hazard (v. 38). Kings are too stupid to tell between what to do and what not because they are blinded by the darkness of wealth; let them stay where they are (v. 50). These kings are murderously cruel like hunters (v. 51).

It is not just on the basis of so many verses where the king is directly scolded that this work appears as strong political criticism aimed at the king himself. There are a number of verses where the king is equated with a buffalo and the buffalo is addressed as king. It will be agreed that this is not exactly panegyric. There are two ways in which the buffalo is equated with the king: (1) by direct addresses and (2) by attributing royal features in the buffalo. The buffalo is addressed in the following ways:

mahiṣādhirāja (vv. 26, 30, 33, 54, 57, 64, 66, 79, 83); *sairibhapati* (vv. 8, 27, 35, 38, 49, 84); *mahiṣendra* (vv. 17, 34, 39, 52, 53, 61, 67, 70); *kāsarapati* (vv. 21, 51, 58, 78, 99); *kāsareśvara* (vv. 41, 72, 80, 86, 97); *kāsarendra* (vv. 37, 40, 81); *kāsarasārvabhouma* (vv. 29, 56); *mahiṣakṣitīśvara* (vv. 69, 92); *kāsarakṣmāpati* (vv. 90, 98); *lulāyarāja* (vv. 48, 60); *mahāsairibha* (vv. 71, 96); *sairibharājarāja* (v. 20); *śrīkāsarādhīśvara* (v. 62); *sairibhamaṇḍaleśvara* (v. 46); *sairibhamaṇḍalendra* (v. 68); *kāsaramaṇḍaleśvara* (v. 63); *mahiṣeśvara* (v. 7); *rājaśrīmahiṣa* (v. 9); *mahiṣābhikhya prabhu* (v. 23); *mahiṣāvatamsa* (v. 45); *lulāyaprabhu* (v. 6); *mahiṣādhīśa* (v. 77); *lulāyādhīśa* (v. 95).

At another level, all attributes of royalty are seen in the buffalo. He who protects people is himself the king. If a king is a king only after he is duly anointed, O, buffalo, please come to the pond. I shall pour pitchers of water on your head (v. 50). The next two verses end with the refrain, 'you alone are our king!'[14] Thus, no matter how one looks at it, the attributes of royalty are unmistakably present in the buffalo.

It does not end there. If the poet had to wait upon wicked kings, it was because he refused to follow Lord Buffalo (v. 7). His guardian is now His Royal Highness, the Buffalo (v. 9). I shall consider the buffalo, who protects people with grain and [other forms of] wealth, as the one who is worthy of respect; what are other kings good for? (v. 16) O, Buffalo, the overlord, poverty does not occur even in dreams to those who seek refuge in you. Be it well for you, the friend of the scores of poor people (v. 30). Scholars do not unfortunately go to my king, the buffalo, who grants all wishes (v. 32). Cattle-shed is verily a palace for the buffalo and dung, musk; the dust on the floor is fresh silk cloth (v. 33). The buffalo looks like one who is initiated to perform the *aśvamedha* (v. 58). When kings of purāṇic fame such as Bhīṣma (the terrible), Anala (one who is never satisfied), Nṛga (approachable to men), Hrasvaroma (with short hair), Bharata (weighty), Pṛthu (with a huge body), Marutta (faster than wind) are present in the buffalo, the poet would not go to the wicked kings any more (v. 82). In another verse which uses the *double entendre* in an equally brilliant way, the poet sees in the buffalo the presence all major kings of the *Mahābhārata* fame (v. 85).

The political criticism contained in the poem does not end with seeing a buffalo in the king and the king in a buffalo. The poet does not spare a chance to scold the agents of the king, both the bureaucrats and the lords. The reference to the 'vulgar urchins who look upon knowledge as so much of poison' in the very third verse is as much to the ministers as to the king. Ministers of the king are traitors and are intent on stealing everything (v. 12). Wicked fellows amass grains and wealth by competing with one another. Then, pretending to be enterprising, they aspire for political power and, finally, by bribing those close to the king, appropriate everything by force. Death upon them (v. 13)! The poet says he took to agriculture as it was impossible to make a living through learning. When the crops become ripe, however, wicked officers such as *subedār*, *havaldār*, *majumdār*, etc., mercilessly encircle the field. 'Alas, what do I say?' (v. 15). Drunken with arrogance bred by prosperity, these corrupt followers of mammon get into the company of wicked friends and indulge in gluttony and sex (v. 16). These rich fellows are evil and drunk with the pride of wealth. They are greedy. They are mean whoresons. They always speak harsh words. It is better to look at the huge testicles of the buffalo than seeing their face; by doing so, one is assured of a sumptuous meal (v. 17)!

A few verses that follow are exclusively devoted to excoriate a category of officers known as the *subedārs* who seem to have earned the special wrath of the poet. As is well known, the *subedār* was in charge of collection of revenue under the Marattas. It is natural that they were the object of hatred, not only because of the excessive extortions but also for the excesses they committed. The poet pulls no punch in rebuking them. Whatever the buffalo produces is taken away by the *subedārs*: obviously, what parents produce is taken away by children, whether for love or by force (v. 18). By an expert use of paronomasia, the poet finds out similarities between the *subedārs* and the buffalo and sees that they are his brothers. His only doubt is: are they elder or younger? (v. 19). The poet has been serving the buffalo long by giving him bundles of grass, washing him clean and massaging his body. Will he do a favour in return? Will he take the God of Death, riding on his back, to the *subedārs* sooner? (v. 20). O buffalo, are you hungry? Go and eat those *subedārs* whom we consider as so much of grass. How does it help the world if you eat the dry, innocent, hay everyday? (v. 21).

Mahiṣaśatakam is not just political criticism alone. Kuṭṭikavi exposes and laughs at the social and cultural decadence that had swallowed the country. We saw that the rulers of the day are described as 'vulgar urchins who look upon knowledge as so much of poison'. This deterioration which had affected knowledge pains the poet. The statement that Śrīdhara had become an expert merchant of the commodity of knowledge and that the good food of Ambu Makhin had become gold itself shows how knowledge had become a saleable commodity (v. 7). He does not conceal his strong disapproval of it. Although he is pained about the way in which it has become difficult to make a living through learning, he expresses the pain clothed in cutting humour (v. 15). The poet's accusing finger points to other areas where society is decadent. He has only contempt, bordering on intolerance, for institutionalized religion. The meaninglessness of sacrificial rites, pilgrimage and various yogic practices is the subject of one verse (v. 36). The way in which Vedic scholars made a fetish of their expertise (v. 54), Madhvācārya (v. 55), Śrīvaiṣṇavas (v. 57), the ways of *yoga* (v. 56), the activities of a *yajamāna* in a sacrifice (v. 58)—all this is the subject of the poet's ridicule.

The expertise of the poet in various branches of knowledge is remarkable. He shows considerable awareness of agricultural practices. He is a keen observer of things around him as just one *svabhāvokti* will testify to.[15] His scholarship ranges from *kāmaśāstra* to *mīmāṃsā*, and includes subjects as varied as *tarka*, *vyākaraṇa*, prosody, poetics, *dharmaśāstra*, *purāṇa*, *itihāsa* and so on. And he attributes the details of an expert in each one of these in the buffalo, with the help of his mastery of the *double entendre*. He is quite an Emperor of Paronomasia, *Śleṣacakravartin*. Thus we have in the buffalo *brahman* (v. 59), Indra (v. 60), *sālagrāma* (v. 61), the ocean (v. 63), the mountain (v. 81), Hanūmat (v. 64), Kārtavīrya Arjuna (v. 65), a poet (v. 66), a poem (v. 67), Bharatācārya (v. 68) eleven incarnations of Viṣṇu including the Buddha (vv. 69–79), Śiva (v. 80), kings of purāṇic fame (v. 82), Arjuna (v. 83), Karṇa (v. 84), the *Mahābhārata* (v. 85), Droṇa (v. 86), Laṅkālakṣmī (v. 87), Rāvaṇa (v. 88), a Muslim chief called Chanda Khan (v. 89), a grammarian (v. 90), a logician (v. 91), a philosopher of the *mīmāṃsā* school (v. 92), a poetic treatise (v. 93), the nine *rasas* (v. 94), a *bon vivant* (v. 95), a womanizer (v. 96), Vāli (v. 97), the guardians of directions (v. 98), the great gifts (*mahādānas*) (v. 99) and a contended Śrīrāma (v. 100). All this is achieved by an expert use of *double entendre*. No amount of appreciation will be too much for this aspect of the literary ability of the poet. So also, in the field of aesthetics and rhetoric, the poet achieves great heights, particularly employing different figures of speech. These are largely in the form of suggestions as are references to points of grammar, prosody, poetics, philosophy, logic, *dharmaśāstras*, *kāmaśāstra*, Purāṇas and so on. In fact, it will take a separate study to appreciate the literary and scholarly aspects of the poem.

My purpose here is to argue that this poem has to be seen primarily as expressing social and political protest. At a time when corruption and debauchery had overtaken the rulers and their agents, when the countryside lay prostrate with war, famine and pestilence, when social and religious practices had become decadent, when foreign powers of different descriptions were making a bid to establish economic and political control, when foreign faiths were making inroads, the poet comes out strongly with his protest. What we find here is not one of those 'weapons of the weak'. In dealing with the intellectual history of the 'early modern' period of Indian history, historians have not given sufficient attention to such reactions of the intellectuals of the likes of Vāñcheśvara Dīkṣita. It is only after their work is appreciated that a fuller appreciation of how intellectuals reacted to changing times will be possible.

NOTES

1. I am extremely grateful to Pierre-Sylvain Filliozat for not only drawing my attention to this great work but also the many delightful hours and e-mail messages discussing it. I have used his Introduction to the French edition of the work in a big way, although I respectfully disagree with him on certain points of opinion and interpretation. His edition of the work is impeccable: Pierre-Sylvain Filliozat, Edition et traduition, *Mahiṣaśatakam: Vāñcheśvarakavipraṇītam, La Centurie de buffle* de Kuṭṭikavi, *Bulletin d'Études Indiennes*, Association Française pour les Études Indiennes, Paris, no. 21.2, 2003 (hereafter *MŚ*). Script: Nāgarī (and Roman for the French part). There are two earlier editions of it: (*a*) *Mahiṣaśatakaṃ* by Kuṭṭikavi, resident of Śahajimahārājapura or Tiruviśanallūr in the district of Tanjore, with the commentary entitled *Śleṣārthacandrikā* of Vāñcheśvara, edited by Rāmakṛṣṇamācārya of Vaṅgipuram with the assistance of Mahāliṅgaśāstrin of Śahajimahārājapura, published by Raṅgācārya of Vaṅgipuram at Sarasvatīnilaya Press in 1875 *samvat* (AD 1932). Script: Telugu. (*b*) *Mahisha Śatakam of Sri Vanchesvarakavi, with the Commentary 'Slesharthachandrika' of his Great-grandson Sri Vanchesvara Yajva*, with Sanskrit Prastavana by K.S. Venkatarama Sastri and an English introduction by R. Krishnaswami Iyer M.A., B.L. Advocate, Tinnevelly, edited by Gurubhaktasikhamani, Sastraprasarabhushana T.K. Balasubrahmanya Aiyar, B.A., Dharmadhikari, Sri Sankaragurukulam, Srirangam, 1946. Script: Nāgarī. I have subsequently brought out an edition with an introduction and prose translation in English. *Śrī Vāñcheśvara Dīkṣita's Mahiṣaśatakam with the Commentary Śleṣārthacandrikā by Vāñcheśvara Yajvan, the Poet's Great-grandson*, edited, translated into English and introduced by Kesavan Veluthat, Kottayam: Mahatma Gandhi University, 2011. Script: Nāgarī (and Roman for the English part).
2. See Prologue to the Commentary by Vāñcheśvara Yajvan, vv. 2–7.
3. The following details about the family are from *MŚ*, Introduction, pp. 3–5.
4. These verses are part of a letter that Melputtūr Nārāyaṇa Bhaṭṭa wrote to two great scholars from the Cōḻa country, Somadeva Dīkṣita and Yajñanārāyaṇa Dīkṣita, enclosing his *Apāṇinīyaprāmāṇyasādhanaṃ*.

The ones referring to Yajñanārāyaṇa Dīkṣita are:

yuṣmadvaiduṣyadhūtaṃ khalu kaṭakabhuvi trāyatē bhogirājaṃ
vāṇīveṇīvidhūtāmapi surasaritam kaṅkaṭīko jaṭāyāṃ |
ityevam yajñanārāyaṇavibudhamahādīkṣitāḥ śatruvarga-
trāṇāddevasya tasyāpyapaharata dhiyā sādhu sarvajñagarvaṃ ||
yuṣmādeva kṣitīśo vipulanayavidhistiṣṭhate rājyadṛṣṭau
tiṣṭhadhve yūyameva prathitabudhajane sandihāne samete |
yuṣmabhyam tiṣṭhate kastridaśagurusamāno'pi yuṣmādṛganyaḥ
prajñālūn yajñanārāyaṇavibudhamahādīkṣitān vīkṣate kaḥ ||
asvasthāḥ keraḷīyāssvayamatimṛdavastatra cāham viśeṣā-
tsārve dūrapracāre khalu śithiladhiyaḥ kim punardeśabhede |
evam bhāvye'pi daivāt kuhacana samaye kalyatā kalyate cet
prajñābdhīn yajñanārāyaṇavibudhamahādīkṣitānīkṣitāhe ||

The letter was discovered and published by Paṇḍitar E.V. Raman Namboodiri in *Mathrubhumi Weekly*, 5 February 1939, and is reproduced by Vaṭakkumkūr Rājarājavarma Rājā in his monumental *Kēraḷīya Samskṛta Sāhitya Caritram*, vol. III, revised second edition, Kaladi, 1997, p. 27.

5. These details are taken from *MŚ*, Introduction, pp. 9–11.
6. For some of these details, see William Jackson, *Tyāgarāja: Life and Lyrics*, 1991; repr., New Delhi: Oxford University Press, 2002, pp. 76–91.
7. Quoted in ibid., p. 87.
8. Ibid.
9. Jackson, *Tyāgarāja*, pp. 90–3.
10. *MŚ*, Introduction, pp. 11–12.
11. *anena rājñaḥ prāmāṇikatve'pi tatparisaravartino'dhikāriṇaḥ khalā iti sūcyate. tathā ca rājño'pi hitopadeśarūpatvānnaitat prabandhe rājño dveṣa iti bhāvaḥ.* Commentary on v. 11.
12. *śrīmadbhosalavamśadugdhajaladheḥ sampūrṇcandropamo*
yaḥ śāsti kṣitimakṣati kṣitipatir mūrtaḥ pratāpaḥ svayam |
dīrghāyurjitaśatrurātmajayuto dharmī prajārāgavān
ullāgho'stu sa nistulairnijasabhāstāraiḥ kramādāgataiḥ ||
rājā dharmaparaḥ paramparadhṛtasnehāśca tanmantriṇo
rājanyatvanī vanīpakajanā āḍhyā bhavantu kṣitau |
puṣñāïgāḥ paśavaścarantu bhajatām durbhikṣvārtā layam
vāñchānāthakaveḥ kṛtiśca kurutām nirrmatsarāṇām mudam || vv. 101–2,
13. *sugrīvo'si mahān gajo'si vapuṣā nīlaḥ pramāthī tathā*
dhūmraścāsi mahānubhāva mahiṣa tvam durmukhaḥ kesarī |

ittham te satatam mahākapiśatākārasya sāhāyyataḥ
sītām prāpya vilaṅghya duḥkhajaladhīm nandāmi rāmaḥ
svayam || v. 100.

14. *bhūpo bhūpa itīva kim nvanugatā jātirghaṭatvādivad-*
bhūmāvasti ya eva rakṣati janān raja sa eva svayam |
kim bhūmīpatayaḥ śarārava ime krūrāḥ kirātā iva
prāyaḥ sārvajanīna kāsarapate rājā tvamevāsi naḥ ||
sānandam mahiṣīśatam ramayase mūrdhābhiṣikto'nvaham
tvam vālavyajanāvadhūtimasakṛt prāyeṇa śṛṅgānvitaḥ |
kim ca svām prakṛtim na muñcasi tṛṇaprāyam jagat paśyasi
svasti śrī mahiṣendra te'stu niyatam rājā tvamevāsi naḥ || vv. 51–2.

See also the commentary on v. 52:

. . . *rājapakṣe: mahiṣīṇām kṛtābhiṣekāṇām strīṇām. 'kṛtābhiṣekā mahiṣī' ityamaraḥ. śate sahasre vā parigaṇite ramayase. antaḥpurastriyaḥ yathā sambhogādinā tuṣyanti tathā kalāśāstroktaprakāreṇa tāsām prītyatiśayam janayati. 'mūrdhābhiṣikto rājanyaḥ' ityamaraḥ. vālam cāmaram vyajanam tālavṛntādikam tayoravadhūtim. śṛṅgeṇa prabhutvenānvitaḥ. 'śṛṅgam prabhutve'iti viśvaḥ. svām prakṛtim svakīyarājyāṅgam svāmyamātyādikam. 'rājyāṅgāni prakṛtayaḥ' ityamaraḥ. jagadbhuvanam. tṛṇaprāyam tṛṇasadṛśam yathā bhavati tathā paśyati. janeṣvaiśvaryādyalpatvena tatra rājñaḥ tṛṇabuddhirbhavatītyarthaḥ.*

15. *kedāre mahiṣīmanojagṛhamāghrāyonnamayyānanam*
dantān kiñcidabhipradarśya vikṛtam kūjan khuraiḥ kṣmām khanan |
pratyagrāyitasūraṇāṅkuranibham yatkiñcidujjṛmbhayann—
ānandam mahiṣeśa nirviśasi yat tadṛaṣṭunetrotsavaḥ || v. 39.

CHAPTER 5

Regional History in the Making of Regions

'REGION', BY DEFINITION, being a part, 'part of what?' is a natural question that raises itself when we begin to talk about 'regional history'. Historians take up different units for purposes of their study: ranging from vast entities such as the whole world itself or more romantic ones such as civilizations; they go to study smaller and smaller units such as regions, localities, villages or even less. It is not as if these units offer themselves as so many 'natural' objects of historical study. It is the historian, with his own agenda, who identifies his units. Those of us who are doing 'regional history' will do well to bear in mind the constituent-constituted relationship between the region and the larger unit which it is part of, as also the changing nature of both. Taking the Malayalam-speaking region as a case study, I presume to show how the two categories—the 'local' and the 'global'—are constituted, and interact with each other, from when evidence expressing these ideas is available in literature.

When we talk of regional history in India, what we have in mind is the history of a part of our country, India or Bhārata. It is a truism to say that this is a post-Independence compulsion, brought about largely by the ideology and practice of nationalism before and after 1947. Even otherwise, the historiographical notion of regional history is an assumption within the framework of nationalism, perhaps all over the world. When Indian historians, in response to the imperialist writings of the nineteenth and early twentieth centuries, wrote history with clear nationalist predilections, they were also writing history of regions as a complement to their writings. Thus K.M. Munshi, R.C. Majumdar, Nilakanta Sastri and others, while making loud and clear statements about Indian nationalism, also began to write regional history by laying bare the history of regions such as Gujarat, Bengal and Tamil Nadu. True, the colonial masters in their administrative reports, manuals and gazetteers had collected a mass of information and arranged them in their vertical and horizontal formations so that they could legitimately claim that the master knew the colony better. An inadvertent by-product of it all was a widening database in relation to understanding the regions. There was an element of one-upmanship in the writings of Indian nationalist historians who used precisely this data in their writings; and the repertoire for writing regional history got enriched in the process. The way in which this grew and has been helpful in the development of a sense of both nationalism and regionalism has been discussed in some detail in the past.

However, neither the colonial masters nor the nationalist champions seem to have been bothered by the question, 'when and how did regions come of age in Indian history?' There was a fashion in Indian historiography which appears to have followed the pattern of a carom board. Accordingly, everything was centralized once upon a time, be it under the Mauryan Empire or the Gupta Empire or the Mughal Empire or what have you. Then the striker struck and the regions went and took their respective positions. My concern is not the validity or otherwise of the assumptions of centralization of these empires and the uniform nature of the structures over which they are thought to have presided. An alternative view is that of looking at the process of the development of regions as *sui generis*. In economy, society, polity, language, literature, artistic style, sculpture, architecture—almost every field—the regions start coming of age in roughly the second half of the first millennium of the Common Era, give or take a couple of centuries here or there. The significant work of scholars like B.D. Chattopadhyaya, Hermann Kulke, B.P. Sahu, Chetan Singh, Sheldon Pollock and others has contributed considerably to this changed perspective.

Here the question, namely, 'what exactly do we mean by region?' will come up again. The lexical gloss that we saw earlier being still valid, one has to recognize that even the parts vary in their features:

size, boundary, constituents and so on. To take the example of my own home state of Kerala, we can see at least three ways in which Kerala is constructed in history. First, there is the territory of the Cēra kingdom of the early historical period, consisting of the present-day Palakkad, Thrissur and Malappuram districts of Kerala and the Coimbatore, Tiruchchiṟāpaḷḷi and Salem districts of Tamilnadu. The second construction is the land that Paraśurāma is said to have retrieved from the sea: the coastal districts of Karnataka, the whole of present-day Kerala and the Kanyakumari district of Tamilnadu. The third is the present-day state of Kerala, which is sought to be historicized in much of recent writings. What are we seeking to historicize? An attempt to answer this question can be made in two ways. One can try and find out the forces that went into defining a region, with clearly identifiable constituents and equally clear causalities working towards it. A second way is to examine the way in which the region was constituted historically from time to time as a discursive formation.

I presume to take up the second aspect in this paper, as I had treated the former at some length earlier.[1] I do it with the clear understanding that it is hard to differentiate the two: it is increasingly recognized that to distinguish history and historiography is well-nigh impossible. The discourse constituting Kerala as a separate region with its own identity can be seen to have been articulated, to begin with in a text called *Kēraḷōlpatti*, or Origin of Kerala. The date of its composition itself is problematic.[2] This text is crucial as arguably the first attempt to historicize Kerala as a separate unit, with its own defined territory and peculiar institutions. It opens by giving an account of Paraśurāma's creation of Kerala, the land between Gōkarṇa and Kanyākumāri, by claiming it from the Arabian Sea with a fling of his axe and settling it by brāhmaṇas brought from the North in 64 *grāmas*, of which 32 are in Tuḷunāḍu and the remaining in present-day Kerala. The first thing we notice is the definition of territory: 160 *kātams* of land between Gōkarṇa and Kanyākumāri. Even here, the text makes a further nuanced understanding. While the whole stretch is Kerala, the land from Gōkarṇa to Perumpuḻa is Tuḷunāḍu (where Tuḷu is spoken) and the land between Perumpuḻa and Kanyākumāri is Malanāḍu (where Malayalam is spoken).

Speaking about the way in which Paraśurāma peopled the land

of Kerala after raising it from the sea, the *Kēraḷōlpatti* says that the brāhmaṇas, who were brought and settled in the first instance, would not stay; they returned to their original home in Ahicchatra for fear of serpents in the new land. Paraśurāma brought a second wave of brāhmaṇas, again from Ahicchatra. In order that they would not be accepted back 'home' if they returned, he had their hair style and dress code changed. So, the people of Kerala here are shown as distinct from the rest of the country with their own hairstyle and dress code. He also persuaded them to accept the mother right so that he could expiate for his own matricidal sin; but only those of one village, namely Payyannūr, obliged by following matrilineal descent. Patterns of descent and inheritance, too, therefore distinguish the people of Kerala. Paraśurāma also established 108 temples each for Śiva, Śāstā and Durgā. He chose 36,000 brāhmaṇas from the different *grāmas* and conferred on them the right to arms (*śastrabhikṣā*), so that they could protect their land themselves.

The difference between the situation in Kerala and the land immediately to north, viz., South Canara, is crucial in this regard. It is a significant indication of the way in which the text seeks to constitute the region in contradistinction with the neighbouring land. The major factor behind this is apparently the role of the brāhmaṇical groups in the two societies. The landed wealth in South Canara was not under the control of the brāhmaṇical groups as much as it was in Kerala and, therefore, the importance that the brāhmaṇas of Kerala had in polity and society was not matched by what their counterparts in South Canara had. As it was much greater in the case of Kerala, Paraśurāma is invoked as not only the creator of the land but also the donor to the brāhmaṇa groups. So also the exceptional importance attached to the arms-bearing brāhmaṇas called *śastra-Brāhmaṇa*s or *cāttirar* and their group meetings is another instance of the use of the past in seeking validation of the brāhmaṇical groups in Kerala society. Paraśurāma established a *brahmakṣatra* in Kerala, where brāhmaṇas did the work of the kṣatriyas, with every arrangement for the welfare of the people, including religion, administration and law. The brāhmaṇical authority in Kerala was so great that it took Viṣṇu as Paraśurāma, a brāhmaṇical *avatāra* with kṣatriya pretensions, to do the job. And, that underlined the distinctiveness of Kerala with reference to the Tuḷu country, too.

If these are the geographical, ethnographical and cultural constituents of Kerala according to *Kēraḷōlpatti*, the political-historical constituent too is clearly defined there in an unequivocal manner. Representatives of the brāhmaṇical establishment governed the land gifted to them by Paraśurāma as *brahmakṣatra*. In course of time, however, they realized that the business of governance corrupted them, and they themselves decided to get a kṣatriya as their ruler. Accordingly, a kṣatriya and his sister were brought; the brother was anointed king who was made to swear habitual allegiance to them. A monarchical state was established in Kerala. The sister was married to a brāhmaṇa and it was agreed that the progeny would belong to the kṣatriya caste according to the matrilineal system of succession. The descendants of this sister would be the successors to the throne. The conviction that government was not the brāhmaṇas' cup of tea and that it belonged to the kṣatriya is very much in tune with the brāhmaṇical principles and the theory of *varṇāśramadharma*. And the upper-caste, brāhmaṇical character of it all is hard to miss, both in the narrative and in other contemporary records. At the same time, there is no attempt to latch the origin of the dynasty on either to one of the reputed kṣatriya lineages of Purāṇic fame or to those celebrated in the Tamiḻ tradition; nor is an origin myth in the tradition typical of the medieval court literature in Sanskrit invented or the heroic deeds of the ruler or his ancestors recited. All this would show that Kerala had arrived as a separate political entity and that the *Kēraḷōlpatti* was historicizing it.

At this point, contextualizing this portion of the narrative will be in order. The history of the Cēra kingdom of Mahōdayapuram (*c.*AD 800–1124) is now fairly clearly known. A close examination of *Kēraḷōlpatti* shows that this first 'historical' portion of it is an attempt to historicize this Cēra kingdom, sources describing the territory which it presided over by the name of 'Kerala' for the first time. To be sure, the word 'Kerala' does occur in the sources of an earlier period starting from Aśokan edicts and the Graeco-Roman accounts and going through Cāḷukya and Rāṣṭrakūṭa inscriptions. But it has been demonstrated that all these early references are to the lineage of the Cēras, known to early Tamil sources as 'Cēral', 'Kerala' being a Prakrit-Sanskrit from of this expression. In fact, even after Kerala came to be used as the name of a land, the alternative expression for

Kēralaviṣaya was '*Cēramāṉ nāṭu*', i.e. 'the Land of the Cēras', which clearly proves this point.

This post-Cēra narrative, historicizing the political entity realized under the Cēras, is conscious of the identity of the region that it crafts, which is demonstrated by the fact that even the social divisions of Kerala that it speaks about have a character distinct from the rest of the country. It speaks about the temples of Śiva, Durgā and Śāstā that Paraśurāma had consecrated in the land. Moreover, the most authentic thing of Kerala is its peculiar system of caste, with its own norms of purity and pollution. Certain castes are considered as so low that their approach and even very sight is thought to be polluting. In fact, the *Kēraḷōlpatti* is very elaborate in its treatment of *jātis* in Kerala.[3] Interestingly, *Kēraḷōlpatti* attributes the ordering of the caste system in Kerala to the ubiquitous Śaṅkarācārya, a means of achieving legitimacy for the institution, notwithstanding the contradiction involved in it. The narrative is emphatic about the distinctiveness of Kerala here: 'in other countries (*paradeśa*) there is no distance pollution among castes. It is as if they all belong to the same *varṇa*. That would not suffice. It is only with rituals that this *karmabhūmi* can be pure. Hence things were ordained like this'.[4] Apart from being an apology for the great *advaita* savant doing things against his credo, this is emphasizing that Kerala is a land different from its 'others'.

After Kerala was so constituted historiographically, we see that this entity with its new identity had acquired the necessary self-confidence in the post-Cēra period. *Keraḷabhāṣā*, or the language of Kerala, had come of age, although the word 'Malayalam' by which it is now known is not used to describe it in sources from the region.[5] In any case, Malayalam had arrived as a distinct language, with its own vocabulary, grammar, syntax and morphology. What is more, a text of grammar, prosody and poetics called *Līlātilakam*, which announces this arrival, was composed by the fourteenth century.[6] The self-confidence that Kerala exudes in that text is so much that it looks upon its others such as the Tuḷuvas and the Tamils as so many inferiors. This derives from the literary expressions and practices, where Kerala is represented as the best of lands.[7] Even after the Cēra kingdom had long become a thing of the past, Mahōdayapuram was still nostalgically thought of as the capital of Kerala, its ruler as still ruling over *Kēraḷaviṣaya* or *Cērmāṉnāṭu*. All this is to be seen as following the experience in the Cēra kingdom, which *Kēraḷōlpatti* was seeking to historicize.

At a different level, however, there was another statement that formed part of the discursive formation constituting the same region considerably differently, using a particularly manufactured image of the past as its sustenance here as well. That was the identity of Malabar, and it was particularly a subject for the Arab, and later European, traders. It had the same geographical reach as the Malanāṭu or Kerala of *Kēraḷōlpatti*. One such statement articulating a clear consciousness of this Malabar is in an Arabic text by Shaykh Zainuddin Makhdum.[8] Written primarily as a call for a holy war against the Portuguese, the full title of the work is suggestive: *Tuḥfatal-Mujāhidīn fī ba'd Akbār al-Burdughāliyyīn* (Tribute to the Holy Warriors in Respect of a Brief Account of the Portuguese).[9] Its primary purpose is to give a call for *jihad* or holy war against the perpetrators of atrocity against Muslims; but it presents a short history of Islam in Malabar and also describes a few strange, 'detestable' customs of the people of Malabar. It articulates the consciousness regarding Malabar, with not only a characterization of its internal sociopolitical features but also a clear definition of its boundaries. Accordingly, Malabar is the 'whole territory . . . with Kumhuri (Kanyakumari) as its boundary in the south and Kanjirakut (Kasaragod) in the north'.[10] Places like Calicut, Weliancode, Tirurangadi, Tanur, Ponnani, Parawanna; the localities surrounding Chaliyam port, Kakkad, Tiruwangad, Mahe, Chemmanad; the localities surrounding Dharmadam; on its south, Walpattanam and Nadapuram; on the south of Koṭuṅṅallūr, Kochi, Vypeen and several other areas are said to have become 'thickly populated and grew into towns with thriving trade and commerce, all because of Muslims'.[11] The Malabar that the Shaykh constitutes is the one centred on Muslim trading groups. The other inhabitants of the land are described, as also their customs, in great detail, with a view to defining this land authentically.[12] This description also enables the identification of the Muslim groups with the local population—they are not mentioned as the oppositional other in an attempt to constitute the self. The antagonistic elements there are the Portuguese, no swearword being spared in describing them. Thus we have a Malabar from Kasaragod to Kanyakumari in this Arabic text, which is synonymous with the

Kerala of other sources and which represented how the Muslim scholar wanted to constitute it in his own way.

In this context, the way in which the Portuguese saw Malabar is interesting. One of the most detailed, and extremely authentic, accounts of the Malabar Coast is contained in the *Book of Duarte Barbosa.*[13] Barbosa had acquired considerable familiarity with the land he was describing, and he had cultivated the local language 'so well, that he spoke it better than the natives of the country'.[14] According to Barbosa, the 'Land of Malabar begins from the place called Cumbola (modern Kumbla in Kasaragod District), and in all from the Hill of Dely (Ezhimala in Kannur District) and ending at the Cape Comorin in it is one hundred and thirty leagues along the coast'.[15] Barbosa repeats the tradition of the rule of Cēramān Perumāḷ[16] and shows how the constitution of Kerala through that kind of a historiography has been achieved in this case also. He knew that 'in this land of Malabar all men use one tongue only which they call Maliama'. Barbosa too, like Shaykh Zainuddin, gives a detailed account of the different castes of the inhabitants of Malabar, and demonstrates that a 'region' is not just a geographical expression: it is constituted by people who speak one language, share in common cultural traditions and distinguish themselves from others. The description of the castes in Kerala, both indigenous and foreign, is so vivid that it is clear that he knew who was *in* it and who, *of* it. The customs of both the natives and the sojourners are described, not as 'detestable', as in the case of the descriptions of the Shaykh. If there is less than accommodation shown to any community, it is to the Muslims and that too on a scale much smaller than the way in which the Muslim scholar represents the Portuguese.

The difference between the Muslim and Portuguese perceptions is brought out clearly by a comparison between the sense of belonging that the Shaykh shows and the Portuguese writer does not show. For *Tuḥfatal-Mujāhidīn*, Malabar was a land of Muslims; the people of Malabar 'had accepted Islam willingly'.[17] Even when the 'strange' and 'detestable' customs of Malabar are described, what informs such descriptions is a curiosity, and eagerness to report the exotic. The land of Malabar was 'theirs' and 'they' had to protect it by waging a *jihad* against the accursed Portuguese. On the other hand, the Portuguese writer does not have any such commitment: he just describes the land which he was very familiar with. Even when he does not make a secret of his dislike for the Muslims,[18] he does not take up any commitment of cleansing the land of them. In other words, he had not made the land his own whereas the Muslims had.[19]

At the same time, the eagerness to participate in the tradition of a larger whole can be seen too. At one level, it was the attempt to affiliate this region to a larger unit of civilization, depending on the point of view of the agency of imagination. Identifying Kerala as a *janapada* in *Bhāratavarṣa* can be seen from the period of the Purāṇas on;[20] but that is as vague as it is inconsequential. The attempt to achieve affiliation to the larger unit from this side can be seen, again, in the *Kēraḷōlpatti*. One of its recensions from Kōlattunāḍ in the northern part of Kerala has a pretentious beginning, with a claim to narrate *jambudvīpōlpatti* in *bhāṣā* (Malayalam).[21] Kerala is clearly situated within the geographical horizon familiar to the Purāṇic world and its 'origin', naturally, is part of the origin of Jambudvīpa. This attempt in a narrative that seeks to constitute Kerala is extremely significant. But it goes beyond such technical texts. One of the medieval *Maṇipravāḷam* texts, *Candrōtsavam*, has a verse which seeks to participate in this tradition and include Kerala within this geographical locus. It says that 'there are eight other khaṇḍas around and that the southern one of Bhārata is more charming than them; even in it, the Land of the Cēramāns [is] like the auspicious mark on the forehead of the goddess of prosperity and god of love'. By the time we come to Pūntānam Nampūtiri, a poet who wrote in simple Malayalam in the sixteenth century, we see this Purāṇic geography was accepted without even an attempt to bring in any distinction for Kerala within Bhārata. He is happy that he was just living in Bhārata and that it was in the present age that he was doing it.[22]

The idea of Bhārata or Bhāratavarṣa, which evolved through centuries in the expressions of high culture in India, particularly in the period of and after the Guptas, was something that Kerala came to know about in the age of the Cēramān Perumāḷs. To begin with, Tamiḻakam, of which present-day Kerala was an inseparable part, did not have much consciousness of this idea. The copious literature in Tamiḻ, although containing stray influences of the Vedic-Sastraic-Purāṇic elements,[23] does not participate in this tradition at all. It was only in the age of transition from the early historical to the early medieval that such an idea itself makes its appearance in south India, perhaps through what Pollock has described as the 'Sanskrit Cosmopolis'. However, in spite of the knowledge of this idea of Bhārata, there is nothing in the records to show that Kerala sought affiliation to it even at this stage. What it did at this stage was to wean itself away from the old affiliation to Tamiḻakam. Gradually, however, Kerala began to participate in the common traditions of this larger unit of Bhārata as an affiliate. The post-Perumāḷ era in Kerala thus found itself as an integral part of Bhāratavarṣa, and it was the brāhmaṇical agency that achieved it. The land created by Paraśurāma was already part of the land of Bhārata.

In the case of Shaykh Zainuddin, however, we see that he looks at Malabar as part of the Islamic cosmopolis (*Dār al-Islām*).[24] In fact, the Shaykh is convinced that it was to the Muslim rulers of the world that appeals had to be sent for help when this Dār al-Islām was under threat; it was such Muslim rulers as the Sultan of Jazrāt (Gujarat), the Adil Shahi Sultan of Deccan, the Sultan of Miṣr (Egypt), the Sultan of Turkey and so on who were appealed and variously helped or refused to help.[25] This is obviously an Islamic Commonwealth—nothing especially Indian about it. No wonder he dedicates the book not to the Zamorin, king of Calicut, of whom he speaks so kindly and with respect, but to the Sultan of Bijapur far afield: Sultan Ali Adil Shah,

> the noblest and most respected of all rulers, one who takes delight in the struggle against disbelievers and regards fighting to uphold the divine word as a great honour. He sets his mind towards the service of the servants of Allah. His lofty courage disposes him to destroy the enemies of Allah.[26]

In the case of Barbosa, there is no such attempt to affiliate the land of Malabar to any larger whole such as the Christendom. Even the later attempt of the Portuguese in the Synod of Diamper was only to make the Christians of Malabar part of the Roman Catholic Church; not Malabar itself. That is another story.

Our purpose is to show how a particular region in the Indian subcontinent was constituted with the help of a particularly manufactured image of the past. That the three different statements which went into the making of the discursive formation more or less agreed with one another, despite the totally different moorings of each, shows the strength of the discourse that had been created as a result. It should not, however, be taken to mean that the identity of Kerala was just discursively constituted. It had the backing of historical factors. An identity that was crafted under the Cēra kingdom of Mahōdayapuram was represented in the first of these statements. Even while that identity continued, new elements that were introduced both continued and changed the identity and affiliation.

I do not mean to say that Kerala was a matter of 'discourse' and that there was no reality at all. On the contrary, that discourse was based on an emerging reality and went a long way in defining the contours of the image of Kerala in centuries that followed. That is why even in the modern period, with three distinct political divisions, there was a Kerala in the minds of the people, and a movement for a united Kerala or *Aikya Keralam* invoked these sentiments.

NOTES

1. Kesavan Veluthat, 'The Evolution of a Regional Identity', in *The Early Medieval in South India*, New Delhi: Oxford University Press, 2009.
2. The date of this text is a matter of debate among historians; there is no agreement regarding its validity as a 'source' of history either. For a discussion, and a plea to look at it as an expression of the historical consciousness rather than as a source of history, see Kesavan Veluthat, 'The *Keralolpatti* as History' , in *The Early Medieval in South India*, New Delhi: Oxford University Press, 2009. There are many versions of the text, with a large number of them available in print. I have used the edition of Hermann Gundert: *Kēraḷōlpattiyum Maṟṟum: Eight Works Published during 1843–1904*, ed. Scaria Zacharia, Kottayam, 1992.
3. Gundert, *Kēraḷōlpatti*, pp. 182–7.
4. Scaria Zacharia, ed., *Kēraḷōlpattiyum Maṟṟum*, pp. 182–7.
5. The word 'Malayalam' to describe this language seems to have been used for the first time in Telugu, in Śrīnātha's *Śrībhīmēśvarapurāṇamu*, I, 72, 73. Quoted in Velcheru Narayana Rao, David Shulman and Sanjay Subrahmanyam, *Textures of Time: Writing History in South India 1600–1800*, Delhi: Permanent Black, 2001, p. 20. However, there are Cōḻa inscriptions of the ninth and tenth century that use the term 'Malaiyāḷar', referring to soldiers belonging to the chiefly houses of Kerala. They included Malaiyāḷan Māḷuvaccār Aṭṭaṅkan Cāttan, Malaiyāḷan Neṭuṅkālāynāṭṭu Iyāṉimaṅkalattu Mānavallan Kaṇṇan, Malaiyāḷan Iravi Kōtai and Malaiyāḷan Neṭumpuṟaiyūrnāṭṭil Vakkāṇattu

Maṇkarai Kaṇṭan Kāman. See *South Indian Inscriptions*, vol. VII, nos. 958, 960, 967, 971 and 973, pp. 466–71. For a discussion of the political context in which they are mentioned in a Co̱la inscription, M.G.S. Narayanan, 'Early Wars and Alliances', in *Perumals of Kerala*, Calicut, the author, 1996. It is a moot point whether these Malaiyāḷar were so described on account of the language they spoke or the country from which they came.

6. For a discussion of the early literary practices in Malayalam, Rich Freeman, 'Genre and Society: The Literary Culture of Premodern Kerala', in *Literary Cultures in History: Reconstructions from South Asia*, ed. Sheldon Pollock, Berkeley and Los Angeles: University of California Press, 2003, particularly pp. 437–86. Freeman had earlier discussed this textbook on grammar in his article 'Rubies and Coral: The Lapidary Crafting of Language in Kerala', *The Journal of Asian Studies*, vol. 57, no. 1, February 1998, pp. 38–65. M.R. Raghava Varier has shown how this text also announces the confidence that Kerala and Malayalam had gained by the fourteenth century. 'Līlātialakattinṟe rāṣṭrīyam', in *Mathrubhumi Weekly*, vol. 71, no. 43, pp. 23–8, reproduced in M.R. Raghava Varier, *Vāyanayuṭe Vaḻikaḷ*, Thrissur: Current Books, 1998, pp. 9–19.
7. For details, Veluthat, 'The Evolution of a Regional Identity'.
8. This work has been relatively well-known to historians, particularly because it was used by Firishta in the seventeenth century. Lt. M.J. Rawlandson translated it into English in 1833 and a more authentic translation by S. Muhammad Husayn Nainar came out in 1942. I have used this translation, as reprinted in Shayk Zainuddin Makhdum, *Tuḥfatal-Mujāhidīn: A Historical Epic of the Sixteenth Century*, translated from the Arabic with annotations by S. Muhammad Husayn Nainar, Calicut and Kuala Lumpur, 2006.
9. Shayk Zainuddin, *Tuḥfatal-Mujāhidīn*, p. 6.
10. Ibid., p. 30.
11. Ibid., pp. 44–5.
12. Ibid., pp. 39–46.
13. *The Book of Duarte Barbosa: An Account of Countries Bordering on the Indian Ocean and their Inhabitants*, translated from Portuguese into English by Mansel Longworth Dames, 1918; repr., New Delhi: Asian Educational Services, 1989. M. Gangadharan has published excerpts concerning Malabar from the book with detailed annotations: *Duarte Barbosa's The Land of Malabar*, Kottayam: Mahatma Gandhi University, 2000. I have followed this edition here.

14. Gaspar Correa, *Lendas da India*, vol. I, Lisbon, 1858–60, p. 379, quoted in Gangadharan, *Duarte Barbosa*, p. 2.
15. Gangadharan, *Duarte Barbosa*, p. 13.
16. Ibid., pp. 13–18.
17. Makhdum, *Tuḥfatal-Mujāhidīn*, p. 4.
18. He describes them as 'this evil generation'. Gangadharan, *Duarte Barbosa*, p. 73n147.
19. However, towards the end of the sixteenth century, the Portuguese were exercised about the 'Christians' of Malabar having gone to heathenism and attempted to impose the Law of St. Peter on the St. Thomas Christians through the notorious Synod of Diamper. For an account, from the Catholic Point of View, see K.J. John, *Road to Diamper: An Exhaustive Study of the Synod of Diamper*, Cochin: Kerala Latin Catholic History Association, 1999. By the time of the Synod in 1599 it was already a whole century after the Portuguese had been here while Barbosa had come in about 1500 itself.
20. S. Muzaffar Ali, *The Geography of the Purāṇas*, 2nd edn., New Delhi: People's Publishing House, 1973, p. 153.
21. M.R. Raghava Varier, ed., *Keralolpatti Granthavari: The Kolattunāḍ Traditions*, Calicut: University of Calicut, 1984, pp. 54–5. The document describes itself as 'Jambudvīpōlpatti'.
22. *Lavaṇāmbudhi madhyē viḷaṅṅunna | jambudvīporu yōjana lakṣavum ||*
    ē̲ḻu dvīpukaḷiṅṅaneyuḷḷatil | uttamam i sthalam ennu vāḻtthunnu ||

    . . .

    itil onpatu khanṇḍaṅṅaḷ uṇṭallō | atil uttamam bhāratabhūtalam ||
    Pūntānam, *Jñānappāna*, in *Añcaṭi, Jñānappāna, Ōṇappāṭṭu*, ed. Manoj Kurur, Changanasseri, 1996, p. 96.
23. M.G.S. Narayanan, 'The Vedic-Sastraic-Puranic Element in Tamil Sangam Literature', *Proceedings of the Indian History Congress*, Aligarh, 1975.
24. Makhdum, *Tuḥfatal-Mujāhidīn*, p. 55.
25. Ibid., pp. 52–5.
26. Ibid., pp. 6–7.

CHAPTER 6

Of Ubiquitous Heroines and Elusive Heroes

The Cultural Milieu of Medieval *Maṇipravāḷa Kāvyas* from Kerala

In this chapter, I wish to make a plea for a literary (re)turn in the context of the talk of the 'anthropological turn' and the 'linguistic turn' that we are hearing about. Of course, the mutuality between history and literature has always been recognized; there is nothing new in this. Literature has been the historian's mainstay, particularly of those working on the earlier periods. Over time, the use of other sources of information such as archaeology, epigraphy and numismatics propelled the development of the discipline of history. Indeed these sources came to be regarded as central to historical knowledge of the ancient world. Literature lost its earlier position—histories based principally on literary sources came to be regarded as less 'scientific'. Happily, there has been a renewed awareness of the importance of literature in recent years, and alternative ways of using literature for historical writing have been developed. Apart from the time-tested way of using literature as a 'source' to study an event or an individual mentioned in a text, literature is also used to capture the climate, the spirit, of an age. The ambience within which a text was produced or the very sensibility of an age may be the subject-matter of the historian who wants to look at texts, including the visual images, in this way. While accepting the importance and legitimacy of these, I believe that there is a third way: reading texts with a sense of history. That is what I presume to be doing here—a literary *re*-turn.

I thus seek your indulgence for making use of this opportunity to present a preliminary report of an attempt to read literary texts from medieval Kerala once again, particularly poetry in what is called *Maṇipravāḷam*. *Maṇipravāḷam*, literally 'ruby-and-coral', was an amalgam of Malayalam and Sanskrit, a new 'language', evidence of the use of which for purposes of literary production is available from Kerala from the thirteenth-fourteenth centuries.[1] It was also used for writing scientific treatises on subjects like astronomy and medicine. *Līlātilakam*, a fourteenth-century work on the grammar, poetics and rhetoric of *Maṇipravāḷam*, defines it as 'the union of *bhāṣā* and Sanskrit', *bhāṣā* being used specifically in the sense of 'the language of Kerala' (*Keraḷabhāṣā*).[2] To be sure, using a blend of Sanskrit and the regional language for purposes of literary expression was not unique to Kerala. There are examples of such blending from many regions both in India and South-East Asia where Sanskrit had been popular. Bharata in his *Nāṭyaśāstra* calls such blendings *miśrabhāṣā* and *ardhasaṁskṛtam*.[3] A verse in the *Kāmasūtra* states that 'by telling stories at gatherings in a language which is neither too heavily Sanskritic nor too much in the local tongue, one earns esteem among people'.[4] This mixed language was known as *Maṇipravāḷam* itself in the Tamil- and the Telugu-speaking regions.[5] However, it acquired a certain autonomy in Kerala. I shall concern myself here with the world represented in that literature, making occasional references also to contemporary works in Sanskrit from Kerala. In fact, there is hardly any difference between the two in any respect except the language: *Kokilasandeśa* of Uddaṇḍa or *Śukasandeśa* of Lakṣmīdāsa might as well have been written in *Maṇipravāḷam*; alternatively, *Kokasandeśam* or *Uṇṇunīlīsandeśam*, both by anonymous authors, might have been written in Sanskrit.

Scholars in the past approached the corpus of *Maṇipravāḷam* literature mostly from the perspective of 'history of literature', looking at it as a 'movement' in Malayalam literature.[6] Their concern was largely with fixing the chronology of individual works as well as the identity of their authors where clues to it were available. A few also undertook some literary appreciation of these works. Writing commentaries on these has been, and is, a flourishing industry ever since their discovery by the turn of the last century.[7] There have also been attempts to use these as 'sources' for the economic and social history of Kerala.[8] However, reading these texts with a sense of history or placing them within the larger context of literary practices within the subcontinent is still a desideratum. It is in this context that I venture to make a fresh reading of these texts.

Earlier scholars writing about *Maṇipravāḷam* poetry in Kerala seem to have missed the extremely important fact that it is very much in the *kāvya* tradition in Sanskrit, both in form and content. I should even go to the extent of saying that it *is* Sanskrit poetry, written in *Maṇipravāḷam*. In fact, the very first sentence in *Līlātilakam*, the significance of which has not been appreciated properly, reads: 'What is stated to be the use as well as motive of Sanskrit *kāvya* itself is to be regarded as those of *Maṇipravāḷa kāvya*.'[9] It is not just in a prescriptive text that this identification occurs: *Candrotsavam*, one of the texts taken up for study here, looks upon *Maṇipravāḷam* (poetry) as of a piece with the Sanskrit *kāvya*s such as *Śākuntaḷa*, *Māḷavikāgnimitra*, *Kādambarī*, etc.[10] The failure to appreciate this has obscured the central features of *Maṇipravāḷam* poetry, namely, its urban life-world, the definitive influence of *Kāmasūtra* on the one side and the literary theories in Sanskrit starting with the *Nāṭyaśāstra* on the other, and other matters of detail. This putative urban world of *Maṇipravāḷam* was inhabited by the *gaṇikās* ('public women') and their *ceṭis* ('servant-maids'), the *nagarakas* ('men-about-town'), the *viṭas* ('libertines'), the *lampaṭas* (the 'profligate') and so on, apart from the celestial *apsarās*, *gandharvas*, *cāraṇas*, *siddhas*, *yakṣas*, *kiṁnaras*, *vidyādharas*, et al., who frequent these *kāvyas* on various missions.[11]

In looking at *Maṇipravāḷam* poetry in this manner, I beg to differ substantially from earlier scholars who took it primarily as a 'movement' in the history of Malayalam literature. They saw it as the expression of cultural and moral decadence, the product of the 'season when the Nampūtiris went into heat' (*Nampūtirimāruṭe poḷappukālam*).[12] The causality behind this statement was apparently two-fold: a preponderance of eroticism in the poetry, with courtesans as the central characters, on the one side, and the growth of the brāhmaṇical establishment in Kerala on the other. It is a fact that many brāhmaṇa settlements had come up and started controlling huge agrarian tracts with their corporations centred on temples by the time of the establishment of the Cēra kingdom of Mahōdayapuram in the ninth century. The corporate character of these bodies was gradually giving way to the domination of individual brāhmaṇa households as 'owners' of the substantial property of the temples in the post-Cēra period.[13] The growth of what is called the *janmi* system of landlordism was a concomitant of this,[14] which resulted in the emergence of a powerful class of brāhmaṇa landlords with considerable leisure. At the same time, the practice of only the eldest male member of Nampūtiri families marrying from within the caste, while the junior members went in for loose liaison with women of the various matrilineal castes, made the Nampūtiri morals less rigid than elsewhere.[15] It was this that prompted scholars to link the salaciousness in *Maṇipravāḷam* poetry with the rise of Nampūtiri landlordism. The literature, however, does not associate itself particularly with Nampūtiris. There is nothing in the texts to show that their authors, who were mostly anonymous, were Brāhmaṇas; and in at least one case where the authorship is known, it is a Cākyār, a caste of professional performers of Sanskrit drama as *kūṭiyāṭṭam* in temple-theatre. Another occasion for propounding *Maṇipravāḷam* was that of the *pāṭhaka*, a different form of story-telling in temples. A verse in the *Padyaratnam* states: 'This art of *Maṇipravāḷam* stays in *pāṭhaka*s. It is accompanied by [the performer with] hanging head-gear and is based on women.'[16] This Cākyār association is of particular importance as we shall presently see.[17] So also, the men represented in these texts are less often the landed Nampūtiris than members of other groups such as traders, fighters and even ruling elites. The context is rarely Nampūtiri *grāmas* and more often urban centres, marketplaces and even 'royal' households. In the circumstances, it becomes necessary to look at the evidence from this literature afresh.

The corpus that I seek to look at once again includes three *campūkāvyas*,[18] two *sandeśakāvyas*,[19] a *sargabandha* in five parts,[20] a collection of verses supposed to embody lessons given by a veteran courtesan to her daughter in their hereditary craft (*vaiśikatantra*),[21] a poem describing a city[22] and several shorter *kāvyas* and stand-alone verses (*cāṭu* or *muktaka*) brought together in one volume by modern scholars,[23] apart from several verses quoted as illustration in *Līlātilakam* mentioned previously. All these are generally centred on courtesans.

One thing that stands out clear and unmistakable about these texts is the heavily Sanskritic *kāvya* stamp they bear. The genres are mainly *campū* and *sandeśa*, with one single work that can be described as a *sargabandha*. There are several smaller *kāvyas*, *cāṭus* and *muktakas*. The narrative style, too, is comparable. *Nāṭakas* as such are absent; but the bulk of the *muktakas* and *cāṭus* brought together in the *Vaiśikatantram* and *Padyaratnam* as well as several of the illustrations given in *Līlātilakam* are from the stage manuals for the performance of Sanskrit *nāṭakas* in the *kūṭiyāṭṭam* mode known as *āṭṭaprakārams*. The metres used are invariably Sanskrit metres such as *Sragdharā*, *Śārdūlavikrīḍita*, and smaller ones like *Vasantatilakā*, *Anuṣṭubha* and *Āryā*. Interestingly, the *sandeśakāvyas* use *Mandākrāntā*, the metre that Kālidāsa has used in his *Meghasandeśa*, as if the use of any other metre would make it less than a *sandeśakāvya*! Dravidian metres, which are used in the Malayalam *pāṭṭu* that had become a popular genre by then, are scrupulously avoided in the verses, although the 'prose' (*gadya*) in the *campūs* is highly rhythm-bound, where the rhythm of some Dravidian metres could be identified.

The *kāvya* character of these works is not confined to their form. Their structure is entirely of the *kāvyas* in Sanskrit. This is clearest in the poetics and rhetoric of these works. We are singularly fortunate in getting a detailed contemporary discussion of its poetics and rhetoric in *Līlātilakam*. A word or two about the nature of this remarkable text may not be out of place here. It is divided into eight chapters, each of which is called a *śilpa*. They deal with (1) the general features of *Maṇipravāḷam*; (2) the 'body'[24] of the language where grammatical features like cases, person, gender, etc., are taken up for discussion; (3) *sandhi*; (4) the poetic flaws (*kāvyadoṣas*); (5) the merits (*guṇas*) of poetry; (6) 'embellishment of the sound' (*śabdālaṁkāra*); (7) 'embellishment of the meaning' (*arthālaṁkāra*); and, finally, (8) consideration of the 'flavour' (*rasa*). It will be clear from this list of contents itself that the anonymous author follows Sanskrit rhetoricians to the last detail, and this is important because there is evidence in the text that he is familiar with not only the somewhat well-developed literature on the subject in Tamil but also contemporary writings in

Kannada and Telugu. At the face of this, his clinging on to Sanskrit theories is of great interest and importance.

In fact, Chathanath Achyuthan Unni has, in a thoroughgoing study of rhetoric in Malayalam, shown convincingly that the poetics and rhetoric that *Līlātilakam* sets out are, to the last detail, from Sanskrit.[25] He has shown how deftly the text uses theories of earlier masters such as Bharata (*Nāṭyaśāstra*), Bhāmaha (*Kāvyālaṁkāra*), Daṇḍin (*Kāvyādarśa*), Vāmana (*Kāvyālaṁkārasūtra*), Bhaṭṭa Tauta (*Kāvyakautuka*), Udbhaṭa (*Kāvyālaṁkārasaṁgraha*), Ānandavardhana (*Dhvanyāloka*), Abhinavagupta (*Abhinavabhāratī* commentary on *Nāṭyaśāstra* as well as *Locana* commentary on *Dhvanyāloka*), Rudraṭa (*Kāvyālaṁkāra*), Bhaṭṭa Nāyaka (*Hṛdayadarpaṇa*), Ruyyaka (*Alaṁkārasarvasva*), Kuntaka (*Vakroktijīvita*), Rājaśekhara (*Kāvyamīmāṁsā*), Bhoja (*Sarasvatīkaṇṭhābharaṇa*) and Vidyānātha (*Pratāparudrīya*), thus crafting a rhetoric of *Maṇipravāḷam* entirely on their basis. To be sure, the author of *Līlātilakam* does not propound any new theory; nor does he set out to defend one particular school against other competing schools. His purpose was different—it was to examine the existing corpus of texts in *Maṇipravāḷam* and define, on the basis of this examination, the purpose and meaning of it. In doing so, he does it exclusively on the lines of his exhaustive knowledge of the literature on the subject in Sanskrit. In spite of his acquaintance with what is available in other south Indian languages such as Tamil and Kannada, *Līlātilakam* does not use their details there. This is not without significance.

Maṇipravāḷam's total dependence on the *kāvya* tradition does not just begin or end with these external features or the prescriptive aspects of prosody, poetics or rhetoric—it goes beyond both form and theory. A reading of the texts shows that these texts are permeated through and through with the urban sensibility that *kāvyas* in Sanskrit express. This is based on a real urban experience that Kerala went through in the medieval period. True, historians have not so far made a detailed study of the urban processes or experience in Kerala in this period. There is, however, strong reason to believe that trade and urbanization had reached a relatively high level in Kerala in this period. The texts describe towns very elaborately. Thus, *Uṇṇiyaccīcaritam* has a lengthy passage on the town of Tirumarutūr.[26] In describing Tirumarutūr, the poet says that it is superior in all respects to not only towns like Aḷakā, Laṁkā, Bhogavatī, Amarāvatī (which may have existed only in the poet's imagination) but also Kollam, Koṭuṅṅallūr, Vaḷḷuvanagarappaḷḷi, Kuṇavāy, Maṁgalapuram and Dōrasamudram (of which he may have had first-hand knowledge). Similarly, *Uṇṇiyāṭīcaritam*'s description of the town of Śrīparvatam with its busy marketplace concludes by saying that it was equal to Kōḻikkoṭu, Kollam, Vayaṉāṭu, Mutukōṭṭūr, Kuḷamūkku and Māṭāvi,[27] each of which was a prosperous trading centre in medieval Kerala. *Uṇṇunīlīsandeśam* describes Kollam as putting even the town of Indra to shame. In the port there are ships big and small, coming from far and near, crossing the ocean like the fame of the ruler of Vēṇāṭu. In short, there is no place equal to it in the fourteen worlds.[28] The market of Kariyanāṭṭukāvu is described as unequalled even by Kōḻikkōṭu and Kollam, although the goddess of prosperity along with all people gathered there withdraw from there by evening and not a child will be seen there after that![29]

This growth in trade was the fallout of two developments. Much of the wetland in Kerala had been utilized for rice cultivation by the time of the Cēra kingdom of Mahōdayapuram (AD 800–1124). Dry land, known as *paṟampu* or *purayiṭam*, was gradually being exploited, particularly for purposes of cultivating what are known as 'cash crops' or 'commercial crops' such as coconut, areca nut, pepper, betel leaves, etc. Raghava Varier and Rajan Gurukkal have described this as the '*paṟampu-purayiṭam* system of economy'.[30] Inscription from the twelfth century onwards point to the increased use of such dry land,[31] which later came to be known as 'garden land'. A verse in *Śukasandeśa*, a Sanskrit *kāvya* from Kerala in this period, introduces Kerala as 'rich in coconut and areca palms on which climb pepper and betel vines'.[32] Accounts of trade contained in the writings of Arab, Chinese and European travellers mention precisely these as the items that were traded in from the port towns of Kerala. Apart from this development of the production of tradable surplus, there was also a growing demand for these products in the international market. West Asian trade continued in the hands of Jewish, Syrian Christian and Muslim traders. Chinese trade opened up in a big way by the twelfth to thirteenth centuries. European travellers were visiting the coast of Kerala, trade being one of their primary interests.[33] This growth in trade brought in its train the rise of urban centres and urbanism.

Apart from mentioning the names of these towns and making comparisons among them, the texts contain detailed descriptions of marketplaces in individual towns. True, many of these descriptions are stereotypical in nature; but it can hardly be denied that the stereotype itself is based on the reality of a marketplace in a town. Thus, we have elaborate accounts of the marketplace of Tirumarutūr in *Uṇṇiyaccīcaritam*,[34] of Kaṇṭiyūr in *Uṇṇiyāṭīcaritam*,[35] of Āyāṉārciṟa in *Uṇṇiccirutēvīcaritam*,[36] and of various towns in *Uṇṇunīlīsandeśam*.[37] In the descriptions of these marketplaces are accounts of the various articles that were bought and sold in these markets. They included local products as well as items that were imported from places far afield such as China and Arabia. Nearly every text, describing a market, speaks about the quarrels among the vendors gathered there, the acrid tongue of the fishwives, the unintelligible speech of people from far-off places and so on.[38] The price of an Arabian horse is mentioned in one place.[39] Ships from China as well as the Coromandel Coast are described in the *Uṇṇunīlīsandeśam* as docked in the port of Kollam.[40] Texts abound in motifs of ships. Thus, a ship approaching the port is used as metaphor to describe a woman going to a man.[41] The *Candrotsavam* advises the heroine to behave with prudence, which is likened to a ship steered properly.[42] Similarly, another verse in the same text uses the motif of a ship in the ocean to describe the circumlocution of a woman.[43]

Incidentally, Chinese and Arabic pottery dating from this period (thirteenth to sixteenth centuries) have been discovered in huge quantities from Kollam and other coastal towns of Kerala.[44] This has to be read with descriptions of these towns by Arab and Chinese travellers in this period. So also, the texts give detailed accounts of the varieties of coins transacted in these marketplaces. It is interesting that, apart from local issues such as *kāśu*, *kaḻañcu*, *kāṇam*, *accu*, *āṉayaccu*, etc., even foreign coins such as *tiramam* (for Dirham) and *aśaravi* (for Ashrafi) find a place in the lists.[45] On the whole, therefore, there is reason to believe that there was brisk trade and a concomitant urban atmosphere in many centres in Kerala in this period. The towns and marketplaces in the *Maṇipravāḷam* texts are not just matters of imagination, although the image of the urban, as carried in the *kāvya* literature in Sanskrit, may have heavily influenced the authors.

Urbanism was not just about the existence of trade and marketplaces. Although it is argued that marketplaces constituted the 'core' of the urban space structure,[46] there were other parts of the town which were no less of 'cores', depending upon the point of reference from which one is looking at it.[47] The *Maṇipravāḷam* texts describe other aspects of the towns as well, such as the 'royal' palaces, the temples, other residential mansions, the roads, gardens, tanks and so on in relation to the towns, references being too many to be quoted. Towns were also the places where the *nagarakas* ('men-about-town') lived. The description of one of the paramours of Uṇṇiyaccī is as if it is copied from the *Nagarakavṛtta* in the *Kāmasūtra*: 'wearing sandals, smearing his body with musk and vermilion, exuding fragrance of sandalwood and aloe. . .'.[48] Similar descriptions are available in *Uṇṇiyāṭīcaritam*,[49] *Candrotsavam*,[50] etc. So also, there is the presence of other kinds of profligate libertines that the *Kāmasūtra* speaks about, although they do not play any central role in the texts.[51]

We have descriptions of the courtesans which answer, to the last detail, what the Sanskrit *kāvyas* see in them. There is, however, a major difference. While the *gaṇikā* is generally the female counterpart of the *nagaraka* in Sanskrit literature,[52] they are the central figures in *Maṇipravāḷam*. This is no contradiction; but it is important that the *nagaraka* hero's presence is much less visible than that of the *gaṇikā* heroine who is ubiquitous in the texts. This may be explained against the peculiar social reality in Kerala. Most non-Brāhmaṇa upper castes were matrilineal and women had a much stronger presence in Kerala. Marriage as an institution was not very deeply entrenched, with *sambandham* or a somewhat loose liaison being the accepted practice. It was not just that the *Nampūtiri Brāhmaṇas* courted such alliances—members of other castes too entered into such alliances from one's own caste or from other, upper, castes. Women in such a situation had a greater presence than men. Thus it may be said, even at the expense of using an oxymoron, that the *nagaraka* hero had only an absent presence in *Maṇipravāḷam*.

In fact, as I mentioned earlier, it is this celebration of women and looking upon them as so many instruments of pleasure that attracted the ire of modern scholars who were brought up within the tradition of Victorian prudery. While there is no denying that these poems are a 'little warmer than necessary',[53] it is equally important that the debt that they have to the *kāvya* tradition in Sanskrit should not be lost sight of. In fact, there are *kāvyas* in Sanskrit which are equally warm or warmer.[54] In seeing these heroines as cast in the same mould of their counterparts, namely the courtesans of the *kāvya* literature in Sanskrit, we should also be able to appreciate similar expressions of art such as sculpture, dance in the *Mohiniyāṭṭam* style and so on. Rather than recognizing them as expressions of an urban sensibility, to say that they mark moral degradation or cultural decadence is passing unnecessary judgements.

The courtesans of the *Maṇipravāḷam* texts belong largely to the elite category of *gaṇikās*, courtesans *de luxe*; they are no ordinary prostitutes. This distinction is very significant. Courtesans, it may be remembered, form an important urban phenomenon. In fact, the courtesans of *Maṇipravāḷam* texts are cast in the same mould of their counterparts in the Sanskrit *kāvyas*, where they are part of the urban setting. It will be interesting to compare the descriptions of the details of the palatial residential houses of the *gaṇikās* in the *Maṇipravāḷa kāvyas* such as *Uṇṇiyaccīcaritam*, *Uṇṇiyāṭīcaritam* and *Uṇṇunīlīsandeśam* with the descriptions of the houses of *veśyās* in the *bhāṇas* like *Dhūrtaviṭasaṁvāda*.[55] Our heroines answer to all the details in the descriptions of the *gaṇikā* in the narrative texts as well as the prescriptions in normative ones like the *Kāmasūtra*.[56]

The debt to *Kāmasūtra* that *Maṇipravāḷam* acknowledges is so much that there are many direct references and indirect allusions to the work in the poems. Speaking about the arrival of the rainy season, the poet says in a verse in the *Padyaratnam* that the time is most opportune for making an exegesis of the *advaitaśāstra* of Manmatha.[57] *Kāmaśāstra* is spoken of as dealing with Vedānta in another verse as well.[58] Elsewhere in the same collection, it is stated that a few youngsters had composed a commentary on *Vātsyāyana* on the wall the previous night.[59] Another verse almost copies the prescriptions of foreplay in the *Kāmasūtra*.[60] *Candrotsavam* says that Candrikā entertained Moon with the different *karaṇas* such as *praṇayakalaha* (love-quarrel), *alpahāsa* (reserved smile), *adharadāna*, *cumbana* (kiss), etc.[61] The heroine's mother prays to Kāmadeva for a girl child and takes a vow that if she is blessed with one, she would have her perform the whole of *Vātsyāyanam* every day![62] *Śukasandeśam*, a Sanskrit *sandeśakāvya* from contemporary Kerala, refers to young prostitutes (*veśakanyāḥ*) being teased by libertines of house-parrots (*śukaviṭa*) when they reach late for lessons in *Kāmasūtra*.[63]

The image of the courtesan in *Maṇipravāḷam* poetry seems to have had its prototype in that of the *apsarās* of Sanskrit literature.

A courtesan in many cases is an *apsarā* fallen as human following a curse. Uṇṇiyāṭī, the heroine of the *campū* bearing her name, was Prāvṛt, an *apsarā*, reborn following a curse of Rōhiṇī. Naṅṅaippiḷḷa, the grandmother of the heroine of *Uṇṇiyaccīcaritam*, was of *apsarā* extraction. Uṇṇiyaccī herself is described as 'stealing the charm of *cāraṇa*, *siddha* and [other] celestial women'.[64] Medinīcandrikā, the heroine of *Candrotsavam*, was born on earth following a curse of the Moon provoked by Menakā, the *apsarā*. In a similar fashion, celestial beings are the cause of separation between the heroes and heroines in the *sandeśakāvyas*. This *apsarā* connection is extremely important because, when their images got crafted in Sanskrit literature, it was the model of the *gaṇikās* that fired the poets' imagination. M.P. Sankunni Nair has demonstrated that the *apsarās* are *gaṇikās* in celestial guise.[65] The *gaṇikā* of Sanskrit *kāvyas*, very much part of the urban setting that saw the production of these *kāvyas*, inspired the image of the *apsarā* and the *apsarā* inspired the *gaṇikā* of *Maṇipravāḷam* literature. A full circle!

These courtesans were well-educated. Even here, there is a close correspondence between the descriptions of the education of the courtesan in the *Maṇipravāḷam* texts and the prescriptions in the *Vidyāsamuddeśa* section of *Kāmasūtra*.[66] The curriculum seems to have included music, dance, painting, story-telling, versification, *kāvyas* in both Sanskrit and *Maṇipravāḷam*, juggling, chess, different games played during the Oṇam festival, gambling, and so on.[67] So also, they were adept in the different ways in which they could entertain their patrons (or clients?).[68]

In this context, special mention may be made of the *Vaiśikatantram*. The title of the work, if it was in the original and if indeed an 'original' existed, demands special attention for the strong association it has with the title of a whole section in *Kāmasūtra*, namely *Vaiśika*.[69] It is in the form of advices given by an experienced *gaṇikā* to her daughter, based on what she in turn had acquired from older generations. It shares all features with the *Kuṭṭanīmata* of Dāmodaragupta. As indicated by the title, the text aims at exposing the secrets of the whole craft of prostitution. It is significant that many of the verses contained in it as well as those in the *Kuṭṭanīmata* are used by Cākyārs in the performance of Kūṭiyāttam. In fact, modern scholars depended heavily on the stage manuals used by the Cākyārs for constituting the text of

Vaiśikatantram. Whether a single work called *Vaiśikatantram* existed or not, the verses in it were in circulation in the period that we are concerned with, particularly among the Cākyārs who performed in the theatre.

This Cākyār factor gives a clue to not only the origin and development but also the specific character of *Maṇipravāḷam* in Kerala. The *Padyaratnam* verse quoted previously unequivocally states that the art of *Maṇipravāḷam* obtains in *pāṭhaka* performances, which in turn was inspired by the *bhāṇas* in Sanskrit. A Sanksrit *bhāṇa* from Kerala, the *Rasasadana*, though slightly later in date (sixteenth century), has the following description of the performer of the *bhāṇa*:

> On the stage with a lighted lamp in the middle, with the *Naṅṅyār* women on the side [marking the rhythm], with the front glittering with brāhmaṇa connoisseurs, and with the *Nambyār* playing on the earthenware drum behind, a *naṭa* acts a *prabandha* with clear expressions.[70]

This is a realistic description of a Cākyār performing *kūttu*. In other texts, too, there are similar statements. Three verses in *Uṇṇiyāṭīcaritam*, on the heroine, are stated to have been recited by the Cākyār during a performance.[71] Indra overhears a *Maṇipravāḷa śloka* that a paramour sings in the *Uṇṇiccirutēvīcaritam* and promptly falls in love with the heroine.[72] The *vidūṣaka* in the *kūṭiyāṭṭam* used to explain the theme and the progress of the story in *Maṇipravāḷam* and even recited parodies (*pratiśloka*) of the verses recited by the main characters.

So, it is not unlikely that *Maṇipravāḷam* poetry as it developed in Kerala had its origin in the Sanskrit theatre. Starting with the *miśrabhāṣā* and *ardhasaṁskṛtaṁ* that Bharata advised in performances and the *goṣṭhīs* that *Kāmasūtra* speaks of where the *nagaraka* is advised to tell stories in a language 'which is neither too heavily Sanskritic nor too much in the local tongue', it grew through the *pāṭhaka*, *kūttu* and *kūṭiyāṭṭam* performances. *Maṇipravāḷam* gradually became a 'new language' in Kerala. The process was slow, complex and interesting. The earliest literary compositions from Kerala, such as the *Āścaryacūḍāmaṇi* of Śaktibhadra (eighth-ninth centuries) or *Tapatīsamvaraṇam* and *Subhadrādhanañjayam* of Kulaśekhara (ninth century) were not only *nāṭakas* but were also used in a big way by Cākyārs for the performance of *kūṭiyāṭṭam*. The Cākyārs made improvisations to suit local sensibilities, which were duly resented by purists.[73] The Cākyārs, however, carried on. The *vidūṣaka*, who has only a marginal role in the original plays, began to take the centre-stage. He claims four full nights all for himself in the plays as his *nirvahaṇa* which purports to be expounding the '*puruṣārthas*'—*puruṣārthas* in this case being *aśana*, *rājasevā*, *veśyāvinoda* and *vañcana* in the place of *dharma*, *artha*, *kāma* and *mokṣa*. They regaled the audience with ribald jokes and erotic poems from well-known texts such as *Kuṭṭanīmata* and so on as well as verses composed *de novo*. Such verses became part of the Cākyārs' repertoire. Whole new *kāvyas* were composed on these lines. In this way, a *Maṇipravāḷavidyā* came to be established, which was 'based on women'—*mahiḷāḷimahāspadā*—all the way. If it is permeated through and through with the *kāvya* tradition in Sanskrit, it is because it had its basis in Sanskrit *nāṭakas*. The ambience, too, was comparable.

A question may raise itself here. Why did the poets choose to write in *Maṇipravāḷam* if they were expressing things Sanskritic all the way? The explanation is found in the verse quoted from *Kāmasūtra*: a language which is too Sanskritic would fail to communicate to an audience of considerable variety; and telling stories exclusively in the local tongue will be too pedestrian. This was a strategy that had been suggested by Bharata, commented on by Abhinavagupta and followed by Vātsyāyana and others, perhaps all over the country and even outside. The only difference is that it saw its fulfilment in Kerala, taking the *kāvya* tradition in Sanskrit to *Maṇipravāḷam* in a consummate manner. The reason for this is to be sought in the preponderance of the brāhmaṇical element in society with a heavy dose of Sanskrit *kāvya* in the education, not only of the Nampūtiris but of the upper sections of society who were under their influence. This combination did not obtain in other parts of south India where, in spite of the presence of *Maṇipravāḷam*, we do not find its development along the lines it took in Kerala.

This examination shows that the literary practice in medieval Kerala in what was called *Maṇipravāḷam* was actually a continuation of the *kāvya* tradition in Sanskrit. The *kāvya* reached Kerala mainly through the *nāṭakas* and took root there through their performances. This is not to deny the presence of other kinds of *kāvyas* that are explicitly mentioned. A second aspect that comes out of this examination is the urban ambience of the poems, contrary to what earlier scholars had thought about them. True, we have beautiful vignettes of the rural in them; but they are as seen by a townsman. It did express the sensibility that had developed in Kerala by this period; but the cultural baggage that it had carried with it was what it had carried from the larger cosmopolis of which it had become part by the tenth century. Was it really a case of the cosmopolitan world of Sanskrit disintegrating,[74] or was it that even the literature in the regional languages started behaving like 'the vernacular form of the cosmopolitan' rather than 'the cosmopolitan form of the vernacular', where it indicates not exactly the disintegration of the cosmopolitan? Alternatively, it may be possible to speak about the phenomenon more meaningfully in terms of the emergence of a regional identity—the self-confidence that the region of Kerala had acquired by now, defined in its own terms as well as in contradistinction with its 'others'.[75] The identity that Kerala had acquired by the time of the Cēra kingdom of Mahōdayapuram had its special features including a heavy brāhmaṇical character. Those sections of society which were responsible for this identity were representing the region that had taken shape by then in a particular way; in so representing, they were making use of the tools available in the Sanskrit *kāvya* tradition with which they were familiar from the period from which the identity and its affiliation had been articulated.

APPENDIX

I give below brief outlines of the texts used here for the benefit of those who are not familiar with Malayalam, particularly as none of these is available in English translation.

The *Campūs*

Uṇṇiyaccīcaritam

The earliest of these, *Uṇṇiyaccīcaritam* (The Story of Uṇṇiyaccī), is a *campūkāvya* set in the northern parts of Kerala, in what are today the Kannur and Wynad districts. The surviving portion of the work opens with the description of Ardhanārīśvara in the temple of Tiruccaḷari. After praising the local king, Puṟakiḻār, who got the roof of the temple covered with copper, the work goes on to describe the different deities and *tīrthas* in the temple. It proceeds to the nearby temple of Tirunelli where Viṣṇu is worshipped. An elaborate description of the town of Tirumarutūr follows. There is the temple of Śiva in that town, where the Aṣṭamī festival is being celebrated with much pomp. All beautiful women of the region are assembled there. A gandharva youth who was watching the festival from above happens to see Uṇṇīyaccī, a vivacious damsel: Is she Lakṣmī? Śacī? Rōhiṇī? The Goddess of Light? Moonlight that has taken feminine form? Or another arrow that Brahmā created for Kāmadeva? The Gandharva youth forgot his station in this trance and descended on the earth taking human form. He met a *caṭṭa* (Brāhmaṇa student) whom he asked: 'Who could this lady be, who has stolen at once the lovely charm of *cāraṇa*, *siddha* and [other] celestial women as well as my heart?' The *caṭṭa* gave him details about the lady. A beautiful woman of the race of *apsarās*, called Naṅṅaippiḷḷa, was born in Atiyamānallūr. She had a daughter, Acciyār by name, through the chief of Aḷḷariṭam house and the girl whom the Gandharva saw was Uṇṇiyaccī, the younger of Acciyār's two daughters. She has taken up residence in the town of Kōlam, the capital of Puṟakiḻārnāṭu.

The Gandharva stays awake all night, thinking of Uṇṇiyaccī. Accompanied by the *caṭṭa*, he proceeds to her house in the morning. Then follows an elaborate description of the prosperous marketplace on the way, where he sees merchants from far and near. The poet gives a detailed account of the merchandise of different varieties. He reaches Uṇṇiyaccī's palatial residence, the description of which answers to all prescriptions of architectural treatises. There is a hilarious description of those who have assembled there just to have a glance of Uṇṇīyaccī. They include merchants, sorcerers, physicians, astrologers, brāhmaṇas, students and others, their boastfulness being particularly the butt of the poet's laughter. The Gandharva's day is made when he is able to see Uṇṇiyaccī at last. Following an elaborate description of her from tip to toe, the poet closes with a prayer to the Goddess of Paḻañcēri that she protect us.

Uṇṇiyāṭīcaritam

Uṇṇiyāṭīcaritam sings in a similar fashion the praise of Uṇṇiyāṭī, daughter of the ruler of Ōṭanāṭu in what later was central Travancore, and a danseuse called Kuṭṭatti of the Ceṟukara house. The poem tells us that she was actually a Gandharva woman born on earth on account of a curse that had befallen her. It opens with the description of Udayaparvata and two Gandharva lineages that lived in its valleys. One of them worshipped Sun while the other were worshippers of Moon.

Into the lineage of the Sun-worshippers was born the extremely beautiful girl, Prāvṛṭ. Once when Prāvṛṭ was playing with her friends, Moon happened to see her and was overtaken by lust. He spent some time with her; but was not entirely satisfied. He approached Rohiṇī, still fired by the urge for sex. Realizing the background, Rohiṇī cursed Prāvṛṭ that she be born as a human. However, on the supplication of Maṇiśekhara, her father, it was granted that she would retain her charm and vivacity as well as accomplishments in dance, music and poetry.

One day Moon heard a song in a captivating female voice from the earth. He was promptly stricken with love. He asked Suvāka and Matidīpa, descendants of the Moon-worshippers living on Moon's path, to go and find out whose song it was. They went, taking an aerial route. They saw the earth surrounded by the oceans and centred on the Meru. They go on to describe the most beautiful Kerala, celebrated in all three worlds, and the town of Tṛśśūr, famous for the Śiva temple, and Mahōdaya, the capital of the kings of Kerala. In that blessed country was the principality of Ōṭanāṭu, where there were many houses of great men, prosperous with grain and wealth as well as accomplished in all arts including sweet music. The city of Kaṇṭiyūr, its capital, was 'celebrated in all ten directions and destroying the pride of Indra's capital'. The description of the marketplace of Śrīparvata there is very elaborate and so is that of the other quarters of the city. In that city are the two palace complexes of the ruler of Ōṭnāṭu, comparable to Aḷakā and Indrapurī. Even poets like Bhāravi would find it difficult to describe these.

Here they descend on the earth. They worship at the temple of Kaṇṭiyūr, which is described in great detail. In an exquisitely decorated hall, a performance was going on. The actor was elaborately dressed and commanded respect. The verses he recited were on Uṇṇīyāṭī. When they enquired who this performer was, they were told that it was Damōdara, a Cākyār, accomplished in all branches of knowledge. Paying their respects to him, they introduced themselves as from *paradeśa*, and told him the purpose of their visit. He told them that a number of verses have been composed on her and took them to her place. Asked about her lineage and other details, the Cākyār tells them, in several verses, about her parents, the ruler of Ōṭanāṭu and the danseuse of the Ceṟukara house. He goes on to describe the birth of Uṇṇiyāṭī and then dwells upon the beauty of Uṇṇiyāṭī. They reach her house and see the variety of people gathered to see Uṇṇiyāṭī, whose description is highly sarcastic. Passing the *ceṭīs*, they wade through the several halls and rooms in the house to finally see Uṇṇiyāṭī. The Gandharvas pay their obeisance to her and then follows an elaborate description of her beauty, where the text ends abruptly as the last leaves of the manuscript have not survived.

Uṇṇiccirutēvīcaritam

Uṇṇiccirutēvīcaritam has a similar theme. It opens with a description of the beautiful brāhmaṇa *grāma* of Cōkiram in the present-day Malappuram District, the accomplished Somayājins there and the temple of Dakṣiṇāmūrti. This is followed by the description of the place called Poyilam within Cōkiram, where the garden takes the central place. *Viṭas* (libertines), danseuses and several others live there, where it is noisy with the galloping sound of horses and even rulers approaching. The poet describes the other temples, and the house of the heroine, Tōṭṭuvāypaḷḷi, and the gardens, tanks and paddy fields attached to it. There, a poet composed and sung a *śloka* in *Maṇipravāḷam*, hearing which Indra approached the poet and asked who she was. He told Indra that in the vicinity there was the house of the accomplished danseuses of Poyilam which surpassed the fame of Laṁkā, Aḷakā and Amarāvati. A great danseuse by the name of Naṅṅa Ayya was born into that house. Her daughter was Rāyirampiḷḷa. Uṇṇiccirutēvi (about whom the *śloka* was sung) was her daughter. Then follows an elaborate description of the beauty of Uṇṇiccirutēvi. Accompanied by the poet, Indra goes to the house of Uṇṇiyccirutēvi and then there is the regulation description of the marketplace, the vendors there and the female servants. Indra sees the house of Uṇṇiccirutēvi, which is described very elaborately. There were, he says, men-in-attendance as well as paramours of different descriptions. At the end of these hilarious descriptions, the poem ends abruptly as the last few leaves have not survived.

The *Sandeśakāvyas*

There are two *sandeśakāvyas* in *Maṇipravāḷam*, both using the structure and theme of *Meghasandeśa*. *Līlātilakam* alludes to a third one, *Kākasandeśam*, and quotes one verse from it; but it has not come down to us. The Sanskrit *sandeśas* from Kerala produced in this period, viz., *Śukasandeśa* of Lakṣmīdāsa and *Kokilasandeśa* of Uddaṇḍa too can be included in this category.

(a) *Uṇṇunīlīsandeśam*

Uṇṇunīlīsandeśam, like its exemplar, has two parts: the *pūrvasandeśa* and the *uttarasandeśa*. It has for its theme the separation of a paramour from his love and a message of love he sent to her through a messenger. A *yakṣī* kidnapped the hero when he was sleeping with his love and took him away through the aerial route. When the *yakṣī* reached Thiruvananthapuram, the hero woke up on the strength of the *mantra*s. Dropped by the *yakṣī*, he landed softly inside the temple of Padmanābha. He was stricken with the pain of separation when Ādityavarman, the crown price of Tṛppāppūr, appeared before him. The hero requested Ādityavarman to take his message of love to his parted heroine away in Kaṭatturutti. A detailed description of the route from Thiruvananthapuram to Kaṭatturutti follows, with the important chieftains, temples, towns, marketplaces and, of course, courtesans en route getting due attention. The *uttarasandeśa* contains an elaborate description of the town of Kaṭatturutti, the heroine's house, the message of love and closes with the regulation prayer that this mission be no cause for separation between the messenger and his beloved.

(b) *Kokasandeśam*

Kokasandeśam is slightly different in theme. The hero, who was sitting with his heroine in Dēśiṅṅanāṭu, suddenly faints. The reason was that he was separated from the heroine in a dream as a celestial being (*khecara*) carried him away and dropped him on the banks of a tank. He comes across a *cakravāka* (*Anas casarca*) bird, and sends a message to his separated heroine, all in the dream. The route from Tṛpraṅṅōṭu in Malappuram District to the destination is described with all the usual details. Unfortunately, as the manuscript is incomplete, it stops with Eṭappaḷḷi and the remaining part of the *pūrvasandeśa* and the whole of *uttarasandeśa* have not come down to us.

Other *Kāvyas*

There are a few other *kāvyas* as well in the corpus of *Maṇipravāḷam*.

(a) *Candrotsavam*

Candrotsavam is a *sargabandha* in five cantos. The poem opens with a *gandharva* falling in love with a *kiṁnarī*. She is attracted, a la *Kalyāṇasaugandhika*, by the strange fragrance of a flower which she had not seen so far and asks the *gandharva* to get her the flower and the *gandharva* promptly sets out. After wandering in different places he returns on the sixth day and tells his love that the fragrance was not of any particular flower but that which emanated from the 'moon festival' that was celebrated on the earth. Apologizing for the delay caused by his being detained by the moon festival, he goes on to describe it and the circumstances leading to its celebration.

The moon festival is something that the gods used to celebrate. Once when Indra was celebrating one, Moon was present there with his wife, Candrikā. Menakā, the *apsarā*, who came to attend the festival fixed a rendezvous with Moon with a gesture through the corner of her eye. Candrikā got scent of this and reached the appointed spot earlier in the guise of Menakā. They engaged in all love-sports, when Menakā reached there. Feeling cheated, Moon cursed Candrikā that she be born a human on earth. When Candrikā applied for *śāpamokṣa*, it was granted that she would be redeemed after celebrating a moon festival.

There was a celebrated family of courtesans in the territory of Ciṟṟilappaḷḷi. Into that family was born a beautiful girl, named Medinīveṇṇilāvu (Moonlight on Earth). Her childhood was described appropriately as a preparation for the days to come. When she came of age, she decided to celebrate the moon festival. She conferred with the major courtesans of Kerala about its desirability with which all concurred. A priest was consulted and he prescribed the details of the conduct of the festival.

The festival is described in elaborate detail. Residential quarters for the distinguished guests are erected and so is the hall where the festival is to be celebrated. Nothing is wanting in luxury in these. The local ruler arrives, followed by the courtesans *de luxe* all over Kerala. Many rich men, the *cāttira* troupes for entertainment, poets, scholars and many other respectable invitees arrive. The poem closes with the blessing that Moon be pleased by the offering of the flowers that are descriptions of the story of Medinīveṇṇīlāvu.

(b) *Vaiśikatantram*

Vaiśikatantram is not quite a *kāvya.* It is a collection of verses supposedly containing advice from a veteran courtesan to her daughter in the craft of prostitution. All tricks that the courtesan has to play to keep her customers in good humour are described. Many verses are repetitive and there is no single theme that informs the work. Many of these verses are available in the *āṭṭaprakārams* of *Kuṭiyāṭṭam*. Scholars have doubted whether this is a single 'work' or a collection of stand-alone verses. In any case, the debt it has to similar texts like the *Kuṭṭanīmata* of Dāmodaragupta from early medieval Kashmir is striking.

(c) *Padyaratnam*

Padyaratnam is a collection brought together by modern scholars. It contains several short *kāvyas* about courtesans, containing one, two, eleven, etc., verses about individual heroines, the longest being on Kauṇōttarā, where 50 verses are devoted to her. There is considerable intertextuality in these, where the heroine of one *kāvya,* such as *Candrotsavam* or *Uṇṇunīlīsandeśam* finds mention here. A whole verse is common between this collection and *Candrotsavam*. The world of courtesans is brought out authentically in these verses.

(d) *Anantapuravarṇanam*

This is a dry account of the city of Thiruvananthapuram with its famous temple.

NOTES

1. I may be allowed to clarify here that I am concerned with the early stages of *Maṇipravāḷam*. Even the works of later writers such as Kaṇṇaśśan, Ceṟuśśēri and Tuñcatt Eḻuttacchan, which are *Keraḷabhāṣāgānams*, use this amalgamated language. The still later *Śrīkṛṣṇacaritam* calls itself *Maṇipravāḷam* although it is very different from the early *Maṇipravāḷam* texts in terms of content. The term *Maṇipravāḷam* was a synonym for Malayalam [literature] even in nineteenth and early twentieth centuries. For instance, *Naḷini* of Kumāran Āśān, which can be said to have inaugurated the modern in Malayalam poetry, used to be called a *Maṇipravāḷa-kāvyam*! The late nineteenth-century translation of *Abhijñānaśākuntala* into Malayalam by Keraḷa Varma Valiya Kōil Taṁpurān was known as *Maṇipravāḷa Śākuntaḷam* (1898). Statements such as 'Our Malayalam language that is *Maṇipravāḷam*' (*maṇipravāḷam enna nammuṭe malayāḷabhāṣa*) were very common in the twentieth century.
2. *Bhāṣā-saṁskṛta-yogo maṇipravāḷam*: *Līlātilakam*, *śilpa* 1, *sūtra* 1, p. 284 (my translation). I have used the edition by Elamkulam P.N. Kunjan Pillai, *Līlātilakam* (*Maṇipravāḷalakṣaṇam*); repr., Kottayam, 1990. The anonymous author explains in the *vṛtti* to this *sūtra* that *bhāṣā* is used here in the sense of the language of Kerala: *bhāṣā cātra keraḷabhāṣā*. There is some contemporary discussion whether *maṇi* is pearl or ruby, even while it is accepted that *pravāḷa* is coral. *Līlātilakam* is clear: 'Sanskrit [used in *Maṇipravāḷam*] should be delicate and well-known and *bhāṣā* should be acceptable to the learned. *Maṇipravāḷam* is so designated on account of a harmonious synthesis of these two. When ruby and coral are strung together by means of the same thread, the two will go well as if they were one on account of the similarity of colour—not ruby and pearl nor coral and sapphire': *atra bhāṣāvad atiprasiddhaṁ sukumārākṣaraṁ saṁskṛtaṁ. bhāṣā ca prāyaśo 'pāmarajanaprasiddhā. tathāvidhayoreva anayoḥ saṁśleṣo bhavet. tatsauṣṭhava pratipādanārtham idaṁ maṇipravāḷam iti samjñā. māṇikyavidrumayorhi samānasūtre protayostulyajātivarṇatayā aikyamiva ābhāti. na punar māṇikyamuktayōḥ pravāḷanīlayorvā.* *Līlātilakam*, *śilpa* 1, *sutra* 1, *vṛtti* 1, p. 285 (my translation). Apart from this prescription, the authors themselves knew that they were composing poems in a language where elements of both *bhāṣā* and Sanskrit were present: *madhuramadhurabhāṣāsaṁskṛtānyonyasammeḷanasurabhilā*

kāvyavāṇīvibhūtiḥ: Elamkulam P.N. Kunjan Pillai, ed., *Candrotsavam*; repr., Kottayam, 1983, v. 23, p. 26.

3. Such blended language was known by the name *Maṇipravāḷam* itself in most of south India. This is attested by the Kashmirian polymath Abhinavagupta, who lived in the latter half of the tenth century and the first two decades of the eleventh century AD. He explains, in his *Abhinavabhāratī* commentary on Bharata's *Nāṭyaśāstra*, that the *miśrabhāṣā* and *ardhasaṁskṛta* that Bharata speaks about were used in different parts of the country and that what obtained in *Dakṣiṇāpatha* was 'famous' as *Maṇipravāḷam*: *anyat trivargaprasiddhaṁ padamadhye saṁskṛtaṁ madhye deśabhāṣādiyuktaṁ tadeva kāryaṁ. Dakṣiṇāpathe maṇipravāḷamiti prasiddham, kaśmīre śāṭhakulamiti. anye tu sakalalokaprasiddhairvyākhyānāpekṣibhiḥ saṁskṛtaiḥ kṛtam ardhasaṁskṛtam āhuḥ apare vararucyādinā praṇītā prākṛtalakṣaṇānvitam śaurasenyādi deśabhāṣādyadhikṛtam prākṛtam evārdhasaṁskṛtam iti manyante.* Ramakrishna Kavi, ed., *Nāṭyaśāstra of Bharatamuni with the Commentary of Abhinavabhāratī by Abhinavaguptācārya*, vol. IV, Baroda: Oriental Institute, 1954, p. 379. I thank Chathanath Achyuthan Unni and Manu Devadevan for drawing my attention to this passage.
4. *Nātyantam saṁskṛtenaiva, nātyantam deśabhāṣayā | kathāṁ gōṣṭhīṣu kathayaṁloke bahumato bhavet ||* *Kāmasūtra*, 1.4.37 (my translation). The reference is to the version available on the Göttingen website: Vātsyāyana, *Kāmasūtra*, Göttingen Register of Electronic Texts in Indian Languages, Georg-August-Universität Göttingen, http://gretil.sub.uni-goettingen.de/gretil/1_sanskr/6_sastra/6_kama/kamasufu.htm, accessed 27 February 2017. Bhoja quotes this verse approvingly in his *Sarasvatīkaṇṭhābharaṇam*. Significantly, Pillai, ed., *Līlātilakam*, p. 285, too quotes it with approval.
5. *Maṇipravāḷam* was used mainly for composing Śrīvaiṣṇava exegeses in the Tamil-speaking region while it did not go much beyond religious literature in Telugu, too, as in the writings of Pālkurki Somanātha. It is clubbed with *citrakāvyas* and riddles in Tamil grammatical tradition. For a discussion, see K. Ramachandran Nair, *Early Manipravalam: A Study*, Trivandrum: Anjali, 1971, pp. 67–72. Inscriptions from South-East Asia too used a free mixture of Javanese and Sanskrit. Nair quotes a verse from Java: *samar divārātri nekaṅ surālayā/deniṅ prakāśātmaka sarvabhāsvarā | aṅiṅ sekārniṅ kumadā jariṅkulam/ muaṅ cakravākin papaśaḥ lavan priyaṁ ||* Nair, *Early Manipravalam*, p. 70. It was in Malayalam that it gained the status of mainstream as a part of a strategy of asserting independence from the Tamil tradition. For this 'declaration of independence', as it were, see M.R. Raghava

Varier, 'Līlāthilakaththinre Rāṣṭrīyam' (The Politics of Līlātilakam), in *Vāyanayuṭe Vazhikal*, Thrissur: Current Books, 1998, pp. 9–19.

6. See, for example, Ulloor S. Parameswara Aiyer, *Bhāṣācampukkaḷ*, Trivandrum: Ulloor Publishers, 1954; Aiyer, *Kēraḷasāhityacaritram*, vol. I, Trivandrum: University of Travancore, 1953; Aiyer, *Kēraḷasāhityacaritram*, vol. II, Trivandrum: University of Travancore, 1962; Aiyer, *Vijñānadīpika*, vol. IV, Trivandrum: Ulloor Publishers, 1938; T.M. Chummar, *Padyasāhityacaritram*, Kottayam: National Book Stall, 1960; K.M. George, ed., *Sāhityacaritram Prasthānaṅṅaḷilūṭe*, Kottayam: National Book Stall, 1968; Elamkulam P.N. Kunjan Pillai, *Keraḷabhāṣayuṭe Vikāsapariṇāmaṅṅaḷ*, Kottayam: National Book Stall, 1955; Pillai, *Uṇṇunīlīsandeśam Caritradṛṣṭiyil Kūṭi*, Kottayam: National Book Stall, 1957; Pillai, *Bhāṣayum Sāhityavum Nūṟṟāṇṭukaḷilūṭe*, Kottayam: National Book Stall, 1958; etc.
7. *Candrotsavam* was published in the year 1900 in a monthly, *Kavanodayam*. T.K. Krishna Menon reported the discovery of a *sandeśakāvya* on *Uṇṇunīlī* in 1903. Kotuṅṅallur Kuññikkuṭṭan Tampurān published the work in the *Rasikarañjini* in 1906. Āṟṟūr Krishna Pisharody republished the same in 1923. P.K. Narayana Pillai published an anthology of 291 *Maṇipravāḷam* verses with the title *Padyaratnam* in 1949. He also serialized a *campūkāvya* named *Uṇṇiccirutēvī* in the *Bhāṣātraimāsikam* in 1949, which he later published as a book in 1954. E.V. Raman Nambudiri reported *Uṇṇiyāṭī*, another *campūkāvya*, and P.K. Narayana Pillai published it. Ulloor S. Parameswara Aiyer mentioned a *campūkāvya* on *Uṇṇiyaccī* in his book *Bhaṣāacampukkaḷ*. P.K. Narayana Pillai edited and published it in *Bhāṣātraimāsikam*. Kuttamasseri Narayana Pisharody published the *Kokasandeśa* in the *Sāhithyapariṣat Quarterly* in 1954. Later, the work was republished by University of Kerala in 1954. K. Ramachandran Nair edited and published a text called *Vaiśikatantram* containing 266 verses in 1969. There have been a large number of commentaries on most of these, particularly after one or the other text was prescribed as compulsory reading for the Master's degree programmes in Malayalam in the universities in Kerala and outside. See also Notes 18–23 in this chapter.
8. Foremost among these is Elamkulam P.N. Kunjan Pillai, *Keraḷabhāṣayuṭe Vikāsapariṇāmaṅṅaḷ*; *Uṇṇunīlīsandeśam Caritradṛṣṭiyil*; *Bhāṣayum Sāhityavum Nūṟṟāṇṭukaḷilūṭe*. There is a brilliant introduction to one of the *Maṇipravāḷa-kāvya*s in Chathanath Achyuthan Unni and M.R. Raghava Varier, ed., *Kōkasandēśaṁ*, Edapal: Vallathol Vidyapitham, 2007, pp. 5–31, who have, apart from looking at the entire corpus of creative literature in *Maṇipravāḷam* within the structuralist tradition,

brought to bear on them a sense of history. Raghava Varier has a couple of important papers: 'Līlātilakattinṟe Rāṣṭrīyam' and 'The Image of "the Other" in the Early *Manipravalam* Texts' (unpublished), both of which are informed by a clear sense of history. Similarly, Freeman, 'Rubies and Coral', has interesting observations informed by insights from anthropology. See also Rich Freeman, 'Genre and Society: The Literary Culture of Premodern Kerala', in *Literary Cultures in History: Reconstructions from South Asia*, Berkeley and Los Angles: University of California Press, 2003, pp. 437–502.

9. *Yat saṁskṛtakāvyasya prayojanam kathyate nimittam ca asyāpi maṇipravāḷakāvyasya mantavyam*. Pillai, ed., *Līlātilakam*, p. 283 (my translation). I should, however, like to make a distinction here. Sanskrit *kāvyas* are much more varied and have reached a height which was never the case with *Maṇipravāḷam.* Sanskrit *kāvyas* have their own central themes or subjects which differ from *kavya* to *kavya*, and also from the theory that it is all ultimately concerned with the enjoyment of the *rasa*. There is no comparison, for instance, between *Kirātārjunīya* and *Meghadūta* or between *Kumārasaṁbhava* and *Rāvaṇavadha*. This diversity at different levels is not seen in the *Maṇipravāḷam* works. All centre on the courtesan; everything seems to gravitate towards her. What are borrowed from the Sanskrit *kāvya* tradition are those words and expressions, similes and metaphors, motifs and tropes, which can represent the *bhoga* (enjoyment) ideal of the urban life that *Maṇipravāḷams* represents. I thank Manu Devadevan for suggesting that I make this important distinction.

10. *śākuntaḷam tadanu māḷavikāgnimitram*
kādambarīcaritamadbhutabandhahṛdyam |
maṟṟum marandamoḻi vaikiṉakūṟudārā
*śuśrāva bhāvamadhuraṁ ca maṇipravāḷa*m || Pillai, ed., *Candrotsavam*, Canto 2, v. 18, p. 55.

11. I owe a debt to Shonaleeka Kaul, *Imagining the Urban: Sanskrit and the City in Early India*, Ranikhet: Permanent Black, 2010, which it is a pleasure to acknowledge. This book prompted me to read the *kāvya* literature in Sanskrit afresh as articulations of an urban sensibility, which in turn enabled me to read *Maṇipravāḷam* poetry in the way in which I seek to do here. I thank Kaul also for the many hours of interesting discussion we had on the subject. So also, M.P. Sankunni Nair's exceptionally brilliant studies (in Malayalam) of Sanskrit *kāvyas* in general and Kāḷidāsa in particular have influenced me in a big way. M.P. Sankunni Nair, *Chatravum Cāmaravum*, Calicut: Mathrubhumi, 1988. It will also be interesting to compare the entire world of the *kāvyas* with

representations of the urban sensibility in the visual arts. For a fleeting suggestion to this effect, see Devangana Desai, 'Social Dimensions of Art in Early India', Presidential Address, Section I, Ancient Indian History, *Proceedings of the Indian History Congress*, Gorakhpur, 1989, pp. 21–56.

12. The expression is used by Elamkulam P.N. Kunjan Pillai, 'Tēvaṭiccisthānam', in *Keralacaritrattinṟe Iruḷaṭañña Ēṭukaḷ*, reproduced in Pillai, *Iḷamkuḷam Kuññan Piḷḷayuṭe Tiraññeṭutta Kṛtikaḷ*, Thiruvananthapuram: University of Kerala, 2005, p. 523. He reiterated it in Pillai, 'Introduction', in *Candrotsavam*, p. 11. He also believed that there was moral decay among Nampūtiris during the period when these texts were composed. Later scholars, such as K. Ramachandran Nair, *Early Manipravalam*, and P.V. Velayudhan Pillai, *Malayāḷa Sāhitya Caritram Kṛṣṇagātha Vare*, Kottayam: National Book Stall, 1989, largely followed the construction of Elamkulam. However, N. Gopinathan Nair, who more or less shares the same tradition of scholarship, has struck a dissenting note in his Introduction to *Uṇṇiyaccīcaritam*, where he expresses doubt whether they were all Nampūtiris. Unni and Varier, *Kōkasandēśaṁ*, pp. 5–31, look at these on a different plane altogether.
13. For a detailed study of the process, see Kesavan Veluthat, *Brahman Settlements in Kerala: Historical Studies*, Calicut: Sandhya Publications, University of Calicut, 1978.
14. For Elamkulam P.N. Kunjan Pillai's understanding of the *janmi* system, see *Janmisampradāyam Kēraḷattil*, Kottayam: National Book Stall, 1953. For a critique and a fresh analysis, see Kesavan Veluthat, *The Early Medieval in South India*, New Delhi: Oxford University Press, 2012, pp. 277–94.
15. It should be noted that the 'looseness' in marriage was not just a Nampūtiri feature. All marriages among the matrilineal castes were of this kind, called *sambandham*, to begin and terminate which was very easy. For some reason, this got associated with Nampūtiris in the nineteenth and twentieth centuries, which has no factual foundation.
16. *Maṇipravāḷavidyeyam pāṭhakeṣvavatiṣṭhate | lambaśipriparīvārā mahiḷāḷimahāspadā* || P.K. Narayana Pillai, ed., *Padyaratnam*; repr., Trivandrum: University of Kerala, 1982, v. 2, p. 76 (my translation). The resonance that this has with the *Kāmasūtra* verse quoted earlier is too important to be missed.
17. It was members of this caste who performed *kūṭiyāṭṭam*, Sanskrit plays as well as *kūttu*, the mono-act form of *prabandha* exposition. They used to call themselves *naṭa*, *śailūṣa*, etc., as well as *sūtas* and *māgadhas*. The collapsing of the *sūta-māgadha* tradition with that of the *naṭa-*

śailūṣa tradition is of great significance for understanding the process of amalgamation of the *mārgi* and *deśi* traditions.

18. *Campū*, by definition, is a *kāvya* where both prose and verse are used: *gadyapadyamayam kāvyam.* The 'prose' (*gadya*), however, is highly metrical.

    There are various editions of the early Maṇipravāḷam *campūs*. The ones that I have used for the present purpose are N. Gopinathan Nair, ed., *Unniyaccīcaritam*, Calicut: University of Calicut, 2005; P.V. Krishnan Nair, ed., *Unniyāṭīcaritam*; repr., Kottayam: National Book Stall, 1976; Aymanam Krishna Kaimal, ed., *Unniccirutēvīcaritam*, Kottayam: National Book Stall, 1984.
19. These *kāvyas*, too, have seen several editions and commentaries. The ones used here are: Elamkulam P.N. Kunjan Pillai, ed., *Uṇṇūnīlisandēśam*; repr., Kottayam: National Book Stall, 1983; Unni and Varier, *Kōkasandēśaṁ.*
20. Pillai, ed., *Candrotsavam.*
21. K. Ramachandran Nair, ed., *Vaiśikatantram*, Trivandrum: S.B. Press, 1969. M.R. Raghava Varier and K.P. Sankaran reject the idea that this is a single 'text' by any one author. M.R. Raghava Varier and K.P. Sankaran, 'Illātta Oru Kṛtiyeccolli' (In the Name of a Nonexistent Work), *Mathrubhumi Weekly*, 19–25 October 2006, pp. 30–3. They argue that these are largely stand-alone verses, used by Cākyārs in their *kūttu* and *kūṭiyāṭṭam* performances, many of these being part of the *āṭṭaprakāram*s ('stage manuals') of *kūṭiyāṭṭams*, particularly *Mantrāṅkam*, which is the third Act of the play *Pratijñāyaugandharāyaṇa* by Bhāsa. Even accepting this very valid argument, there is no gainsaying that the verses contained in them represent the world of courtesans.
22. K. Rathnamma, ed., *Ananthapuravarṇanam*, Trivandrum: University of Kerala, 2007.
23. Pillai, ed., *Padyaratnam.*
24. The practice of Sanskrit theoreticians looking at *kāvya* as consisting of body and soul is followed here as well.
25. Chathanath Achyuthan Unni, *Alaṁkāraśāstram Malayāḷattil*, Trivandrum: State Institute of Languages, 1984.
26. Gopinathan Nair, ed., *Unniyaccīcaritam*, pp. 95–8.
27. Krishnan Nair, *Unniyāṭīcaritam*, p. 50.
28. Pillai, ed., *Uṇṇunīlīsandeśam*, vv. 68–71, pp. 69–71.
29. Ibid., v. 124, pp. 98–9.
30. M.R. Raghava Varier, *Madhyakālakeraḷam: Sampattu, Samūham, Samskāram*, Trivandrum: Chintha Publications, 1997, pp. 23–32. This

article, 'Paṟampupurayiṭasampadvyavastha', is written jointly by him and Rajan Gurukkal.

31. See, for instance, Kesavan Veluthat, 'The Perunchellur Copper Plates of AD 1145', in *Sāhityavum Caritravum: Dhāraṇayuṭe Sādhyatakaḷ*, Kozhikode: Mathrubhumi Books, 2013, pp. 151–9.
32. *yaṁ medinyāṁ ruciramaricottālatāmbūlavallīvellatkerakramukanikar ān keraḷānudbaṇanti||* in N.P. Unni, ed., *Śukasandeśa of Lakṣmīdāsa*, Delhi: Nag Publishers, 1985, I, v. 34, p. 30 (my translation).
33. Vasco da Gama found two Berbers from Tunis, who spoke Castilian and Genoese in Calicut in 1498. Sanjay Subrahmanyam, *The Career and Legend of Vasco da Gama*, New York: Cambridge University Press, 1997, p. 129. Still earlier, there were travellers like Athansius Nikitin, Niccolo Conti and many others who visited the coasts of Kerala.
34. Gopinathan Nair, ed., *Unniyaccīcaritam*, pp. 125–33.
35. Krishnan Nair, ed., *Unniyāṭīcaritam*, pp. 47–50.
36. Krishna Kaimal, ed., *Unniccirutēvīcaritam*, pp. 33–4.
37. Pillai,, ed., *Uṇṇunīlīsandeśam*, vv. 63–5, pp. 68–9; vv. 79–85, pp. 75–6. The editor thinks that there is no place for such elaborate description of marketplaces in a *sandeśakāvya* and that nothing will happen if we read the *kāvya* leaving out these descriptions! Pillai, , ed., *Uṇṇunīlīsandeśam*, p. 76.
38. Pillai, ed., *Uṇṇunīlīsandeśam*, vv. 63–75; pp. 68–79; Gopinathan Nair, *Unniyaccīcaritam*, pp. 125–33.
39. Gopinathan Nair, ed., *Unniyaccīcaritam*, p. 150.
40. Pillai, ed., *Uṇṇunīlīsandeśam*, v. 70, p. 71.
41. Narayana Pillai, ed., *Padyaratnam*, v. 35, p. 134.
42. Pillai, ed., *Candrotsavam*, Canto 3, v. 52, p. 93.
43. Ibid., Canto 3, v. 65, p. 96.
44. Noboru Karashima, ed., *In Search of Chinese Ceramic-sherds in South India and Sri Lanka*, Tokyo: Taisho University Press, 2004, esp. pp. 44–54.
45. *Tiramam* is mentioned in Pillai, ed., *Uṇṇunīlīsandeśam*, v. 63, p. 68; it is mentioned with a variation in spelling (to suit the metre) as *tramam* in Krishnan Nair, ed., *Uṇṇiyāṭīcaritam*, p. 49. *Aśaravi* is mentioned in Pillai, ed., *Candrotsavam*, Canto 1, v. 105, p. 48.
46. B.D. Chattopadhyaya, 'Urban Centres in Early Medieval India: An Overview', in *Situating Indian History: For Sarveppalli Gopal*, ed. Sabyasachi Bhattacharya and Romila Thapar, Delhi: Oxford University Press, 1986, p. 28.

47. Kaul, *Imagining the Urban*, p. 109n131.
48. Gopinathan Nair, ed., *Unniyaccīcaritam*, pp. 148–51 (my translation). Compare this with what the *Kāmasūtra*, 1.4.5, expects the *nagaraka* to do: *sa prātarutthāya kṛtaniyatakṛtyaḥ, gṛhītadantadhāvanaḥ, mātrayānulepanaṁ dhūpaṁ srajam iti ca gṛhītvā* . . . .
49. Krishnan Nair, ed., *Unniyāṭīcaritam*, vv. 164–70, p. 69.
50. Pillai, ed., *Candrotsavam*, Canto 5, v. 11, p. 153.
51. They are mentioned as making a beeline to see the courtesan in all the three *campūkāvyas* we have taken up. So also, they figure in the verses in *Vaiśikatantram*.
52. Kaul, *Imagining the Urban*, p. 144; Sankunni Nair, *Chatravum Cāmaravum*, pp. 63–75, 103–16; Desai, 'Social Dimensions of Art'.
53. This is the title of a chapter on Khajuraho in John Keay's book, *India Discovered*, London, 1981; repr., New Delhi: Rupa, 1989, Chapter 8. Keay quotes Captain Burt, one of James Prinsep's rowing engineers, to have reported in the *Asiatic Journal* that he 'saw seven Hindoo temples, most beautifully and exquisitely carved as to the workmanship, but the sculptor had at times allowed his subject to grow a little warmer than there was any absolute necessity for his doing; indeed some of the sculptures here were extremely indecent and offensive'. Keay, *India Discovered*, p. 99. This kind of disapproval informs the understanding of *Maṇipravāḷam* poetry in the writings of earlier scholars.
54. Such 'warmth' can be felt in the eighth canto of Kāḷidāsa's *Kumārasambhava*. For works that are almost entirely of this category, see the four *bhāṇas* of Vararuci, Īśvaradatta, Śyāmilaka and Śūdraka included in the *Caturbhāṇi*. I have used the edition by D.G. Sharma and Krishna, ed., *Caturbhāṇi*, Trichur: Mangalodayam Press, 1922.
55. For the references in the *Maṇipravāḷa kāvyas*, Gopinathan Nair, *Uṇṇīyaccīcaritam*, 'prose' 17, pp. 143–7; Krishnan Nair, ed., *Uṇṇīyāṭīcaritam*, vv. 126–7, pp. 61–2; Pillai, ed., *Uṇṇunīlīsandeśam*, II, vv. 33–8, pp. 121–3. For *Dhūrtaviṭasaṁvāda*, see *Caturbhāṇī*, p. 7. (Each of the four *bhāṇas* included here is separately paginated). There are similar correspondences between the descriptions of the *cēṭīs*, in both the *Maṇipravāḷa kāvyas* and the *bhāṇas*.
56. *Kāmasūtra*, 6.1.
57. Narayana Pillai, ed., *Padyaratnam*, v. 161, p. 114.
58. Ibid., v. 175, p. 119.
59. Ibid., v. 168, p. 117.
60. Ibid., v. 171, p. 117.
61. Pillai, ed., *Candrotsavam*, Canto 1, v. 92, p. 46.

62. Ibid., Canto 2, v. 23, p. 57.
63. Unni., ed., *Śukasandeśa*, op. cit., II, v. 12, p. 69.
64. Gopinathan Nair, ed., *Unniyaccīcaritam*, p. 112.
65. Sankunni Nair, *Chatravum Cāmaravum*, pp. 103–16. This brilliant piece by Sankunni Nair provides rare insights into the world of Sanskrit *kāvyas*.
66. *Kāmasūtra*, 1.3. Bharata enjoins that the *gaṇikā*s speak Sanskrit and recommends Sanskrit education for them.

    rājñyāśca gaṇikāyāśca śilpakāryāstathaiva ca |
    kāryāvasthāntarakṛtaṁ yojyam pāṭheṣu saṁskṛtam ||
    krīḍārtham sarvalokasya prayoge ca sukhāśrayaṁ |
    kalābhyāsāśrayam caiva pāṭhyaṁ veśyāsu saṁskṛtaṁ ||
    kalōpacārajñānārthaṁ krīḍārthaṁ pārthicasya ca |
    nirdiṣṭaṁ śilpakāryāstu nāṭake saṁskṛtaṁ vacaḥ ||

    Nāṭyaśāstra, Chapter 18, vv. 37, 40, 41. See Babulal Shukla Sastri, ed., *Nāṭyaśāstra*, Varanasi: Choukhamba Sanskrit Sansthan, 1978, pp. 339–40. I am grateful to Chathanath Achyuthan Unni for drawing my attention to this.
67. Many texts give indications of this. A very good representative is the education that Medinīcandrikā got in Pillai, *Candrotsavam*, Canto 2, vv. 59–66, pp. 67–8.
68. Ramachandran Nair, ed., *Vaiśikatantram*.
69. *Kāmasūtra*, *Adhikaraṇa* 6.
70. *madhye dīpajvalanamadhure pārśvataḥ pāṇighastrī-*
    citrībhūte sarasahṛdayairbhūsurairbhāsitāgre |
    pṛṣṭhe mārdaṅgikavilasite raṅgadeśe praviṣṭaḥ
    spaṣṭākūtam naṭayati naṭaḥ ko'pi kañcit prabandhaṁ ||

    Quoted in N.P. Unni, ed., *Prabandhamanjarī*, New Delhi: Rashtriya Sanskrita Sansthan, 1998, p. xlvi (my translation).
71. Krishnan Nair, ed., *Uṇṇīyāṭīcaritam*, vv. 118–20, p. 59.
72. Krishna Kaimal, ed., *Unniccirutēvīcaritam*, v. 3, and *gadya* 14, pp. 27–8.
73. A whole treatise chastising the Cākyārs for the freedom they took came to be written in the period around fifteenth century. K.G. Paulose, ed., *Naṭāṅkuśam*, Trippunithura: Government Sanskrit College, 1993.
74. Sheldon Pollock, *The Language of the Gods in a World of Men: Sanskrit, Culture and Power in Premodern India*, Berkeley and Los Angeles: University of California Press, 2006, p. 410.
75. Kesavan Veluthat, 'The Evolution of a Regional Identity', in *The Early Medieval in South India*, New Delhi: Oxford University Press, 2009, pp. 295–311.

CHAPTER 7

Kāṇa-Janma-Maryādā

Origin and Development of Land Relations in Medieval Kerala

THERE WAS A time when the epigraphist would lament that 'the great bulk of the inscriptions consists of grants to tanks and temples which are of no interest whatever . . . [O]f the condition of the country and the people [they tell] us nothing.'[1] The historian has since tasted the apple and shed some of his innocence. Following a century of epigraphical studies in India after Butterworth and Chetty penned these words, giant strides have been taken towards laying bare the economic and social aspects of our past with the help of the same kind of inscriptions recording 'grants to tanks and temples', particularly in south India. A whole new world of relationships is exposed by a study of the land-grants and other inscriptions—the working of local groups and its implications for society and polity have been worked out systematically with the help of these records. The present paper reports the results of an attempt to see how a structured relationship in land-rights emerged in Kerala in the Medieval period in the light of the author's study of the inscriptions of Kerala.[2] Most inscriptions of Kerala date from the period between the ninth and twelfth centuries of our era. They were, with the exception of a handful, discovered, deciphered and published in the last century. The absence of the typical *dānaśāsanas*, with the usual *praśastis* found in the records of other parts of the country, made it difficult for the early epigraphists to tie these records around a dynasty and work out the details of political history.[3] It was only in the latter half of this century, thanks to the work of Professor Elamkulam P.N. Kunjan Pillai,[4] that these records were incontrovertibly assigned to the Cēra Perumāḷs who ruled from Mahōdayapuram. In the light of the evidence provided by these records, Pillai reconstructed the outlines of the political history of that dynasty and also presented a picture of socio-economic evolution.[5]

Epigraphical records of this period from Kerala are generally resolutions of temple committees. The temples owned vast areas of land and commanded the allegiance of large sections of people. Pillai rightly appreciated the significance of this crucial character of the temples and realized that the key to understanding the pattern of socio-economic evolution in Kerala lay in these records which he studied, for all practical purposes, for the first time. According to him, these temples were managed by committees known as the *ūrāḷar* or *sabhā* which was a body elected from among the entire population of the village (*ūr* or *ūrār*), and subject to its ultimate authority. The *sabhā* or *ūrāḷar* were also further subject to an assembly of the *nāṭu*, which he called the *nāṭṭukūṭṭam* and identified with the 'Hundred' organizations attached to the various *nāṭu* divisions under the Cēras of Mahōdayapuram. These elected committees of the *ūrāḷar* consisted of both brāhmaṇas and non-brāhmaṇas to begin with, when things were going on smoothly in a democratic and egalitarian way. During the period described by Pillai as the 'Hundred Years' War' between the Cēras and the Cōḻas, however, brāhmaṇas came to dominate them. This led to the loss of the democratic and egalitarian character of the *sabhā* of the *ūrāḷar*. This, in turn, led to a concentration of the huge chunks of landed property in the hands of a few brāhmaṇa landlords, giving rise to the peculiar kind of tenurial pattern in Kerala known in later times as the *janmi* system.[6]

This presentation of the evolution of brāhmaṇa landlordism in Kerala is predicated on three major assumptions:

1. The elective, democratic, character of the *sabhā* of the *ūrāḷar* which functioned within a larger unit of the *ūr*, *ūrār* or *ūrkūṭṭam*,

2. The existence of a still larger body known as the *nāṭṭukūṭṭam* identified with the 'Hundred Organizations' and its superordinate authority over both the *ūrkūṭṭam* and the *sabhā* of the *ūrāḷar* within it, and
3. The changes in the character and organization of these bodies brought about by the so-called 'Hundred Years' War' and the resultant domination of the Nambudiri brāhmaṇas.

The first two assumptions flow from an inadequate consideration of the context of the names in the inscriptions and the third, out of a faulty understanding of the political process, which itself is conditioned in part by the first two. We shall consider the first two assumptions in greater detail now.

The inscriptions, most of which are from temples, contain names of a large number of individuals figuring as witnesses to transactions, donees and also members of the managing committees of the temples. The names generally consist of three segments: the name of the family, father's name and the ego's name, e.g. Vaṉṟalaiccēri-Kōtai Iravi.[7] In a few cases there would be one more segment before such three segmented names, e.g. Mūḻikkaḷattu-Kūṟṟampaḷḷic-Cuvākaran-Tāmōtaran[8] where the first segment signifies the village from which the individual originally hailed. There are, however, cases where one or more of these segments are omitted.

In studying these names, Pillai did not distinguish the members of the temple-committees from the donors and witnesses to the transactions. There are certainly names of non-brāhmaṇas, but they figure mostly as donors. In other cases it can be demonstrated that the names are of brāhmaṇas. However, the absence of the brāhmaṇical suffix *śarman*, the total absence of references to *gotra* and the corruption of personal names into unrecognizable Dravidian forms (like Cāttan for Śāstṛśarman, Kaṇṭan for Nīlakaṇṭha, Tuppan for Subrahmaṇya, Uruttiran for Rudra, etc.) led Pillai to assume they were names of non-brāhmaṇas.[9] Thus, for instance, even where Pillai conceded brāhmaṇa status to six out of the ten donees in a Kiḷimānūr record, who constituted the *sabhā* of the *ūrāḷar* there, the unmistakable brāhmaṇa identity of the remaining four was lost sight of.[10] On account of this failure to appreciate the brāhmaṇical character of the *sabhā* and *ūrāḷar*, he was driven to assume that they were popular bodies, organized in an elective and democratic manner, with a heavy representation of non-brāhmaṇas in them.

Apart from the absence of *gotra* names or the *śarman* suffix, what stood in the way of Pillai's appreciating the brāhmaṇical character was the inadequate consideration of the context in which the records appear. His lack of familiarity with conditions in central and northern Kerala, from which regions most of these records come, may have prevented him from appreciating this. In fact, many of these records are from temples which are reputed as *grāmakṣretras* of brāhmaṇas—a tradition that Pillai ignored. Nor did he know that many of the houses mentioned in them do survive to this day and that they are brāhmaṇa houses.[11] This knowledge is essential to realize that the names of those who figure in the records in the capacity of witnesses and members of the *sabhā* are brāhmaṇas. But then, Pillai mixed up all names figuring in records and argued, somewhat theatrically, that a large number of them were non-brāhmaṇas.[12] The reality, however, is that the list included many brāhmaṇa names which he failed to identify as such. Such non-brāhmaṇas as are present are in the capacity of donors or tenants and not as those who controlled the land of temples. It was this failure in the understanding which vitiated his findings in relation to the character of the temple-centred agrarian corporations in Kerala.

A closer examination of the spatio-temporal contexts in which these records occur, or the context within the records themselves where the names figure, would dispel such misunderstandings. As stated earlier, there are practically no *dānaśāsanas* by which a new brāhmaṇa settlement is created. In the absence of such founding charters, we have to depend on the records registering the proceedings of the temple committees for understanding the nature of their organization. However, there are at least three records registering the consecration of new temples and the accompanying endowment of lands and creation of settlements around them. This would serve as an index to the character of the settlements. The Kollūr Maṭham Plates,[13] dated AD 1189, purports to be the renewal of an earlier charter said to be granted in late tenth century AD. It is claimed that the original record had decayed. The record lists names of twenty-three brāhmaṇa families which constituted the settlement around the Dēvīdēvēśvaram temple. An unpublished stone inscription of the early eleventh century from Tiruvaṭūr[14] in the Kannur district gives further details about the composition of the newly created settlement. Twenty-four brāhmaṇas from well-known, pre-existing *brāhmaṇa grāmas*—five from Vaikkam,[15] two from Paṟavūr, six from Āvaṭṭiputtūr, four from Iruṅgāṭṭikkūṭal, and seven from Perumanam (all from central and south Kerala)—were invited and settled around this newly endowed temple in north Kerala with land and other privileges. Details in the record show in an unmistakable way the brahmaṇical character of the temple committee which was charged with the management of the landed properties in the village. Another record,[16] of AD 1168 from Kilimanur in south Kerala, describes the creation of a brāhmaṇa settlement around the newly consecrated temple of Tiruppalkkadal. The record names ten brāhmaṇas drawn from eight well-known brāhmaṇa *gramas* in central and south Kerala as the *ūrāḷar* of the temple in so many words.[17] These records demonstrate the brāhmaṇical character of the temple-centred agrarian corporations in early medieval Kerala. Although these instances form a very small proportion of the extant records, that the pattern suggested by them is applicable to the various regions of Kerala is clear from a study of the working of such committees there.[18] In a few cases the decisions recorded are endorsed by individuals who obviously formed members of the temple-committees; and they can be demonstrated as brāhmaṇas from the names of their houses.[19]

In certain other cases, the follow-up of the decisions is achieved by invoking imprecatory clauses, which includes loss of caste as if involved in one of the five heinous sins (*pañcamahāpātaka*).[20] Sometimes such decisions in Kerala are stated to be modelled on the lines of well-known precedents such as the one at Mūḻikkaḷam, known variously as Mūḻikkaḷak-*kaccam*, Mūḻikkaḷac-*cavattai*, Mūḻikkaḷat-*toḻukkam*, etc. This precedent not only had wide currency but also the force of law in all the temple-centred brāhmaṇical corporations of Kerala. Mūḻikkaḷak-*kaccam* was a typical *vyavasthā* following the prescriptions in the *Dharmaśāstras*; and so was the invocation of the *mahāpātakas*. In fact, it has been shown that the rules of the *Dharmaśāstras* governing the constitution and conduct of the *sabhā* of brāhmaṇa *śiṣṭas* were followed to the last letter in such *sabhās* in south India, including Kerala.[21]

Pillai, however, assumed that the *sabhā* of the *ūrāḷar* was a body elected from among the entire population of the village, partly because he missed its exclusively brāhmaṇa character and was pushed to a corner, as it were, to attribute an elective, democratic character to the body. His political and social commitments provided him with the handy explanation he has offered. There was another factor behind this assumption of an elective, democratic character of such bodies. He assumed that there was a larger body of the *ūrār* at the village level, consisting of perhaps the entire population of the village.[22] The basis of this argument is a faulty interpretation of very slender evidence, taken out of context. In one record, detailing the arrangements for leasing out a piece of land owned by the temple, it is stated that the *ūrāḷar* should not obstruct cultivation.[23] Elsewhere in the same document, it is stated that even a unanimous decision of the *ūrār* could not alter these decisions.[24] These two terms, *ūrār* and *ūrāḷar*, in the same document and in a few other documents in relation to bodies at the village level led Pillai to assume that these were two different bodies. However, if the terms *ūr*, *ūrār* and *ūrāḷar* figuring in inscriptions from Kerala from this period are analysed in their proper context, it can be seen that they are used in the same sense.[25] The honorific plural, *ūrāḷar*, was also used to refer to an individual member of the body.

The second assumption, that the *ūr* and the *sabhā* within it was subject to the superordinate authority at the *nāṭu* level is, in a similar way, the result of a scant consideration of evidence in context. This body, which Pillai called *nāṭṭukūṭṭam* without support in the sources, was identified in the 'Hundred Organizations' figuring in the inscriptions.[26] In many cases, the protection of land and other properties endowed to temples were placed under these 'Hundreds'—'The Three Hundred', 'The Five Hundred', 'The Six Hundred', 'The Seven Hundred', etc. Taking all such records where the 'Hundred Organizations' figure and analysing them in context, M.G.S. Narayanan has demonstrated that they constituted the prototype of the Nayar militia in Kerala who formed the 'Companions of honour' to the local chieftains and the Cēra king.[27] In fact, a short, fragmentary inscription from Tiruvanvaṇḍūr is enough to dispel any misunderstanding about the nature of the *munnūṟṟuvar* ('Three Hundred'). It lists, namely (1) the Three Hundred of Naṉṟuḻaināṭu (2) a certain Cēntan (3) Maṅgalattu Kumaran Kuṉṟappōḻan and (4) Naṇṉṟuḻaināṭṭu . . . yan as 'these four individuals' in connection with some arrangements, the details of which are lost in the record.[28] However, that the Three Hundred is counted as one individual in the record is clear and unmistakable, thereby precluding the idea that it was a larger body with superordinate powers over the bodies at the village level. It is possible that Pillai took in this case the analogy of the situation obtaining in the Cō<u>l</u>a country where a body at the *nāḍu* level, known as the *nāṭṭār*, existed, which was presented to have had superordinate powers over the bodies at the village level.[29] The crucial difference between *nāḍus* in the two situations, namely that while it was a political unit under the chieftaincy of a *nāṭuvā<u>l</u>i* (local ruler) in Kerala, it was a peasant locality, a sociopolitical subregion, in the Cō<u>l</u>a country,[30] was not considered in this case by Pillai.

A contextual examination of these terms makes it clear that the first two assumptions of Pillai are unwarranted. The third one, which seeks to explain changes in the character and organization of the temple-centred agrarian corporation with a predominance of brāhmaṇas there and leading to the rise of brāhmaṇa landlordism, is actually necessitated by the first two—wrong—premises from which Pillai started. Recent research has shown that a 'Hundred Years' War' between the Cēras and the Cō<u>l</u>as had indeed not taken place.[31] The two powers in south India—unequal in all respects—stood in different kinds of relationship over the period and there was no situation of war for any continuous period. Moreover, the supposition that events like an inconsequential war could bring about basic changes in the relations of production is unwarranted.

The fact appears to be that there was no dramatic change in the tenurial pattern in Kerala in the eleventh century, as imagined by Pillai. The rise of the Cēra kingdom in the beginning of the ninth century itself was a function of a major economic transformation, the most important aspect of which was in relation to the opening up of river valleys and clearing of land in other ways for purposes of agriculture. Inscriptions start making their appearance in Kerala from this period, and a vast majority of them are from or related to temples and dealing with the arrangement of landed property. A clear pattern of the land tenures is available from these records.

As suggested here, the temples in relation to which the inscriptions are available owned huge estates of land. The case of the Tiruvalla temple alone is sufficient to show the magnitude of the possessions.[32]

There are other temples as well which commanded similar landed properties. These temples were the nucleus of huge brāhmaṇa settlements and all their affairs were managed by the committee of brāhmaṇas who were put in charge of both the ritual and the properties of the temple. Unfortunately, royal charters 'creating' such big settlements and endowing them with land have not come down to us. In all probability, they do not exist, as we see that most of the influential settlements were already in place by the time state had emerged and royalty had established itself in Kerala. In fact, this has been shown as causative to the emergence of state there.[33] Therefore, to believe that these settlements, with the command of vast tract of agrarian land, owed their existence to a donation by the Cēra king or his 'governors' does not fit in with evidence.[34] There are, to be sure, instances of land-grants to groups of brāhmaṇas in the later period; but all these are made by the local chiefs—and in some cases such land was either purchased or exchanged from the previous owner. If the person who granted the land owned it 'in theory', the question of his having to acquire it by purchase of exchange would not have arisen. What is likely is that when the 'great transformation' that Rajan Gurukkal and Raghava Varier are talking about[35] took place in Kerala, the major brāhmaṇa settlements with their control of land were already there. They were themselves claiming that it was all a gift of Paraśurāma, seeking to legitimize it.

In discussing the structure of land-relations in Kerala, what the *Kēraḷōlpatti* has to say about it is often ignored, primarily because the authenticity of the text as history was always in doubt.[36] According to this tradition, Paraśurāma created the land and donated it to brāhmaṇas. Even here, it is not to be taken that it was Paraśurāma who was responsible for structuring the land-relations as they obtained in the pre-colonial period; but the somewhat detailed exposition of the structure is too important to be dismissed summarily. According to the *Kēraḷōlpatti*, Paraśurāma created the land of Kerala and settled it with brāhmaṇas in 64 grāmas, 32 in Tuḷunāṭu and 32 in Kerala proper. He also ordained that 36,000 of them belonging to 16 grāmas take to the profession of arms. They were exempted from studying the Vedas and were described as *ardhabrāhmaṇas* to distinguish them from the *Vedabrāhmaṇas*. Such arms-bearing brāhmaṇas were given land with libation of water, such land being *rājasvam*. It was worthy of being described as *janmam*, no other tenure being entitled to that description. Subsequently, he made all arrangements so that the inhabitants of Kerala would live like the residents of heaven. The text continues to say that the *Vedabrāhmaṇas* got land donated from the *ardhabrāhmaṇas*. Śūdra cultivators were brought from different places and settled there, and given several rights and prerogatives. They were enjoined to be the servants and tenants. The tenants were allowed a lower share (*kīḻāykkūṟu*) while [the brāhmaṇas] themselves retained the upper share (*mēlāykkūṟu*). The tenants were bestowed with the *kāṇam* right while [the brāhmaṇas] granted themselves the *janmam* right. The system of *kāṇam* and *janmam* (*kāṇajanmamaryādā*) was defined in this way.[37]

It is not our argument here that this account in the *Kēraḷōlpatti* in relation to the origin of the *janmisampradāyam* or landlordism is to be taken as *the* way in which the land tenurial patterns had their origin in Kerala. A two-tier arrangement, with the *janmam*, a superior right vested in the brāhmaṇa lords, and the *kāṇam*, an inferior right in the hands of the tenant-cultivators immediately below them, is clear here. It is exactly this pattern with further elaborations that obtained in Kerala in the pre-colonial days, where *janmam* was defined as the absolute proprietorship and *kāṇam*, an intermediary tenure placed between *janmam* and tenancy-at-will. In practice, the latter was some kind of a usufructuary mortgage, where land was held by the tenant after a certain amount of money was paid to the landlord as security. This interest accrued on such moneys was deducted from the returns of the land, which was to be paid to the landlord as rent.

The picture that emerges from the epigraphical records of the later Cēra kingdom conforms to this. As mentioned here, most of the inscriptions are concerned with the way in which temple-centred brāhmaṇa settlements managed their landed property. They give a fairly clear picture of the land tenures obtaining in Kerala during those days. Accordingly, we see that a major chunk of land where rice was cultivated was controlled by the temple-centred brāhmaṇa settlements, which included both *devasvam*, or the property of god, which was collectively held by the corporate group of brāhmaṇas, and *brahmasvam*, or the property of brāhmaṇa, which was individually held by the brāhmaṇa households. The title they had over such land is described as *aṭṭippēṟŭ*. There are other instances where institutions and individuals received land and other privileges as *viṭupēṟŭ*. The crucial term in both these expressions is *pēṟŭ*, which means, literally, 'birth'. In all likelihood, *janmam* is a Sanskrit translation of this term. In certain other cases, members of the ruling family or other private individuals kept land under the control of temples. Such tenure is described as *kīḻīṭŭ*, amounting to some kind of subordinate lease-hold. There is another kind of tenure called *iṭaiyīṭŭ*, an intermediary lease-hold. In these cases, the crucial term, *īṭŭ*, means 'security'. Was some security taken from the lessee and charged on the land leased out to him where the transaction had clear features of a usufructuary mortgage? If it is so, was the security paid in terms of gold in the absence of coined money? In this context, it may be remembered that the unit of exchange in gold was a weight, *kāṇam*. *Kāṇam* was used as a standard unit of transactions, and stood for 'money' in a general sense.[38] It may, therefore, be suggested that the *iṭaiyīṭŭ* and *kīḻīṭŭ* tenures in the records of the Cēra kingdom answer to the *kāṇam* tenure of later days.[39]

Lower in hierarchy, there were the tenants-at-will, who were described as *kārāḷar*, their right being called *kārāyma*. At a still lower level were occupants called *kuṭi* with the *kuṭimai* rights. It was much more nuanced than a three-tier hierarchy.[40] Thus, it may be proposed that the essential aspects of the landlordism of Kerala, which included what is called the *kāṇa-janma-maryādā*, were already in place in the period of the Cēra kingdom of Mahōdayapuram.

The post-Cēra period witnessed its elaboration and the addition of further nuances in the graded hierarchy, what with greater land-use and the diversification of crops in that period. Inscriptions on stone and copper thin out during this period.[41] A large number of records on palm leaves called *granthavaris*, many of them registering transaction of land, take their place. A few of them have been published; many more await publication. Even those that have been published are not subjected to systematic analysis. But what little has been done is useful. In an excellent study of legal practices and jurisprudence in medieval Kerala,[42] Donald R. Davis, Jr. has obliquely touched upon the land tenures in medieval Kerala. In the large number of documents transferring *aṭṭippēṟŭ* rights, Davis sees the equivalent of the transfer of *janmam* rights. He shows a brilliant flash of insight in taking the terms *aṭṭippēṟŭ* and *janmam* as 'technically synonymous'.[43] He takes up samples of the transfer of such rights in relation to brāhmaṇical temples, brāhmaṇa houses, Nāyar houses and temples under their control. Each of these transfers of *aṭṭippēṟŭ* rights is done with libation of water and for a consideration, a 'price fixed at the current rate determined by four people' or, more simply, 'price at the current rate' (*annu nālar kaṇṭu peṟum vila artham* or *annu peṟum artham*, respectively). It is interesting that the way in which price, *vila* or *artham*, is linked to the property is by the verb *peṟum*, lit., 'bearing'. *Pēṟŭ*, meaning 'birth', is its noun and translates into Sanskrit as *janmam*. Although Davis takes up only a few sample documents of such transfers, the validity of his generalization is borne out by the large number of records transferring *aṭṭippēṟŭ* rights. It turns out that this right answers, in every detail, to the *janmam* right of later days. In fact, a couple of documents, which Davis has not mentioned, use the two terms as synonymous.[44] One document calls itself a *janmakkaraṇam*, '*janmam* document' while other documents of a similar nature are *aṭṭippēṟṟōlakkaraṇam*, '[palm] leaf document of *aṭṭippēṟŭ*'. In the context in which other documents speak about the transfer of *aṭṭippēṟŭ* rights, the term used here is *janmam*. In a similar case, an *aṭṭippēṟṟōla* dated AD 1608, included in the *Vanjeri Granthavari*, transfers typically the *aṭṭippēṟŭ* rights for the 'current' price.[45] At the end of the document, it is stated that a letter each was taken from the senior and junior princes of Veṭṭam (the local chieftaincy) on the day on which this *janmam* was purchased. Unequivocally, thus, *janmam* and *aṭṭippēṟŭ* are synonymous. In this connection, another term used in medieval Malayalam to denote such rights over cultivated land is *ulpatti*, a *tadbhava* of Sanskrit *utpatti*, 'origin'.[46] It can be seen that this term is close to *janmam* and *pēṟŭ* both semantically and contextually. However, *ulpatti* is also used in the more general sense of 'landed property'. Other shades of right over land, which are adumbrated in the Cēra records, are more clearly visible in the records of the post-Cēra period. Of these the most important is one that went between the *aṭṭippēṟŭ* or *janmam* and the actual cultivation, that is to say, the *iṭaiyīṭŭ* and *kīḻīṭŭ* of the Cēra records. This was created and given to intermediaries often in return for a loan or security, the interest of which was adjusted against the proceeds of the land, something of a usufructuary mortgage. The terms used most frequently in the post-Cēra documents are *veppŭ*, *o̱ṟṟi*, and *paṇayam*. The relationship in this case was somewhat complex, combining in it those of a debtor and a creditor as well as a landlord and a tenant. The *granthavaris* contain a large number of documents called *veppōlakkaraṇam* and *oṟṟiyōlakkaraṇam* creating and transferring such rights.[47] In a few documents, the money taken as loan/security is described as *kāṇam* in so many words.[48] Although different terms are used, the details in the documents show that there was no difference whatever among the *kāṇam*, *veppŭ*, *oṟṟi* or *paṇayam* tenures, where the tenancy is on the condition of a deposit of loan/security.[49] This tenure obtains immediately below the *janmam* or *aṭṭippēṟŭ* tenure. The holder of the *aṭṭippēṟŭ* tenure, which was the closest to absolute property rights, reserved a superior right over the *kāṇam*, *veppŭ*, *oṟṟi* or *paṇayam* tenures as indicated by his right to levy an upper share called *mēlāyma* or *mēlāma*, as brought out by the *Koodali Granthavari*.[50] In this context, the statement in the *Kēraḷōlpatti*, that shares of the landlords and tenants were the upper share (*mēlāykkūṟŭ*) and lower share (*kīḻāykkūṟŭ*) respectively, particularly the terminology used, acquires significance.

Further down, at the extreme bottom of the hierarchy, records of the Cēra kingdom show that there were the labourers who worked the land and were transferred along with land when transactions of land took place. In fact, historians have equated this with similar practices in medieval Europe and recognized it as answering to serfdom. Whatever the validity of that description, such labourers are called variously as *āḷ*, *aṭiyār*, etc. The former term means 'man' and the latter, 'the lowly, subservient, one'. So also, the occupants of the land called *kuṭis*, who had only the right of possession of land, are mentioned in the records of the Cēra kingdom. In fact, the ubiquitous Malayalam word for 'tenant', *kuṭiyān*, is derived from this. An inscription from Kumāranallūr speaks about those śūdra cultivators of the settlement (*matilakattu kutiyirikkum Śūdrar*).[51] It may be recalled that the *Kēraḷōlpatti* too describes the cultivators as śūdras.[52] This pattern continues in the later records as well. It is these two shades at the lowermost rungs of the hierarchy that can be seen by the terms *aṭima* and *kuṭima* in the later records and the *Kēraḷōlpatti*.[53] Donald Davis, although his central concern is not with the structure or evolution of land-rights, has shown how there were other shades of rights vested in the *aṭiyār* and *kuṭiyār*—rights to perform labour services and to cultivate the land respectively—which consolidated themselves in this period.[54] What emerges, therefore, is that the peculiar kind of land tenures obtaining in Kerala had their origin in the Cēra kingdom. There were no cataclysmic changes taking place towards the time of the decline of that kingdom or in the period immediately following it. What is seen is the congealing of a tradition that was already under way in the Cēra kingdom.

Another feature of the post-Cēra period was a loss of the corporate character of the bodies of brāhmaṇas at the level of the villages. In the age of the Cēras, the brāhmaṇical bodies in the *sabhā* of the *ūr* functioned as corporate entities with great solidarity. The remarkably jealous way in which the corporate interests of this body were guarded is brought out by the documents.[55] In the subsequent period, however, they lost this well-knit corporate character. This can be seen from a large number of features such as the non-insistence of full attendance, lack of unanimity in decisions, the practice of attendance by proxy, decrease in the numerical strength of the *sabhā*, the domination of certain individuals in it and their exercise of greater powers, and so on.[56] The result of it all was that individual families came to acquire prominence and in the process started controlling all the properties of the temple, i.e. the *devasvam*, apart from their own *brahmasvam* properties. There are also instances where *devasvam* properties were appropriated as *brahmasvam*.[57] Elamkulam Kunjan Pillai had argued that this appropriation happened through the intermediate stage of *brahmasvamāṉa devasvam*, that is, '*devasvam* that is brahmasvam'.[58] This may very well have been so; but the process was more complex than what could be explained in terms of the cruelty and caprice of individual families in the wake of the uncertainties during a war. Factors such as the expansion of agriculture, changes in the cropping patterns, introduction of new crops, etc., as well as the increase of the new landowning sections of service professionals who were remunerated in terms of land as service tenure are to be considered as causative to the process of the growth of landlordism in the post-Cēra period. The entry of the Portuguese and Dutch players into the political and economic arena also contributed to the process after the fifteenth century. The radical changes in the administration of revenue after the colonial takeover demanded redefinition of tenurial rights and the nineteenth century witnessed solidification of the relations.

NOTES

1. Alan Butterworth and V. Venugopaul Chetty, *A Collection of Inscriptions on Copper Plates and Stones in the Nellore District*, Madras: Government Press, 1905, p. v.
2. The present paper is based on the author's earlier research for his two dissertations: Kesavan Veluthat, 'Aryan Brahman Settlements of Ancient Kerala', Unpublished M.A. dissertation, University of Calicut, 1974, and Veluthat, 'Brahman Settlements in Kerala, AD 1100–1500', Unpublished M.Phil. dissertation, Jawaharlal Nehru University, New Delhi, 1978. Some of the results are available in Veluthat, *Brahman Settlements in Kerala: Historical Studies*, Calicut: Sandhya Publications, University of Calicut, 1978.
3. For a brief survey of the progress of epigraphical studies in Kerala, see M.R. Raghava Varier, 'Epigraphical Studies in Kerala', *Tamil Civilization*, vol. 5, nos.1 & 2, March–June 1987; Kesavan Veluthat, 'Epigraphy in the Historiography of Kerala', in *Archaeology of Kerala: Past and Present*, ed. M.R. Manmathan, Kozhikode, 2007, pp. 126–49.
4. Most of Professor Elamkulam P.N. Kunjan Pillai's writings pertaining to this period are in Malayalam. Translations of some of the crucial articles, however, are available in English. Elamkulam P.N. Kunjan Pillai, *Studies in Kerala History*, Kottayam: National Book Stall, 1971.
5. His studies on the matrilineal system, or *marumakkattāyam*, and landlordism, or *janmisampradāyam*, both appearing in his *Studies in Kerala History*, are of particular interest in this respect.
6. Elamkulam P.N. Kunjan Pillai, *Janmisampradāyam Kraḷattil*, Kottayam: National Book Stall, 1959, pp. 8–44.
7. Kunjan Pillai takes him for a non-brāhmaṇa. Pillai, *Janmisampradāyam Kraḷattil*, p.19. This house figures in later Malayalam poems as a famous Nambudiri house. For a list of 200 brāhmaṇas collected from inscriptions of this period, see Veluthat, 'Aryan Brahman Settlements', Appendix II, pp. 92–102. Many of them are mistaken by Pillai for non-brāhmaṇas.
8. *Travancore Archaeological Series (TAS)*, vol. V, pt. I, no. 24, pp. 63–86, l. 4.
9. It was M.G.S. Narayanan who first challenged this. Narayanan, 'Political and Social Conditions of Kerala under the Kulasekhara Empire *c.*AD 800–1124', Ph.D. thesis, University of Kerala, 1972. This dissertation, a definitive and exhaustive study of the history of Kerala in this period, is not formally published although the author has circulated

a few printed copies. Narayanan, *Perumāḷs of Kerala*, Calicut: Cosmo Books, 1996. Following him the present writer took up the line.

10. Pillai, *Janmisampradāyam Kraḷattil*, pp. 22–3. The four individuals whom he identifies in the record, *TAS*, vol. V, pt. I, no. 24, are from the house of Vaññippuḻa, Vilakkilimaṅgalam, Kamukañcēri and Makiḻañcēri. Vaññippuḻa is an influential brāhmaṇa house to this day. A *bhaṭṭasōmayājin* of Vilakkilimaṅgalam figures in an earlier record from Tiruvalla. *TAS*, II, pt. III, pp. 131–207, ll. 584–5. Elsewhere in the record under reference (vol. ll, pp. 11–12), land assigned to these ten families is described as *paṭakāram*, an exclusively brāhmaṇa privilege. And the names such as Nārāyaṇa and Trivikrama are apparently of brāhmaṇas.
11. I have made an examination of the inscriptions and shown that many brāhmaṇa families mentioned in them survive to this day. Veluthat, 'Aryan Brahman Settlements', Appendix 2. There are other scholars who continue to mistake them for non-brāhmaṇas for obvious reasons. R.N. Nandi, review of Veluthat, *Brahman Settlements in Kerala* in *Indian Historical Review*, vol. VIII, nos. 1–2, pp. 126–8.
12. Pillai, *Janmisampradāyam Kraḷattil*, pp. 19–20.
13. *TAS*, vol. IV, no. 7, pp. 22–65.
14. Nos. 477 and 478 of 1926. I thank Professor M.G.S. Narayanan for permitting me to use his copy of the inscription.
15. There is a traditional list of 32 original brahmaṇa settlements in Kerala which the present writer has identified: *Brahman Settlements*, Vaikkam, however, is not one of them.
16. *TAS*, vol. V, pt. I, no. 24.
17. Ibid. See also *supra*, no. 12.
18. For a comprehensive study of the organization and administration of the temple-centred agrarian corporations in early medieval Kerala, see Veluthat, *Brahman Settlements in Kerala*, pp. 52–67.
19. See Pillai, *Janmisampradāyam Kraḷattil*, pp. 19–20.
20. For a discussion and interpretation, see M.G.S. Narayanan, 'Socio-Economic Implications of the Concept of Mahapataka in the Feudal Society of South India', *Journal of Kerala Studies*, vol. VI, 1979, pp. 453–60.
21. Veluthat, 'The *Sabha* and *Parisad* in Early Medieval South India', pp. 75–82.
22. Pillai, *Janmisampradāyam Kraḷattil*, p. 21.
23. *TAS*, vol. V, no. 2, p. 6.
24. Ibid.
25. Pillai, *Janmisampradāyam Kraḷattil*, pp. 19–20.

26. Pillai, *Janmisampradāyam Kraḷattil*, p. 38. The expression *nāṭṭukūṭṭam* which Pillai uses does not occur in the records.
27. M.G.S. Narayanan, *Reinterpretations in South Indian History*, Trivandrum: College Book House, 1977, pp. 99–112.
28. *TAS*, vol. V, no. 10, p. 34.
29. This is the general picture on local government in south India under the Cōḻas. K.A. Nilakanta Sastri, *The Colas*, 1955; 2nd edn., Madras: Madras University Press, 1975, pp. 503–6; for a recent re-examination, see Y. Subbarayalu, *Political Geography of the Chola Country*, Madras: State Department of Archaeology, Government of Tamil Nadu, 1973.
30. For this distinction, see Kesavan Veluthat, *The Political Structure of Early Medieval South India*, Delhi: Orient Longman, 1993, pp. 114, 177, et passim.
31. Narayanan, *Perumāḷs of Kerala*, chapters on 'Early Wars and Alliances', 'Cōḻa Invasions' and 'The Last Phase'.
32. Veluthat, *Brahman Settlements in Kerala*, chapter on 'The Tiruvalla Settlement: A Case Study', pp. 39–51. For information on this temple and the copious epigraphical records from there, see Alex Mathew, 'Political Identities in History', School of Social Sciences, Mahatma Gandhi University, Kottayam, 2006.
33. Narayanan, *Perumāḷs of Kerala*, chapter on 'Early Wars and Alliances' under 'Rise of the Kingdom', 'Influx of Aryans', 'Governors from Outside' and 'Founder of the Kingdom'.
34. 'All land seems to have belonged to the Cēra king in theory. The governors were his feudatories and as such they enjoyed the lands in their districts in return for payment of tribute. These lands possessed by the king or his feudatories and inhabited and cultivated by the native population are known *Cērikkal* in the records of the age. It is from such land that *nagaras* and *grāmas* were carved out and leased out to the foreign and native merchants or the Aryan Brahmin cultivators.'

    This crucial statement by Narayanan is not supported by evidence. There is no such 'theory' ; nor is there any evidence of the 'leasing out' to the 'Aryan Brahmin Cultivators'. It also contradicts his own position here. Narayanan, *Perumāḷs of Kerala*, Chapter on 'Economic Conditions' under 'Land Tenures', p. 174.
35. Rajan Gurukkal and Raghava Varier, *Cultural History of Kerala*, vol. I, Thiruvananthapuram: Department of Cultural Publications, Government of Kerala, 1999, pp. 235 ff.
36. For a recent discussion of *Kerāḷōlpatti* as history, Kesavan Veluthat, 'The *Keralotpatti* as History: A Note on the Pre-colonial Traditions

of Historical Writing in India', in *Culture and Modernity: Historical Explorations*, ed. K.N. Ganesh, Calicut: University of Calicut, 2004.

37. Scaria Zacharia, ed., *Hermann Gundert's Keraḷōolpattiyum Maṟṟum*, Kottayam, 1992, pp. 159–60. Translation by the present author.
38. Narayanan, *Perumāḷs of Kerala*, p. 164. This was one-tenth of a *kaḻañcu*, which was accepted as a unit all over south India. Sastri, *The Colas*, pp. 613–4. A *kaḻañcu* was equal to a *gadyāṇa* figuring in the documents from Karnataka. The term *kāṇam* is used in the sense of 'money' in general in many post-Cēra records. There is at least one place where the term *kāṇam* is used in Malayalam literature in the sense of money. Describing the wedding of Śiva and Pārvatī elaborately, an old song that Nampūtiri women recite calls the dowry which Śiva received *kāṇam*: *. . . kaṇavum nīrumay vāṅṅikkoṇṭaṅṅaṉe / hōmam tuṭaṅṅī namaś śivāya.* I quote this from memory as heard from my grandmother who used to recite it in the evenings.
39. M.G.S. Narayanan, however, believes that *kāṇam* is derived from the verb *kāṇuka*, 'to see', and used in the extended sense of 'to acquire' as used in the Syrian Christian copper plates. Narayanan, *Perumāḷs of Kerala*, p. 174. He takes it to mean 'a kind of proprietorship prevalent in Kerala in later times also' and defines it as a 'perpetual lease', 'as long as the world, sun and moon endure'. He continues to say that the right that the temple-centred brāhmaṇa settlements had over land was such *kāṇam* right. None of these is, however, borne out by evidence that he has himself competently marshalled.
40. Narayanan posits a three-tier hierarchy. Narayanan, *Perumāḷs of Kerala*, p. 174.
41. For a discussion of this pattern, Kesavan Veluthat, 'Storage and Retrieval of Information: Literacy and Communication in Pre-modern Kerala', in *Webs of History: Information, Communication and Technology from Early to Post-colonial India*, ed. Amiya Kumar Bagchi, Dipankar Sinha and Barnita Bagchi, Delhi: Manohar, 2005, pp. 67–82.
42. Donald R. Davis, Jr., *The Boundaries of Hindu Law: Tradition, Custom and Politics in Medieval Kerala*, Torino: Comitato Corpus iuris Sanscriticum et fontes iuris Asiae Meridianae et Centralis, 2004.
43. Ibid., p. 52.
44. K.K.N. Kurup, ed., *Koodali Granthavari*, Calicut: University of Calicut, 1995, Document no. 157, p. 97.
45. M.G.S. Narayanan, ed., *Vanjeri Granthavari*, Calicut: University of Calicut, 1987, pp. 29–30.
46. Hermann Gundert, *A Malayalam and English Dictionary*, Mangalore:

C. Stolz, 1872, s.v., *ulpatti*. The documents contained in Kurup, *Koodali Grandhavari*, use the expression in the same sense. When the *aṭṭippēṟŭ* rights in a piece of land are sold, such land is described as *ulpatti*.

47. Narayanan, *Vanjeri Grandhavari*, passim; Kurup, ed., *Koodali Grandhavari*, passim.
48. For example Kurup, ed., *Koodali Grandhavari*, Document no. 51, p. 53.
49. Davis, *The Boundaries of Hindu Law*, p. 67, believes that *kāṇam* was still a relatively higher tenure [than the other two] in which the holder of the *kāṇam* right receives much of the produce from the land of his (or his family's) supervision. The documents he has used, or the others in the *granthavaris* he has consulted, do not, however, warrant this conclusion.
50. Kurup, *Koodali Granthavari*, passim.
51. *TAS*, vol. III, no. 49, pp. 191–6.
52. Zacharia, *Kēraḷōlpattiyum Maṟṟum*, pp. 159–60.
53. Zacharia, *Kēraḷōlpattiyum Maṟṟum*. It is interesting that the *Kēraḷōlpatti*, like the Kumāranallūr inscription mentioned in note 51 (this chapter), assigns a Śūdra status to those who belong to this category.
54. Davis, *The Boundaries of Hindu Law*, p. 67.
55. Narayanan, *Perumāḷs of Kerala*, pp. 109–20. This is by far the most elaborate and systematic treatment of the problem. For other discussions, see Veluthat, *Brahman Settlements in Kerala*, chapter on 'Organization and Administration during the Later Cēra Period, AD 800–1100', pp. 52–67; Gurukkal, *The Kerala Temple and Early Medieval Agrarian System*, Sukapuram: Vallathol Vidyapeetham, 1992. Neither of these takes it beyond what Narayanan had written.
56. For an elaborate treatment, see Veluthat, *Brahman Settlements in Kerala*, chapter on 'Changes in the Organization and Administration', pp. 86–95.
57. A clear instance of this can be seen in the Peruñcellūr Copper Plate. Veluthat, 'Peruñcellūr Ceppēṭu, Kollam 321 Kanni 21 (1145 September 22)', *AdhAram: A Journal of Kerala Archaeology and History*, vol. 1, 2006, pp. 75–82. This record speaks of how the temple committee of Peruñcellūr and the ruler of the local *nāṭu* together lent a sum of 707 *ānaiyaccŭ* to a private brāhmaṇa individual, taking from him landed properties and the labourers who worked them as mortgage. An additional sum of 300 *ānaiyaccŭ* was lent three years later and charged on the same properties. The whole transaction is described as *paṇayam* and the second instalment of money charged on it is called *brahmasvam*.
58. Pillai, *Janmisampradāyam Kraḷattil*.

CHAPTER 8

Congealing of Castes

The Case of Medieval Kerala

ONE OF THE MAJOR debates in the social history of India has been around the ubiquitous institution of caste. It has baffled all visitors to the country from outside from very early times. So also, from when historical writing on 'modern' lines was inaugurated, the institution lent itself to treatment of varied kinds. Sociologists and anthropologists have been trying to unravel its mystery while political scientists are concerned with the use of the reality in politics, past and present. It needs hardly any emphasis that caste is used as the basis, imagined or real, for rallying people for purposes other than what it is meant for. In spite of this overarching importance of the institution, there has been practically no study of a serious nature examining the processes of its formation and the structure that it took from time to time in the case of Kerala. This chapter seeks to raise a few questions in that direction and tries to look at the evidence from medieval Kerala—inscriptions, palm leaf documents and literary texts—in order to see how occupational groups got congealed into castes in Kerala. Taken up for illustration is the case of what are described as the 'intermediate' 'temple-serving' groups. They perform varied functions, sometimes unconnected with what are supposed to be the duties of the castes they belonged to in later times, in early inscriptions, but start gradually getting congealed as so many castes in later times with all features defining castes such as rituals, patterns of succession through patriliny or matriliny, commensality and connubiality, allotted positions on the scale of purity and pollution and so on. Hopefully, it will throw light on the general pattern obtaining not only in Kerala but elsewhere in the subcontinent as well.

The *Kēraḷōlpatti* has an interesting, and somewhat detailed, account regarding the origin of castes and assignment of status to each one of them in society.[1] Unfortunately, historians who have written about the social history of Kerala have paid scant attention to these statements in this extremely important narrative.[2] It may be worthwhile to summarize what the narrative has to say in relation to the ordering of society on castes, not so much to know how it exactly was as to see how it was perceived by those sections of society that produced it and that it addressed. It was the inevitable Śaṅkarācārya who laid down the elaborate rules concerning castes and their hierarchy, the relative status of each in terms of purity and pollution and suchlike in 24,000 books![3] In any case, there is a late medieval text called *Śāṅkarasmṛti* which was followed in Kerala as a textbook of social conduct including caste rules, although it has nothing to do with the great *advaita* philosopher.[4] Interestingly, the word used for what has come to be known in later times as caste is *kula*, which in Sanskrit means 'a race, family, community, tribe, caste, set, company', etc.[5] The more familiar expression, *jāti*, is used only sparingly, which has its own significance. The greater emphasis on kinship than on the other features identified as defining castes should not be lost sight of.

According to the *Kēraḷōlpatti*, the *ācārya* ordained that there should be four *varṇas*, which would be divided into 18 *kulas*, to be subdivided into 68 *kulavarṇas* and 72 *kulas*.[6] After giving a detailed account of the different 'castes' which were so ordered in Kerala, the text goes on to say that the omniscient Śaṅkarācārya also decided the relative status of each on the scale of purity and pollution, including distance pollution. The text suddenly becomes apologetic about the entire arrangement, particularly the distance pollution and seeks to defend it in the following fashion:

> God, to be sure, does not make any distinction of castes. There is no distance pollution in *paradēśa*; it is as if all belong to the same *varṇa*. That is not to be in this land. Purity of land can be achieved by purity of *karma*. No

distinction is necessary in a Land of Knowledge; but deliverance is possible in this Land of *Karma* only through *karma*. Hence this arrangement.[7]

All the castes mentioned (and more) are known from survivals. Epigraphical records from earlier periods do not speak about all of them. The purpose of inscriptions being what it is, they cannot be expected to speak of these myriad castes. The inscriptions record matters such as a grant of land or assignment of privileges to traders or resolutions of temple committees, and only those sections of society that are parties to such transactions can be expected to be present there.[8] The vast majority of inscriptions from medieval Kerala are from temples and, therefore, the largest number of individuals and groups which find representation in these records are those that are related to temples in one capacity or the other. Although the major concern of the inscriptions is not rituals *per se*, since there are provisions made for the institution and conduct of rituals, groups related to their conduct find a place there. It will be interesting to look at some of these mentioned in the inscriptions and see how they started performing other functions to get congealed as so many caste groups in later times. The statements in the *Kēraḷōlpatti* may be taken up as a starting point.

After mentioning brāhmaṇas and defining the status of the different varieties of them, the text goes on to speak about an *antarāḷa* ('intermediate') group called *ambalavāsis* ('temple-dwellers') who were 'superior to śūdras but inferior to brāhmaṇas'. It gives an elaborate list of such groups:

Of these, there are two varieties of *potuvāḷs*. The *akappotuvāḷ* would carry the idol of the deity for *śivabali*, look after the *dēvasvam*, the deity and the temple, and wash the steps to the *sanctum sanctorum* clean. The *puṟappotuvāḷ* would accept offerings from the devotees and arrange for plantain leaves, ghee, firewood, milk, honey, etc., for the offerings. Those who perform *śaktipūja* in the service of Bhagavatī are called variously as *piṣāran*, *piṭāran*, *aṭiyān*, *aṭikaḷ*, etc. The *puṣpakan* or *nambiaccan* has the work of providing flowers, making garlands and doing other odd little jobs of the temple. His women are called *brāhmaṇis*. His house is called *pūmaṭham* or *pādōdakam* and he is called *pūnambi*. The *brāhmaṇi's* livelihood is by singing at the steps [of the *sanctum sanctorum*]. The *piṣārōṭi* is assigned the conduct of an ascetic as well as sweeping inside the temple and making garlands. The 'Dweller of Kailāsa' was assigned jobs in the temple. His women, to be called *vāriyatti*, were to sweep the temple. Those who belonged to the *jāti* of *vāri* should have the pattern of pollution [on birth and death] for the kṣatriya and the occupation of the *puṣpakan*. It is said that all those who are born into this [group] are of Āḻvāñcēri Tamprākkaḷ. The males among the *śḷāghyār* are called *cākyār* and the females, *naṅṅyārs*. Their function is to tell divine stories in performances, play and recite *kūttu*, read *vyākaraṇa*, *nāṭakas* and *purāṇas*. A group called *cārnnavar* was assigned to assist them: they are *nambiyārs*. Among them, *iḷayatŭ* would cook and accept rice for the *śrāddha* of *śūdras*. The *mūssatŭ* is the *pariṣa* of the village. As they have incurred a curse from Paraśurāma, they do not perform any rites of brāhmaṇas. Close to them are *celampāṇṭis* who are servants of the deity of Thiruvananthapuram. There is another set of *cārnna pariṣa* called *teyyampāṭi* who perform *kūttu* for Śāstā. They propitiate gods by drawing their images on floor [*kaḷam*] and singing songs in their praise. Where there is *pūjā* of Bhadrakāḷi, two groups, namely *mānāri* and *puttillam*, were installed for the *kaḻakam* there. These and *uṇittiris* are the highest among the *ambalavāsis*. Mārāyar are not counted as *ambalavāsis*. They are drummers. As *asthikuṟicci* or *asthivāri*, they participate in funerary rites and hence are included among the *pariyarattavar*.[9]

This somewhat long but elaborate and clear account is highly dependable as it preserves the details and hierarchy among the castes referred to as *ambalavāsis* in later-day Kerala. In fact, colonial ethnography as represented by the writings of Edgar Thurston,[10] L.K. Ananthakrishna Iyer[11] and the like have presented a similar picture, following field studies and personal knowledge of what obtained here at the time of their writing. It is also attested by survivals. As such, the statements in the *Kēraḷōlpatti* may be taken as documenting the situation when these had emerged as so many castes, as when the ethnographers recorded what they experienced in the nineteenth and twentieth centuries. As this text cannot be much later than the eighteenth century, this may be taken as the picture as it obtained in that period of time. How far back can we go in documents in our attempt to find out how they got defined in this way? To what extent do inscriptions and literary texts help us in the matter?

The earliest documents giving us some evidence of these groups are the inscriptions dating from the age of the Cēras (AD *c*.800–1100). These inscriptions are largely from, or concerned with, temples and therefore deal with regulating the rituals of the temples as also the arrangements for the conduct of these from out of the proceeds of land or other assignments that the temple received as offerings from different sources. However, it is interesting that these records do not help us to identify these sections as so many castes; in fact, at least in a couple of cases, there is reason to believe that some of them were brāhmaṇas. A closer examination of the documents will bear this out.

Of the different groups with which our quotation from the *Kēraḷōlpatti* began, the *potuvāḷ* of the two varieties—namely, the *akappotuvāḷ* and the *puṟappotuvāḷ*—heads the list. If the *Kēraḷōlpatti*, colonial ethnography and later survivals represent the former as charged with the duties of 'carrying the idol of the deity for *śivabali*, looking after the *dēvasvam*, the deity and the temple and wash the steps to the *sanctum sanctorum* clean', their function is somewhat different in the inscriptions. They are seen in their capacity of managers of the property of the temple—perhaps the statement in the *Kēraḷōlpatti* that their work included 'looking after the *dēvasvam*' is a faint recollection of this old function. But none of the other functions, such as carrying the idol during processions or sweeping the steps of the *sanctum sanctorum* clean, typically of the *ambalavāsi* castes in modern times, is seen as associated with the *potuvāḷs* of the Cēra inscriptions.

In fact, in most inscriptions of the Cēra period—and there are a large number of them—the *potuvāḷ* is very much part of the managing committee deciding unanimously on the conduct of the affairs of the temple. Historians have identified the *potuvāḷ* as the 'secretary' to the committee.[12] Both semantically and in terms of function, the *potuvāḷ* would seem to answer to the *madhyasthan* in the inscriptions from other parts of south India.[13] In most cases, he is stated as attending the meeting of the committee managing the affairs of the temple, the *ūr*, which historians in the past had taken for the local body looking after what has been called 'village administration'. He is as much party to the decisions of the *ūr* as are its members.[14] What is more, he is seen, at least in some cases, as executing the decisions such as taking land on lease and giving away land on lease on behalf of the temple. Besides, at least in a few cases, he is seen as in charge of the general affairs of the village.

An Āvaṭṭipputtūr inscription of the 20th year of Kōta Ravi (AD 903)[15] says that the decision recorded there was taken unanimously by the Twenty-seven (the *ūrāḷar*) and the *potuvāḷ* of Āvaṭṭipputtūr and that the *ūrāḷar* and the *potuvāḷ* shall redress the grievances of the villagers. It says further that the *ūrāḷar* and the *potuvāḷ* shall not take bribes or seek sexual favours from the women of the villagers or do any other 'good or bad things'. There is also indication in this document that the *potuvāḷ* was a brāhmaṇa: 'if the *ūrāḷar* or the *potuvāḷ* did anything opposed to these decisions, they would be equated with those who violated the Kaṭaṅṅkāṭṭu kaccam, lose their properties, and lose membership [in the assembly of *ūr*] and [eligibility to become] *paraṭai*'. It has been shown that one of the conditions for membership in the *ūr* and eligibility for *paraṭai* was being a brāhmaṇa. Another record, from Kayalkkāṭŭ,[16] is more explicit: if any one of the parties was to violate the decision under reference, taken unanimously by the *āyiram*, the *aṭikaḷmār*, the *potuvāḷ* and the *ūrāḷar*, or if anybody was to misappropriate the property of the temple, such would be equated with one who has killed his father and the teacher who initiated him and taught him the Vedas, eaten that corpse and slept with his mother after that. The brāhmaṇa status of all the parties is brought out unequivocally by this reference to 'the *upādhyāya* who performed the *upanayana* and taught Vedas'.

There is reason to believe that the *potuvāḷ*'s was an office to which incumbents were appointed from time to time. An inscription from Chembra near Mahé discovered and published by M.R. Raghava Varier[17] makes this clear. It records, as usual, a unanimous decision of the *ūr*, *sabhā* and *potuvāḷ* and one of the items decided on was that the son of a certain Ciṟaittalai Tariyanan (Darśana), was to be installed as the *potuvāḷ—potuvāḷ vāḻikkak-kaṭavar*.[18] There are a few other records which speak of 'the *potuvāḷ* in office from time to time'—*aṉṟaṉṟu muṟai potuvāḷ*[19]—or 'the *potuvāḷ* in office'—*muṟaiyuṭaiya potuvāḷ*[20]—which makes it clear that the office was not hereditary or permanent.

This somewhat elaborate examination of the way in which the *potuvāḷ* shows himself up in the Cēra records and immediately thereafter brings out clearly that a *potuvāḷ* caste had not emerged in that period. There are indications that the *potuvāḷ* was a brāhmaṇa. For one thing, it would not have been possible for him to wield such influence in the *brāhmaṇa*-dominated *sabhā* or the 'village assembly' unless he was a brāhmaṇa himself. He seems to do none of the jobs associated with *ambalavāsis* which are considered as infra-dig by pretentious brāhmaṇas in Kerala. However, there are a couple of records of interest in this context. The Māṇiyūr inscription referred to earlier speaks of the *virutti* enjoyed by the *potuvāḷ*, indicating not only that his was a paid job but also that land was given in lieu of salary, the income from which was the reward for his work. With the assignment of land as remuneration for a job, the hereditary nature of the job is not far behind, as land had already become an item of property that was, among other things, inherited. At least in one place we see the *potuvāḷ* engaged in a piece of work which is typically of an *ambalavāsi*; the Veḷḷalūr inscription mentioned previously speaks of the *potuvāḷ* as making garlands—*tiruppaḷḷittāmamuṅ keṭṭi*.

What it all suggests is that the term did not indicate a caste to begin with. An office concerned with the management of the properties of the temple and coordinating the villagers in relation to the temple and its properties, it was generally manned by brāhmaṇas. When the practice of assigning land in lieu of salary for the office emerged, it is likely that the office became hereditary. Marriage and kinship may have been closely associated with this. Gradually, as the *potuvāḷ* became inseparably related to the temple, certain pieces of work in the temple, such as 'carrying the idol of the deity for *śivabali*, looking after the *dēvasvam*, the deity and the temple and wash the steps to the *sanctum sanctorum* clean' were identified as his own. The 'caste' of *potuvāḷ* was being born.

The experience in the case of other groups mentioned in the list is comparable. Another group mentioned in the list in the *Kēraḷōlpatti* with which we began is the *mūssatŭ*. The *Kēraḷōlpatti* hastens to add that he is the *pariṣa* of the village. In fact, the ethnography of colonial times and survivals through the modern period speak of a section of the caste of *mūssatŭ* as *ūril pariṣa mūssatŭ*. The *mūssatŭs* today constitute a caste of *ambalavāsis*, describing themselves as *śivabrāhmaṇas*. The *Kēraḷōlpatti* states that they do not perform any rites of brāhmaṇas as they have incurred a curse from Paraśurāma. In the Cēra inscriptions, however, the *pariṣa* or *paraṭai* are very much brāhmaṇas, constituting the 'executive committee' of the assembly of the *ūr*.[21] In fact, the *paraṭai* or *pariṣad* figures prominently in inscriptions from south India, about which historians have written at great length.[22] The correlation between *Dharmaśāstraic* and epigraphical evidence regarding the *sabhā* and the *pariṣad*, too, has been brought out persuasively.[23] It has been shown that they were brāhmaṇas with all privileges including rights in the temple and claims to property. Occasionally, there is reference to *Mūttōr* or *Mūttavakaḷ*, obviously the plural of *mūttatŭ*, in the place of *paraṭai* in certain places, thereby suggesting that the two terms are interchangeable. A Tṛkkaṭittānam inscription makes it clear that those who perform priestly functions (*śānti ceyyumvar*) or take up lesser functions in the temple and enjoy *virutti* lands from the temple are not eligible for membership in the assembly or the office of the *paraṭai* and that the *paraṭai* should not take the temple's land on lease.[24] An Airāṇikkuḷam inscription is more explicit in giving the caste status of the *paraṭai*: those members of the *ūr* and *paraṭai* who violated the decisions to which they were party would lose their property and privileges, and would be equated with those who have killed the teacher who initiated them into the Vedas and their father and married their mother.

As in the case of the *potuvāḷ*, there is a visible shift in the caste status of the *mūssatŭ* or *mūttatŭ* as well. The statement in the *Kēraḷōlpatti*, that they do not perform the rituals of brāhmaṇas as they had incurred the wrath of Paraśurāma, seems to make an attempt at explaining the fact of a 'fall' in the caste status. How did it happen? There is no way in which we can answer this question. Is it a case of the fall in ritual status following the closer association of the *mūttatŭ* with the temple and their being required to perform 'unclean jobs' such as sweeping, washing vessels, etc.? In any case, they are of an inferior caste status today whereas they are brāhmaṇas of high ritual and social status in the inscriptions.

Even more interesting is the case of the *vāriyan*. The *Kēraḷōlpatti* avers that 'the *Kailāsavāsi* ("Dweller of Kailāsa") was assigned jobs in the temple. His women, to be called *vāriyatti*, were to sweep the temple. Those who belonged to the *jāti* of *vari* should have the pattern of pollution [on birth and death] for the kṣatriya and the occupation of the *puṣpakan*'. Obviously, this is a reference to the caste of *vāriyar* with the details of their function and status as they obtain today. The *vāriyar* claim that they belong to the putative Kailāsa *gotra*.[25] It is tempting to suggest that the Kailātam uṭayanār, who figures in the Vāḻappaḷḷi copper plate of Rājaśēkhara as the donor of some land to the temple,[26] may be a *vāriyar* of this variety.

In any case, inscriptions from the period of the Cēras represent them not as caste but as associated with the managerial functions of the temple and its properties. Like the *potuvāḷ* and *paraṭai*, he is seen as being party to the major decisions of the committee of *ūr*. In fact, a couple of references to *vāriyam uṭaiyān* in Cēra inscriptions compel us to believe that there existed subcommittees called *vāriyams* here also as in contemporary Tamil-speaking areas. The *vāriyam* of the Cōḻa situation has been commented on at length.[27] Even if such subcommittees did not exist in Kerala, the importance of the *vāriyan* cannot be exaggerated. M.G.S. Narayanan has brought out the importance of this office.[28]

However, unlike in the cases discussed here, the process of the 'fall' of *vāriyar* seems to be documented in the inscriptions themselves. The Kollūr Maṭham Plates of AD 1184, which claims to be a reissue of an earlier tenth-century document, speaks of 'the *vāriyans* who sweep [the temple premises]' and the land assigned to them in lieu of their salary. There are also references to the *vāriyar* making garlands and doing similar jobs. These references may throw light on the process of the congealing of the *vāriyar* as a caste group, and the statement in the *Kēraḷōlpatti*, quoted previously, may be taken to show the status and functions that the caste came to acquire in later times.

There are similar, if less prolific, references to other caste groups described as *ambalavāsis* as well. They include *nampi*, *iḷayār*, *aṭikaḷ*, *cākkai*, *naṅgai* and the like.[29] It is difficult to assess their status with the help of inscriptions. However, it is clear that they had not emerged as so many castes, with any fixed function and status in the age of the Cēras. It is in the period that followed that we can see this happening. Even there, it is interesting that some of them, such as the *mūssatŭ* or *puṣpakan/nampi accan*, have the thread and are patrilineal, while some others, such as the *potuvāḷ* and the *vāriyan*, are both matrilineal and have no thread. In the present state of our knowledge, no definite statement can be made about the process through which they got congealed into so many castes. What is likely is that when professions got linked with land given in lieu of salary, jobs too were inherited along with land. This led to the creation of a kinship group, which later became exogamous. Slotting of each of them in a graded hierarchy of purity and pollution followed this. In the end, we have the process of legitimization; when the whole arrangement is attributed to none other than Śaṅkarācārya, in an attempt to seek inviolability to it.

NOTES

1. Scaria Zacharia, ed., *Kēraḷōlpattiyum Maṟṟum:Eight Works Published During 1843–1904 by Dr. Hermann Gundert*, Kottayam, 1992, pp. 182–7.
2. This is a much maligned narrative of the history of Kerala. Historians have treated it variously, their judgement ranging from looking at it as 'a farrago of legendary nonsense' to 'having attained the rank of authentic history'. For a detailed discussion and an alternative reading of *Kēraḷōlpatti*, see Kesavan Veluthat, 'The *Keralolpatti* as History', in *The Early Medieval in South India*, New Delhi: Oxford University Press, 2009, pp. 129–46.
3. Zacharia, *Kēraḷōlpattiyum Maṟṟum*, pp. 182–3.
4. K.K. Tampurān, ed., *Śāṅkarasmṛti (Laghudharmaprakāśikā)*, Trichur: Bharatavilasam Press, 1906. There is a more recent edition of this work: N.P. Unni, ed., *Śāṅkarasmṛti: Laghudharmaprakāśikā*, Torino: Comitato Promotore per la Pubblicazione del Corpus Iuris Sanscriticum, 2003.
5. Monier Monier-Williams, *A Sanskrit-English Dictionary*, s.v. *kula*, Oxford: The Clarendon Press, 1960.
6. Zacharia, *Kēraḷōlpattiyum Maṟṟum*, pp. 182–3.
7. Ibid., p. 187.
8. For a definitive and exhaustive study of the political and social conditions of Kerala based on the inscriptions of this period, see M.G.S. Narayanan, *The Perumāḷs of Kerala*, Calicut: Cosmo Books, 1996.
9. Zacharia, *Kēraḷōlpattiyum Maṟṟum*, pp. 183–4.
10. Edgar Thurston and T.K. Rangachari, *Castes and Tribes of Southern India*; repr., New Delhi, 1993, relevant volumes.
11. L.K. Ananthakrishna Iyer, *The Castes and Tribes of Cochin*; repr., New Delhi: Cosmo, 1981; L.A. Krishna Iyer, *Kerala and Her People*, Palghat: Educational Supplies Depot, 1961.
12. Narayanan, *The Perumāḷs of Kerala*, p. 110, takes the *potuvāḷ* to mean literally a 'public servant' and as one of 'the officers who assisted them [i.e. the executive committee of the village assembly]'. Rajan Gurukkal takes the *potuvāḷ* for the 'secretary' of the committee.
13. Scholars are not unanimous in their interpretation of the term in the context of Cōḻa inscriptions. K.A. Nilakanta Sastri takes the term to

mean 'arbitrator'. Sastri, *The Cōḻas*, Madras: University of Madras, 1955; 2nd edn., 1975, p. 510. T.N. Subrahmanyan takes it to mean 'headman' (*South Indian Temple Inscriptions*, 'Glossary') while K.V. Subrahmanya Aiyar, who edited the Larger Leyden Plates glosses the word as 'arbitrator'. *Epigraphia Indica*, vol. V., no. 22, esp. line 210 ff. For a strange formulation, Burton Stein, *Peasant State and Society in Medieval South India*, Delhi: Oxford University Press, 1980, p. 121.

14. Āvaṭṭipputtūr inscription of Kōtai Iravi, 20th year; Triprangode Inscription of Kōtai Iravi, 23rd year; Poraṅṅāṭṭiri inscription of Kōtai Iravi, 27th year; Chembra inscription; Neṭumpuṟam Taḷi inscription of Indu Kōtai, 17th year; Veṇṇāyūr inscription of Bhāskara Ravi, 2nd year; NeṭumpuṞam Taḷi inscription of Bhāskara Ravi, 13th year; Tṛkkaṭittānam inscription of Bhāskara Ravi, 13th year; Tṛkkaṭittānam inscription of Bhāskara Ravi, 14th year; Perunna inscription of Bhāskara Ravi, 12th year; Tṛkkaṭittānam inscription of Bhāskara Ravi, 26th year; Perunna inscription of Bhāskara Ravi, 33rd year; Kuḷattūr inscription of Bhāskara Ravi, 38th year; Iriṭṭālakkuṭa inscription of Bhāskara Nampirāṉār; Mūḻikkuḷam inscription of Bhāskara Ravi, 49th year; Panniyankara inscription of Ravi Kota; Perunna inscription of Kulaśēkhara, 10th year; Māmpaḷḷi copper plate of Śrīvallavan Kōtai; undated Tiruvanvaṇṭūr inscription; Veḷḷalūr inscription of AD 1124; Cēnnamṅgalam inscription; two Tṛśśivapērūr inscriptions; Tṛprayār inscription; Pūkkōṭṭūr inscription; Kayalkkāṭŭ inscription; Māṇiyūr inscription; and so on.
15. *Bulletin of the Ramavarma Research Institute*, vol. VII, no. 2, pp. 127–30.
16. Puthusseri Ramachandran, *Kēraḷacaritrattiṉṛe Aṭisthanarēkhakaḷ*, Thiruvananthapuram, 2007, pp. 393–4. I have not been able to verify this inscription for want of any details in this publication.
17. M.R. Raghava Varier, *Kēraḷīyata: Caritramānaṅṅaḷ*, 2nd edn., Sukapuram, 2009, pp. 96–117.
18. Ibid., p. 97, lines 20–1.
19. Ibid.
20. Ibid.
21. Narayanan, *The Perumāḷs of Kerala*, p. 110; Kesavan Veluthat, *Brahman Settlements in Kerala: Historical Studies*, Calicut: Sandhya Publications, University of Calicut, 1978; Rajan Gurukkal, *Kerala Temple and the Early Medieval Agrarian System*, Sukapuram: Vallathol Vidyapeetham, 1992.
22. See, for example, Sastri, *The Cōḻas*, passim.
23. Veluthat, 'The *Sabha* and *Parishad* in Early Medieval South India'.
24. Ramachandran, *Kēraḷacaritrattiṉṛe Aṭisthanarēkhakaḷ*, pp. 63–4. I have not been able to verify this inscription either.

25. On the occasion of *śrāddha* and other ceremonies, *vāriyar* invokes the names as 'born into the Kailāsa *gotra*'. I thank M.R. Raghava Varier for this information.
26. Narayanan, *Index to Cera Inscriptions*, no. A. 1.
27. Sastri, *The Cōḻas*, passim.
28. Narayanan, *The Perumāḷs of Kerala*, p. 110.
29. Interestingly, brāhmaṇas, performing the priestly function, are not included in the group of *ambalavāsis* or 'temple dwellers'. They, in reality, are 'temple dwellers' more than others mentioned in the list. It is, therefore, necessary to rethink the meaning of the word *ambalavāsi*. *Ambalam* primarily means 'a hall', both in Tamiḻ and Malayalam. The halls within the enclosure of the temple are even now known as *nālambalam, valiyambalam, cuṟṟambalam*, etc. So, are the 'temple dwellers' really those who were confined to the halls such as the ones mentioned, with no entry to the central shrine, the *sanctum sanctorum*?

CHAPTER 9

Use of 'Hindu' Idioms in Christian Worship and Propaganda in Kerala

IT IS WELL-KNOWN that Kerala, in the south-western coast of India, has been host to Semitic religions such as Judaism, Christianity and Islam from very early times. This plurality and coexistence of religions of a West Asian origin along with the local 'Hindu' traditions of various descriptions has caused writers of the nationalist era to boast that Kerala had offered an illustrious example of religious toleration from very early times.[1] Alternatively, it has been described as an instance of 'cultural symbiosis', the material concerns that enabled or necessitated it receiving greater attention than altruistic considerations of toleration.[2] It is rarely recognized that there have been exchanges of a rich, varied and complex character in this coexistence of different religious groups, which nourished one another with the idioms and expressions borrowed mutually. The use of idioms of the more numerous and hence dominant groups, accepted by those who came from outside, not only made their 'religions' less strange and exotic but also earned for the latter greater acceptability among the local people. This paper tries to make a case study of this process

*I thank Denis Fernandes and Ines Županov for reading a first draft of this paper critically and raising many questions which helped in clarifying a number of issues.

by looking at the way in which the Christians of Kerala adopted the idioms typical of the 'Hindu' Brāhmaṇical religion in worship and, later, for purposes of propaganda, thereby contributing to the making of a composite culture in this part of the country.

The sources for the present study are largely palm-leaf documents in Malayalam preserved in the *Division Manuscrits orientaux* of the Bibliothèque nationale de France (BnF), Paris.[3] These manuscripts are in a good state of preservation, although there are many errors in the catalogue.[4] There are many volumes of Malayalam manuscripts, of which I take up here those which are related to Christian theology and propaganda. These include a few volumes of palm leaf manuscripts related to Christian theology,[5] two of them correctly identified as such but a third one listed as just *Manuscrits en malayalam sur olles* ('Malayalam Manuscripts on Palm Leaves'). Pierre-Sylvain Filliozat, Jean Deloche and Manonmani Filliozat have identified two of them in their work on Anquetil Duperron as among three documents which the latter carried from India.[6] The third one, which Duperron is said to have brought, could be another one listed as *Manuscrits en malayalam sur olles*, which was in the Musée Guimet, Paris, but transferred to the BnF much later.[7] In these three manuscripts, the dates of two of which are given, there is a clear indication that following the famous or notorious Synod of Diamper in AD 1599, there was another council held in Kodungallur in 1606 confirming some of the ideas and actions of the former. Many doctrinal questions are discussed here. A second manuscript is a catechism, where problems of theology such as the Trinitarian concept and the virginity of Mary are discussed in detail. Unfortunately, both these documents are fragmentary. The third one could not be read in its present condition.

There is a document that the catalogue lists as 'Yadjourvedam en malayalam'.[8] This is a palm-leaf manuscript with 95 leaves, written on both sides. It has nothing to do with *Yajurveda* or any other Veda for that matter. The text is an abridged retelling, a free rendering, of the Bible, with emphasis on the story of Jesus Christ. A colophon at the end of the text describes it as *Miśihācaritam*, 'the Story of the Messiah'. It is in verse, largely in the popular Malayalam metre *Pāna*, except for one canto where Sanskritic metres such as *Indravajrā*, *Upendravajrā* and their mixture *Upajātī* are used. Perhaps what prompted the scholar who prepared the catalogue, and even the person who wrote the name of the text on the outer cover, is an invocatory passage at the beginning: *Ēcēśvarāya namaḥ* ('Salutations to Ēśu, the *Īśvara*') for its apparent similarity with *yajuḥ*, if indeed it was not an attempt to claim that the saga of Jesus is part of the Vedic lore. In this context, it is important to remember that the Bible is referred to in Malayalam as the *Vedapustaka* or *Satyavedapustaka* to this day. The scribe, who is obviously not the author, signs his name as 'Koṭiyēn Cheṟiyān Utupp' and puts the date of finishing the copy as 'Kanni the 8th in the Year 1774 After the Birth of the Messiah' and also as 'Kanni the 8th in the Year 950 of Kollam Era', which corresponds to 8 September 1774. This method of dating is interesting. Months of the Christian calendar are represented by the names of corresponding months in the solar Malayalam calendar. Thus, *Makaram* stands for January and they go on like *Kumbham*, *Mīnam*, *Mēṭam*, *Eṭavam*, *Mithunam*, *Karkiṭakam*, *Ciṅṅam*, *Kanni*, *Tulām*, *Vṛścikam* and *Dhanu*, for the next eleven months in that order. Thus the date of the present document is 8 September 1774, with which 'Kanni the 8th, K.E. 950' will correspond.[9] Another instance of giving dates in this fashion is available in the text itself: it gives the date of Jesus's birth as '25th of *Dhanu*' (December). In another version of this work, this date is expressed differently as *vilpañcavimśati*—'Bow the 25th'—*vil* being the Malayalam for the Sanskrit word *dhanuḥ* ('bow')![10] This is an important instance of the use of the local idioms to express Christian ideas. Other documents, too, are dated in the same way.[11]

This work turns out to be the same as the extremely popular Christian liturgical text known variously as *Puttan Pāna*, *Miśihāṭe Pāna*, *Miśihācaritam*, *Kūtāśappāna*, *Rakṣākaravēdakīrtanam*, or *Rakṣācaritakīrtanam*. It was composed by Revd John Ernest Hanxledon, S.J. (1681–1732), a German Jesuit who worked in Kerala in the first three decades of the eighteenth century. He was an accomplished scholar in both Malayalam and Sanskrit and was fondly known to the people of Kerala as 'Arnos *Padre*'.[12] There are at least ten printed versions of this work and a large number of manuscripts in palm leaf and paper.[13] These versions show significant variations that are too serious to be dismissed as errors caused by individual copyists. It, on the other hand, shows that the work was popular as oral tradition for a long time and that, passing through word of mouth from generation to generation and region to region, it typically acquired several variations. It is to be remembered that the Christian community in Kerala had no access to the Bible until the nineteenth century except for what the priest would read out and interpret during services in churches and other sacraments. In fact, Catholic Christians of different denominations to this day recite the *Puttan Pāna* in ritual on the occasion of death of relatives and during Lent, particularly ten days before Easter and on the eve of Good Friday. This practice—followed by a vast section of the non-literate population even after nearly three centuries of its composition, as well as the existence of a large number of copies produced over several points in time—shows, on the one hand, the extreme popularity of the work among the Christians, and, on the other, the fact that it had passed from the literate to the oral tradition in a strange, reverse process. That, then, will explain the existence of a large number of different versions. This is only natural in a society where the major chunk of population had no access to literacy but was in need of the Bible, which was now available to them in verse, easy to remember and easier to render.

There are other works of Arnos *Padre*, too, which have to be read with the *Puttan Pāna*. They include a collection of four separate works, namely, *Maraṇaparvam*, *Vidhiparvam*, *Narakaparvam* and *Mokṣaparvam*, collectively brought together as *Caturantyam*. Besides, there are other works too, such as the *Ummāparvam*, *Ummāṭe Duḥkham*, *Vyākulaprabandham*, *Genovāparvam* and *Ave Maris Stella*.[14] The Malayalam compositions of the *Padre* present a most interesting case of the use of idioms and concepts popular in Kerala and their adaptation into the Christian scheme, even at the expense of sacrificing many doctrinal and theological aspects represented by the Counter Reformation, of which the *Padre* was a product and representative. This is all the more significant because the *Padre* was operating in Kerala just a century after the notorious Synod of Diamper (1599) which sought to cleanse the Christian world here of un-Christian practices. He also represented the agents of the Synod.

I shall take up the *Puttan Pāna* to begin with. It is an abridged retelling of the Bible in verse, in the popular Malayalam metre called *Pāna*. Notwithstanding the subject matter, the debt of the German poet to the textual tradition available in Malayalam and Sanskrit is hard to miss. To begin with, the metre itself is that of the *Jñānappāna* of Pūntānam, which was on the lips of every pious Malayali. As the *Jñānappāna* was the *Pāna*, the *Padre* may have decided to call his own as the *Puttan Pāna* ('the New Pāna'). *Puttan Pāna* was otherwise known as *Kūtāśappāna* ('the *Pāna* of Sacraments') as the *Padre* seems to have thought that the function of *jñāna*, which he took as the best of the ways of realizing God in the Indian tradition, had its counterpart in the sacraments. Chapters are divided as *sargas* in the typical Sanskrit tradition, and at the end of every chapter, it is called an *āśvāsa*, again typical of some Sanskrit texts. These superficial items do not exhaust the debt of the work to typically Indian concepts even at the expense of doing violence to Christian doctrines.

One significant thing that strikes us is the use of a linguistic instrument for distancing of castes. This social distancing is achieved in Malayalam by the use of what is called *ācārabhāṣā*, where people of lower castes are supposed to use a different vocabulary in talking to those of the upper castes. There is difference at the level of the subject of the action as well. Thus, first person singular is *aṭiyen* (the lowly 'I') while second person is *iviṭunnu* (lit., 'here', where you are pleased to be present). When rice that *aṭiyen* eats is *kallari* (rice full of stone pebbles), *iviṭunnu* would eat *paḻayari* (seasoned rice). Your eating is *amṛtēttu* (partaking of the nectar) while mine is *āharikku* (guzzling). The list can be extended to nearly every word, and the subject is an interesting study in itself. The *Puttan Pāna* makes heavy use of this jargon in an attempt to show the distancing at three levels: between man and God, between man and the Son of God and between Son and Father, where the former of the pairs is always located as of a lower caste while the latter is of the higher caste. This shows the extent to which values and usages of caste society had been internalized in the Christian world here.

If the use of idioms and ideas typically of Kerala is somewhat sparing in the very first work of the *Padre*, the *Puttan Pāna*, they are used more liberally and with greater conviction in his later works. His debt to earlier Malayalam poets like Tuñcatt Eḻuttacchan, Ceṟuśśēri and Pūntānam becomes clearer in them as also his greater internalization of Sanskritic Hindu practices, notions and idioms in matters of not only worship but also other details of worldview. In prosody, too, the German poet makes use of Indian conventions. This is clear from the way in which Malayalam metres like *Kēkā*, *Kākaḷī*,

Mañjarī, *Ūnakākaḷī* (*Pāna*), etc., as well as Sanskrit metres such as *Indravajrā*, *Upendravajrā*, *Upajātī*, etc., are employed with masterly felicity. So also, see the use of *śabdālaṅkāras* such as *yamaka*, *ślesā*, alliterations, etc. Even going beyond these external features, one notices the heavy debt to Indian traditions.

As is well-known, the *Mahābhārata* divides its chapters into so many *parvans*. The Malayalam renderings of the epic use the same title, *parvam*, in its *tatsama* form. It is significant that the *Padre* uses the very same nomenclature for his short works, namely, *Maraṇaparvam*, *Vidhiparvam*, *Mōkṣaparvam*, *Narakaparvam*, *Ummāparvam*, *Genovāparvam*, etc. Coming to their contents, too, the debt to the Malayalam epics of Eḻuttacchan is clear. For instance, one of the unmistakable features of Eḻuttacchan is to repeat the different names of his favourite deities, Rāma and Kṛṣṇa, endlessly in making any reference to them in a mood of *nāmajapa-yajña*. Thus we read in the *Padre*'s *Mōkṣaparvam* the following passages:

akhilalōkēśvaram bhāgyakāraṇam dēvam
nikhilaśubhālayam mōkṣadam nirantaram
advayam nirupamam ēkamavyayam vara-
pradamalayam stutyam sakalaguṇadharam
praṇamya sāṣṭāṅgēna sarvēśadānamukhyam
guṇapradhānam nityamaṅgalam bravīmyaham.[15]

sarvēśam mṛtyuñjayam naratrātāram nātham
sarvajñavēdagurum sukṛtajanapriyam
dēvajam mē mātaram martyajam mē pitaram
dēvam ca manuṣyam ca mṛtam cāmṛtam caiva
vēdāntamicchapradam nirguṇam dayākaram
vēdanāharam sākṣād guṇadam mōkṣpradam
duritaharam pīḍitādhāram narāśrayam
svarīśam sarvapālam sāṣṭāṅgam namāmyaham.[16]

It can be seen that they are entirely in Sanskrit although rendered in a Malayalam metre, *Kekā*; that they constitute typically a string of *nāmans* in a worshipful mood; and that, most important of all, they will pass for passages straight from one of Tuñcatt Eḻuttacchan's works.

Even more amazing are direct borrowings and/or adaptations from texts like the *Bhagavad Gītā*, *Nītisāra*, *Manusmṛti*, Bhartṛhari's *śatakas* and other authorities of Indian tradition. For instance, the point that the *Padre* makes in the *Maraṇaparvam*, that one takes this body to live on this earth in the same way as wearing a cloth,[17] is not only reminiscent of the following passage in the *Bhagavad Gītā*:

> *vāsāmsi jīrṇāni yathā vihāya navāni gṛhṇāti naro parāṇi* |
> *tathā śarīrāṇi vihāya jīrṇānyanyāni samyāti navāni dehi* ||[18]

but also participates in the belief in the cycle of rebirths, which is totally opposed to Christian doctrine. The following passage from the *Maraṇaparvam* is interesting for its close similarity with a passage from the *Viṣṇubhujaṅgaprayāta* attributed to Śaṅkara and extremely popular in Kerala:[19]

> *āmayaśaktiyāl balakṣayam koṇṭu*
> *kōḷmayirkkoḷḷunnu vāyumuṭṭi* ||
> *vātapittakaphanilakaḷ nīṅṅippōy*
> *tataślēṣmattālum śvāsam māṟum* |
> *gātram taṇukkunnu nāḍi kampikkunnu*
> *śītasvēdamolikkunnippōḷ* |[20]

The famous statement in the *Nītisāra*—that the father desires education, mother desires wealth, relatives desire a respectable family background and girls desire handsome mien in the matter of alliances for girl children[21]—is repeated verbatim in the following passage in the *Genovāparvam*:

> *nālāgraham nārimārkku vivāhattil*
> *nāludikkilum prasiddhiyallō* |
> *vidvāneyicchikkum tatpitāvennatum*
> *vittatteyicchikkum mātākkanmaar* ||
> *bandhukkaḷ tatkulaśrēṣṭhatvamicchikkum*
> *bandhurarūpikaḷ kanyamārkku* |[22]

The fear that Manu expresses about men getting overwhelmed in the presence of women, presented in the famous passage:

> *mātrā svasrā duhitrā vā na viviktāsano bhavet* |
> *balavānindriyagrāmo vidvāṃsamapi karṣati* ||[23]

finds expression in the following words of the *Padre*:

ārāyālum nārimāruṭe cārattu
svairamāyeppōḻum cennirunnāl |
dhairyam veṭiññu paravaśarāyīṭu-
māryanmār panṭitu collīṭunnu ||[24]

The Indian notion that teacher's wife, king's wife, elder brother's wife, mother-in-law and one's own mother constitute the 'five mothers'[25] is adapted in the following passage in the *Genōvāparvam*:

bhārya tan mātāvu-magrajan bhāryayum
vīryayām jñānasnānamātāvum |
rājākkaḷ patniyum rājabhṛtyanmaarkku
nālum tan mātāvōṭoppamallō ||[26]

Mother-in-law, elder brother's wife, godmother, king's wife—these four are equal to one' own mother. . . .[27]

It is particularly significant here that *jñānasnānamātā*, the godmother, takes the place of *gurupatnī*, teacher's wife, a meaningful substitution in a Christian situation. The debt that the following statement of the *Padre*:

martyakālam kṛśam pādam kaḷiccu pōm
ardhamuṟaṅṅippōm phalam vinā |
pādam kaḷaññupōm sārakāryattinnu
pādakaraṅṅaḷutsāhiccilla ||[28]

One-fourth of human life will be lost in paly; half of it will be lost in sleep; a quarter will be lost in serious business—[my] limbs did not work [for anything godly].[29]

has to a verse in the *Vairāgya-śatakam* of Bhartṛhari[30] where the latter speaks of the way in which time is whiled away:

āyur varṣa-śataṃ nṛṇāṃ parimitaṃ rātrau tad-ardhaṃ gataṃ
tasyārdhasya parasya cārdham aparaṃ bālatva-vṛddhatvayoḥ |
śeṣaṃ vyādhi-viyoga-duḥkha-sahitaṃ sevādibhir nīyate
jīve vārita-raṅga-cañcalatare saukhyaṃ kutaḥ prāṇinām ||

is clear and unmistakable.

Examples of this kind are far too many to be exhausted. Equally interesting is the use of categories such as *caturaṅga sainya* (the four-fold army), *navaratna* (the nine gems), etc., that the poet uses. In describing the education of the European prince in the *Genōvāparvam*, the *Padre* is carried away by Indian categories.[31] The subjects taught included the *śāstras*, *purāṇas*, *vedānta*, *siddhāntas*, *saṅgīta*, *sāhitya*, the *caturupāyas*, the six *nayas* and *rājadharma*! In a remarkable situation elsewhere, the poet makes a reference to *svargaṅgā*, the heavenly Gaṅgā, the crossing of which is taken as leading to heaven since it washes off all sins. Adding to this is the notion that this bath is verily baptism which is supposed to wash off the Original Sin.[32] Both God and Son of God are referred to as *Deva*, *Īśa*, *Bhūtanātha*, *Parātpara*, *Paramātman*, and so on. Even Mary is occasionally described as *Devī*. The idea of *puruṣārtha* is brought in, too, where the European king is described, in the *Genōvāparvam*, as abdicating in favour of his son and taking to the forest in the typical *vānaprastha* style, however much it is alien to the Christian tradition. All this is not to be taken as if the German Padre had shaken off all his European, Christian moorings as Kuryas Kumbalakkuzhi argues after looking at some of these items.[33] On the other hand, it has to be seen as the continuation of a long tradition in Kerala where the local idioms and patterns were used in the worship and even propaganda of Christianity.

Another interesting set of documents in the BnF is in a haphazard collection of leaves from different works, bound together in one volume.[34] It is entered in the catalogue as 'religious texts'. There are several leaves from the *Yuddhakāṇḍa* of the Malayalam *Adhyātma Rāmāyaṇa* of Tuñcatt Eḻuttacchan, and another section from the same book. But after them is a stray leaf from a Malayalam commentary of the *Amarakośa*, all executed in different hands and therefore obviously parts of different books, the stray leaves of which got bound together at some point. These are followed by a heterogeneous collection of fragments of beautiful verses in typical Malayalam metres such as *Kiḷippāṭṭu* (particularly *Kekā*), *Pāna*, and the ones used for *Tuḷḷal*. These are all on Christian doctrines, one being plain vituperations disparaging 'Hindu' beliefs and practices as well as the institution of caste. All are, unfortunately, incomplete. There are a few more manuscripts in paper, containing catechisms, accounts of church affairs, etc.

Despite their being highly haphazard and practically unidentifiable in terms of their contents, the fragments contained in the palm-leaf collection are of extreme significance. One of them appears to contain an extremely abridged rendering of the *Puttan Pāna*. It uses concepts such as *mokṣa*, *vaitaraṇī*, etc., in explicating Christian theology. Another, which begins with the benediction *Ēcēśvaya namaḥ* as in the *Puttan Pāna*, is not only in beautiful *Kēkā* metre but also in the form of a bird being persuaded to tell the story—a technique adopted by Tuñcatt Eḻuttacchan in his *Adhyātma Rāmāyaṇa* and *Mahābhārata*.

A third fragment is even more interesting. It begins with the invocation *Eśasarvēśvarāya namaḥ* (Salutations to Jesus, the Lord of All) and calls itself *Tarkaśāstram*. The contents, however, have nothing to do with Indian logic. It is a rejection of Hindu religion, disparaging Hindu deities in a most vituperative language. It begins by saying that:

> good and evil can be distinguished by human mind when both are presented with clarity. When the Sun of knowledge has risen, the darkness of ignorance will disappear. They say that there are four Vedas; but they are not Vedas, but *bheda*. There is only one *Veda*. When a singular God with a single form created humanity in one image that followed a single path, it is only logical that He should have created one *Veda* alone. Brahmā, Viṣṇu and Śiva are devils of hell; and so are other deities like Kāḷi, Śāstā and so on. 'Do not listen to the brāhmaṇas and worship these devils. It is a pity that you worship these and other devils and disparage the true God.'

The story of the origin of these 'false gods' is given in some detail. After God had created heaven and earth, He also created angels, the word *sumanasaḥ* being used to describe them. They were assigned to heaven where, however, some of them indulged too much in the pleasures and defied God. They were promptly cursed by God to become devils. These devils, revengeful to God, could not, however, take Him head on. So they decided to take it out on men who were, after all, created in His image. Thus they took the form of sages such as Vālmīki, Nārada and others, went to the forests and produced false Vedas.

> And what are gods according to them? Gods have wives, indeed! A few of their gods have many wives—some a thousand and some, 16,008! Some of these gods have children in strange animal forms. Devils are born as children of gods in certain cases. Some of these gods covet the wives of other gods. Indra had the most shameful of results from this. Brahmā fell in love with his own daughter.

The list goes on and on. 'Do you want to worship such gods?' So also, the text makes a scathing attack on matriliny, the form of inheritance among the dominant sections of population in Kerala. The text as it obtains in the BnF is incomplete; but its general character is clear from what survives.

These texts present an interesting pattern. All of them are produced in the period after the Synod of Diamper or Udayampērūr (AD 1599), a watershed in the history of Christianity in Kerala.[35] The Synod sought to purge Christianity in Kerala of the 'heretical' practices followed there. These so-called heresies had long antecedents. It is well-known that Christianity in Kerala claims antiquity dating from the time of St. Thomas, the apostle, himself. Whatever the authenticity of that claim, the West Asian trade in the Malabar Coast had brought the Christian element there sufficiently early, in any case, by the sixth century. A few Christians may have been there, not as a numerous or even identifiable religious group, but as something of a 'clan', that being the available identity in that period.

Relations between the Christians of India and of Persia seem to have existed from very early centuries. This association affected the spontaneous growth of a genuine Church adversely, preventing the evolution of an entirely 'Indian' Christian pattern of thought, worship and lifestyle. Instead, not only did the church leaders begin to come from Persia, but the Kerala Christians were also forced to borrow Persian thought forms and formulas of faith, worship patterns, laws, church customs and practices. It meant that the Kerala Christians had to lead a life not in one world but in two at the same time: the geographical, political and sociocultural environment of Kerala on the one hand, and the ecclesiastical world of Persia on the other. This was somewhat unnatural. It is such a Christian life in Kerala that some writers described as 'Hindu [Indian] in culture, Christian in religion and Syro-Oriental in worship'.[36]

The legends and oral traditions of these Christians claim that they are descendants of converts from 'high castes', particularly Nampūtiri brāhmaṇas, into Christianity. This indicates the worldview of a *jāti* society. By AD 849, the date of the Syrian Christian copper plates, the Christians of Kerala had already become an inseparable part of the local population.[37] The grant shows that the Christians had mingled with local occupational groups like carpenters, blacksmiths, washermen, oil-mongers, toddy tappers, etc. They had even adopted local cultural idioms in religious doctrines and practices. The 'deity' consecrated in the Tarisāppaḷḷi, the church of Tarsa at Kollam, was referred to as *tēvar* (Skt. *deva*). An important offering to the *tēvar* was the sacred oil lamp as in the case of the brāhmaṇical temples in Kerala. The incorporation of the local idioms in Christian religious ideas and practices shows how the local mainstream culture had influenced them.

This incorporation was so comprehensive that records of the sixteenth century present the Christians of Kerala to have had all features of the local people in dress, worship, social practices and other details. They were known as *Nazaranis*, following the 'way and worship patterns of St. Thomas'. The leader of the former was the Archdeacon who was the *jātikku kartavyan* ('head of the *jāti*—caste'). He acted in consultation with the representatives of different parish churches, each of which was looked after by a *yōgam* ('assembly') in the fashion of the brāhmaṇical temples. The priests in the churches were trained in select parishes under an elderly scholar called *malpān* in the typical *gurukula* style. In the matter of dress, the Christians turned out 'like Nairs'. It is interesting that the Christians followed the rules of caste rather rigorously including the practice of untouchability, which should be anathema to Christian principles. They celebrated Malayāḷi festivals like Ōṇam. They consulted astrologers and would not mind resorting to black magic and witchcraft in cases of necessity. They used also to worship in the brāhmaṇical temples. The identification with *jāti* society was so complete that not only did the Christians refer to themselves as one but the others, such as the Muslims, Jews and Nairs, were also described as so many. The word 'Hindu' is not used at all; there is an occasional reference to 'Malayāḷar' and to *kāvyar* (*kafir*) to distinguish the local population from the Muslims, Christians and Jews.[38]

It is such a distinct Malayali Christian society that the initiative of the Portuguese sought to make it a part of the larger Roman Catholic Church in 1599 under the leadership of Dom Menezes, the Portuguese Bishop of Goa. This was obviously an attempt to gain hegemony over the native population. In any case, ruthless decisions were imposed, mostly in a high-handed manner, in what was called the 'Synod of Diamper' (Udayampērūr). All elements that distinguished the Christians of Kerala were looked upon as heresy and sought to be stamped out; and they were henceforth forbidden 'to acknowledge the Patriarch of Babylon or any other Supreme Pastor, but the Pope of Rome, upon pain of excommunication'. This distorted the self-perception of the St. Thomas Christians; it also separated them from the rest of the local population. There was the feeling among a minority of the Christians that they were becoming victims of the missionaries who were agents of the Portuguese colonial state. However, the Christian community in Kerala did not take this attempt at bulldozing lying down. The Oath of Coonen Cross at Mattanchery (1653) is one of the more spectacular expressions of such resistance. A section of the Christians went back to the 'way and worship patterns of St. Thomas' from the newly imposed 'Law of St. Peter'. Even those who started following the 'Law of St. Peter' and paying allegiance to the Roman Catholic Church went back to many of the Indian traditions to which they were heirs.

The documents examined here fall into this pattern. Arnos *Padre*, who was a Jesuit priest brought to India by the same agency responsible for the Synod of Diamper (Udayampērūr), *via* Goa, would have been expected to carry forward the mission of the Synod, namely, freeing the Christians of Kerala of heretical elements, i.e. the ways of the *kāvyar* ('unbelievers'). Using the concepts and idioms of Hindus in worship and propaganda was not exactly the way to achieve this. It will be interesting to compare, and contrast, this with what happened in Tamilnadu, in what is known as the Madurai Mission. The work of the Jesuit priest, Roberto de Nobili, in the Madurai Mission shows how, nearly a century before the time of Arnos *Padre* and in the wake of the Synod of Diamper, a similar attempt was met with heavy opposition within the Society of Jesus.[39] De Nobili had, in fact, adopted an *alias* for himself in Tamil—*Tattuvapōtakar* (the Instructor of the Truth)—and used many more items of the Hindu Brāhmaṇical faith and practices in his missionary work than Arnos *Padre* had done. He wrote many works in Tamil and lived almost like a brāhmaṇa so that he earned the sobriquet of 'Roman Brāhmaṇa'. This had irritated his colleague Gonçalo Fernandes, another Jesuit priest who worked with him in Madurai; but the Church finally upheld de Nobili's ways, for whatever reason.[40]

However, there was a major difference between this and the

experience in Kerala. It is surprising that the Jesuit priest in Kerala was able to get away with what he was doing and writing. True, the question of an *imprimatur* for his work did not arise as there was no 'printing' involved in it in the literal sense of the term. What is likely is that the superiors in the Society of Jesus, either in Goa or in Rome, did not worry overmuch about the details of what the *Padre* did, so long as the primary purpose of his mission, namely, getting converts, was served in an attempt to accommodate native traditions. What he wrote in obscure languages like Malayalam or Sanskrit, in any case, did not bother them too much. Moreover, unlike de Nobili, Arnos *Padre* did not have a Gonçalo Fernandes to complain against his work. And, if the *Padre* was a good theologian, which he must have been, he could have justified his position in any which way he wanted! This conformed to the concept of *adiaphora* (indifferent things) which the Roman Catholic Church followed in the period after Counter Reformation.[41]

While de Nobili's was an innovation in Madurai, what Arnos *Padre* did in Kerala was a continuation of a long tradition. This tradition was the result of many centuries of coexistence between the various local 'Hindu' groups and the Christians. What the Synod of Diamper tried to obliterate did not quite disappear. In fact, it persisted and even influenced, ironically, the very same agencies that attempted to wipe it off. Aspects of a composite culture had evolved through many centuries which the Portuguese imperial state had sought to dismantle. That did not quite happen although fissures were introduced successfully. Things have become different in more recent times, following the large-scale communalization of society and polity; but the factors that have led to this denouement lie not in the past but in the compulsions of the present.

NOTES

1. See, for example, A. Sreedhara Menon, *A Survey of Kerala History*, Kottayam: National Book Stall, 1969, chapter on 'Confluence of Religions'. Menon's is even now the most popular textbook of Kerala history in the universities in Kerala, if by default.
2. M.G.S. Narayanan, *Cultural Symbiosis in Kerala*, Trivandrum: Kerala Historical Society, 1972. See also Rajan Gurukkal, 'Communal Harmony

in Early Medieval Kerala: An Outline of its Material Milieu', *Religion and Society*, vol. 34, no. 1, 1987.

3. Research for this paper was made possible by a two-month stay in Paris under the *programme franco-indienne* in the *Maison des Sciences de l'Homme* in 2002 and another stint of visiting professorship there in 2003. A considerable body of Malayalam manuscripts, mostly on palm leaves, is available in the Bibliothèque nationale de France (BnF), Paris. I thank the authorities of the *Maison des Sciences de l'Homme* for their generosity on both the occasions. I also thank the Indian Council of Historical Research for supporting my travel in 2002.
4. They are listed in A. Cabaton, *Catalogue Sommaire des Manuscrits Indiens, Indochinois & Malayo-polynésiens (in the Bibliothèque nationale)*, Paris: E. Leroux, 1912. One copy kept in the BnF is somewhat updated, with handwritten additions and some corrections made from time to time, the date and authority of such revisions being not known. Even this copy, although it contains many more entries than other copies, is not free from errors of identification of the manuscripts.
5. Cabaton, *Catalogue Sommaire des Manuscrits*, Indien 752, 767, 769, 770, 778, 780 and 1002.
6. Abraham Hyacinthe Anquetil Duperron, *Voyage en Inde 1754–1762: Relation de voyage en preliminaire ā la traduction du Zend Avesta*, présentation, notes et bibliographie par Pierre-Sylvain Filliozat, Jean Deloche and Manonmani Filliozat, Paris: Maisonneuve et Larose, 1993, p. 492, items 104, 5.
7. Listed as Indien 1002 in the handwritten additions to the catalogue of Cabaton, *Catalogue Sommaire des Manuscrits.*
8. Cabaton, *Catalogue Sommaire des Manuscrits*, Indien 765.
9. At present, i.e. after Kerala accepted, sometime in the nineteenth century, the readjustment of the Christian calendar by Pope Gregory, there is a difference of about fourteen days between the dates in that and the Malayalam calendar; but earlier the beginnings of months in both corresponded more or less. I have seen this in inscriptions from Kerala in the twelfth century. Kesavan Veluthat, 'The Perunchellur Copper Plates of AD 1145', in *Sāhityavum Caritravum: Dhāraṇayuṭe Sādhyatakal,* Kozhikode: Mathrubhumi Books, 2013, pp. 151–9.
10. N. Sam, Kuryas Kumbalakkuzhi and D. Benjamin, eds., *Arṇōsupātiriyuṭe Kāvyaṅṅaḷ* (in Malayalam), Kottayam: Current Books, 2002, p. 142.
11. See Scaria Zacharia, ed., *Udayampērūr Sūnahadōsinṟe Kānōnakaḷ* (Acts and Decrees of the Synod of Diamper) (in Malayalam), Etamattam: Hosanna Mount, 1994.

12. Sam et al., *Arṇōsupātiriyuṭe Kāvyaṅṅaḷ*. This contains a scholarly introduction by Kuryas Kumbalakkuzhi giving details of the life and work of the *Padre* in Kerala. The *Padre* was also the author of a *Vocabularium Malabarico Lusitanium* (Malayalam Portuguese Dictionary), several commentaries of difficult Sanskrit texts, a grammar of Sanskrit in Latin and so on. For a brief account of the work of the *Padre*, S. Guptan Nair, 'Introduction', in Arnos *Padre*, *Vocabularium Malabarico Lusitanium*, Trichur: Kerala Sahitya Akademi, 1988.
13. Another version I have consulted, apart from what is contained in Sam et al., *Arṇōsupātiriyuṭe Kāvyaṅṅaḷ*, is K. Raghavan Pillai, ed., *Kūtāśappāna*, Trivandrum, 1960. This version, incidentally, was discovered from the house of a Nambudiri Brāhmaṇa, which is not without significance for the problem at hand. Sam et al., *Arṇōsupātiriyuṭe Kāvyaṅṅaḷ*, gives a list of ten different printed versions and several manuscripts in both palm leaves and paper. Interestingly, neither Sam et al., *Arṇōsupātiriyuṭe Kāvyaṅṅaḷ*, which is an otherwise competent critical edition, nor any of the other editions, makes even a mention of this manuscript from the BnF, suggesting that this has not been used by scholars earlier.
14. Of these, *Ave Maris Stella*, in Latin, has not been recovered, known only from the notices of Father Paulinos, a Croatian priest who did comparable work in Kerala. The other works, some of which exist in different editions, have been brought together in Sam et al., *Arṇōsupātiriyuṭe Kāvyaṅṅaḷ*.
15. Sam et al., *Arṇōsupātiriyuṭe Kāvyaṅṅaḷ*, p. 477.
16. Ibid., p. 513.
17. Ibid., p. 319.
18. *Bhagavad Gītā*, II, 22.
19. *jareyam piśācīva hā jīvato me mṛjāmatti raktam ca māmsam balam ca |*
aho deva sīdāmi dīnānukampin kimadyāpi hanta tvayo'dāsitavyam ||
kaphavyāhatoṣṇodbaṇaśvāsavegavyathāviṣphurat sarvamarmāsthi-bandhām |
vicintyāhamantyāmasahyāmavasthām bibhemi prabho kim karōmi prasīda ||
Viṣṇubhujaṅgaprayātam, vv. 11–12.
20. Sam et al., *Arṇōsupātiriyuṭe Kāvyaṅṅaḷ*, p. 321.
21. *śrutamicchanti pitaraḥ dhanamicchanti mātaraḥ |*
bāndhavāḥ kulamicchanti rūpamicchanti kanyakāḥ ||
22. Sam et al., *Arṇōsupātiriyuṭe Kāvyaṅṅaḷ*, p. 624.
23. *Manusmṛti*, 2.215.

24. Sam et al., *Arṇōsupātiriyuṭe Kāvyaṅṅaḷ*, p. 649.
25. *gurupatnī rājapatnī jyeṣthapatnī tathaiva ca |*
    bhāryāmātā svamātā ca pañcaite mātaraḥ smṛtāḥ ||
26. Sam et al., *Arṇōsupātiriyuṭe Kāvyaṅṅaḷ*, p. 647.
27. Translated by the author.
28. Sam et al., *Arṇōsupātiriyuṭe Kāvyaṅṅaḷ*, p. 337.
29. Translated by the author.
30. Bhartṛhari, *Śatakas*, 3.49.
31. *śāstrapurāṇvum vēdāntayuktiyum*
    siddhāntakarmamāyuḷḷatellām |
    saṅgītasāhityavidyādisarvavum
    onnoḻiyāte grahiccu nannāy ||
    nālupāyaṅṅḷumāṟunayaṅṅaḷum
    nānāvidhavidyayellām maṟṟu ||
    śāstraprayōgaṅṅaḷokkavē śāstrōktam
    yuktipōl sarvavum samgrahiccu ||
    . . . pārthivadharmaṅṅaḷellām grahiccavan
    cittasukhattōṭu mēvi melle ||
    Sam et al., *Arṇōsupātiriyuṭe Kāvyaṅṅaḷ*, pp. 613–14.
32. *maṅgalam siddhippānāy dakṣiṇabhāgapathi*
    gamanam tuṭaṅṅumpōḷ nadiyekkaṭakkaṇam |
    svaragaṅgayuṇṭennatu nirmmulasamsārattil
    ajñānamatamennu satyamāyirikkilum ||. . . .
    snānamaviṭe mumpil kaḻippinaddhvaganmār
    enkilē naṭappatinnupāyamuṇṭāyvarū ||
    maṅgalajñānasnānam kaḻiññōranantaram. . . .

    Sam et al., *Arṇōsupātiriyuṭe Kāvyaṅṅaḷ*, pp. 463–4. Note that here the author speaks of death as 'taking the route to the south', which means nothing in the Christian tradition.
33. Sam et al., *Arṇōsupātiriyuṭe Kāvyaṅṅaḷ*, p. 58.
34. Cabaton, *Catalogue Sommaire des Manuscrits*, Indien 778. In a stray leaf, numbered '32' on the margin, we see the copyist making the following statement: 'Lord help us. The Messiah witnesses this. Know that Akappampil Kuṟupp wrote the four *pādams* of *Māṟallēśin Pāna*. This contains the following four: *Cōttiyāti Miśihāṭe Pāna*, *Paulo Silihāṭe Pāna* and *Māṟallēśin Pāna*. This *grandha* [*sic*] was written for Avaṇamkōṭṭa Kuriyatta Ousepp.' The list gives the names of three although it says it contains four; in any case, this is an indication of the identity of these texts. Because of their fragmentary nature, however, nothing more can

be said about them, including their authorship, date, etc. It is not unlikely that Arnos *Padre* had a hand in their production.

35. Zacharia, *Udayampērūr Sūnahadōsinr̲e Kānōnakaḷ*. For a defensive account of the Synod, K.J. John, *Road to Diamper: An Exhaustive Study of the Synod of Diamper*, Cochin: Kerala Latin Catholic History Association, 1999.
36. For further details, Gurukkal and Varier, *Cultural History of Kerala*, vol. I, pp. 267–71.
37. Narayanan, *Cultural Symbiosis in Kerala*, pp. 31–7; Appendix IV, pp. 86–94.
38. Zacharia, *Udayampērūr Sūnahadōsinr̲e Kānōnakaḷ*.
39. Ines Županov, *The Disputed Mission*, Delhi: Oxford University Press, 1999.
40. De Nobili had not only made bold to write to the Pope openly that he 'professed to be an Italian Brāhmaṇa' but all the Jesuit theologians sided with him espousing his brāhmaṇical conceptualization of the Indian cultural idiom. Županov, *The Disputed Mission*, p. 238.
41. I am indebted to Ines Županov for some of the ideas in this paragraph. Her suggestion that this is accommodation pushed to extremes is more acceptable than that of a slippage into heathenism. Evidence does not allow us to consider the latter. Personal communication by e-mail dated 15 December 2005 and 18 February 2006.

Appendix

Bhakti Movement in South India

DEFINITIONS

The Tamil Bhakti Movement represents primarily a religious phenomenon with a valuable social content—a new wave of Aryan or Hindu influence among the Tamil people.[1] During its lifespan of three-and-a-half centuries, beginning from the middle of sixth century AD,[2] Śaiva and Vaiṣṇava saints along with their followers practised and propagated the cult of *bhakti* in the countryside, and went to pilgrim centres singing and dancing. They received royal patronage, clashed with the Jains and Buddhists in open debate and defeated them, presumably healed the sick, and performed other miracles. Their hymns addressed to several deities constitute the cream of Tamil literature. Although elements of dissent, protest and reform are clear in the movement, these are subordinated to the overall pattern of a greater movement—the consolidation and extension of classical Hindu society in early medieval India.

The Bhakti Movement in south India, in fact, had a two-fold character, i.e. its two main currents of Śaivism and Vaiṣṇavism which, flowing in parallel ways, also mingled occasionally—the Vaiṣṇava saints being known as Āḻvārs and the Śaiva saints, Nāyaṉārs. It is doubtful whether the movement started as a conscious one. It is likely that several *bhaktas* appeared simultaneously in different centres, and the movement developed its

*Jointly with M.G.S. Narayanan. Reprinted from S.C. Malik, ed., *Indian Movements: Some Aspects of Dissent, Protest and Reform,* Shimla: Indian Institute of Advanced Study, 1978, pp. 36–66.

conscious identity by the ninth century. By this time, Sundarmūrti Nāyaṉār, the last of the Nāyaṉārs; and Nammāḻvār, one of the last Āḻvārs indicated in their works a comprehensive understanding of the literature in the respective fields.[3] For the first time an awareness of the group identity of saints and temples has been explicitly mentioned and treated in their compositions. This was carried forward by Nāthamuni (tenth century) who edited the Tamil Vaiṣṇava canon and Nambi Āṇḍār Nambi (eleventh century) who was the earliest compiler of the Śaiva hagiology.

How the terms Nāyaṉār and Āḻvār, employed by their contemporaries, came to refer to the leaders of the Śaiva and Vaiṣṇava movements, respectively, remains a puzzle. The word Nāyaṉār may be a Tamilized form of Sanskrit *nāyaka* (meaning 'a leader'), probably suggestive of the Śaiva belief that the sixty-three leaders were incarnations of the bhūtagaṇas of Śiva. The term Āḻvār has been derived from the root *āḻ* which could imply the act of plunging or immersing oneself and, as such, it has been suggested that the Āḻvārs were persons who delved deeply into devotion. Alternatively, the change from ḷ to ḻ being linguistically admissible, the term *āḷ* is taken to mean 'to rule' or 'to preserve'. In that case, the Vaiṣṇava saints may be said to have enjoyed in *bhakti* literature the chief attribute of Viṣṇu whose function is preservation, as distinct from creation or destruction. A third possibility, which we would support, is that Āḻvār is the literal translation of the Sanskrit word *bhakta*. Since *bhakta* is derived from the root bhaj, meaning 'to divide', 'to apportion', *bhakta* literally means one who enjoys a share.[4] Thus, since the term *bhakta* was originally employed to denote a servant or retainer who shared the wealth of his master, in the course of time the same word must have been used for a devotee in view of the *dāsyabhava* ('attitude of service'). Perhaps the Tamil word may have this meaning since the root *āḷ* also means 'to possess', 'to enjoy', etc.

HISTORIOGRAPHY

Until recently, most of what has been written about this twin movement concerns itself with the chronology, identity of individual saints and some literary and philosophical appreciations. Early scholars treated it chiefly as a literary movement or, at best, an ideological phenomenon with religion as the source of inspiration. The very label, 'Bhakti Movement', conferred by modern writers was based on this literary-philosophical conception, because they had no clear notion about either its chronological sequence or its social significance. Historical studies, initiated by scholars like S. Krishnaswami Aiyangar, R.G. Bhandarkar, T.A. Gopinatha Rao and K.A. Nilakanta Sastri in the twenties, were able to approximately fix the chronological framework, and with it came the inevitable scholarly disputes about the identity and date of individual saints. Mainly because of the uncertainty of its historical outline, and partly due to the lack of emphasis on social history, the correlation between religio-literary aspects and the socio-political background of the movement was not highlighted. Moreover, it was viewed as a pure Tamil movement and, consequently, never in the larger context of Indian civilization. Even today, due to a lack of theoretical perspectives in south Indian historiography, historical works have not yet been able to assess the Tamil Bhakti Movement from a pan-Indian viewpoint. Hence, the present study attempts to analyse the movement not only within the larger framework of the development of society and culture in India, but also in its socio-economic context with special reference to the elements of dissent, protest and reform.

SOURCE MATERIALS

Historical evidence for an analytical study are chiefly found in the literary works of the Nāyaṉārs and Āḻvārs themselves, which are in the form of devotional songs addressed to deities mostly with reference to particular temples. These works which reflect the elegance of classical Tamil verse became the model for much of Tamil poetry in subsequent periods. The source materials may be classified as follows:

1. Songs of the Nāyaṉārs and Āḻvārs.
2. Later compositions by their followers in the form of chronicles and hagiologies.
3. A few references in contemporary and near-contemporary epigraphs to devotional works and the temples connected with them.[5]
4. A few sculptured panels, painting and images representing the incidents in the lives of these personalities.[6]

MOVEMENT IN SPACE AND TIME

A study of the Bhakti Movement suggests that it had its origins on the east coast, in and around such famous temples as Tirupati and Kanchi.[7] Tirupati, the seat of Tirumal or Viṣṇu, otherwise known as Vēṅkaṭam, is mentioned as the northernmost point of Tamiḻakam in early Tamil Sangam literature.[8] In the Sangam period there was a chief called Pulli at Vēṅkaṭam, probably a remote ancestor of the Pallavas, who seem to have used a Sanskritized tribal name as their dynastic title.[9] The relationship between Vēṅkaṭam and the process of Aryanization of Tamiḻakam is significant. The northernmost point of Tamiḻakam was also the point of contact between the Aryan and Tamil ways of life. Since Vēṅkaṭam, the earliest northernmost centre of Vaiṣṇava *bhakti* cult, appears to be closely associated with the Pallavas, we feel that the Bhakti Movement was a by-product of the Aryanizing or Sanskritizing influence. The same point is underlined by the relative precedence and importance of Kanchi, the later capital of the Pallava kingdom. It is well known that the Pallavas were one of the early Dravidian dynasties which were thoroughly Aryanized. For instance, by the close of the third century AD, to the middle of the sixth century, Pallava rulers of the Prakrit and Sanskrit charters acted as the protagonists of Aryanization in the Far South. They adopted the same role as the Sātavahanas of the Deccan. The new Pallava line of Simhaviṣṇu, established in the second half of the sixth century, continued the patronage of brāhmaṇas and brāhmaṇical culture on a much larger scale than before.[10]

Following the first phase of the movement in the late sixth and early seventh century under the patronage of the Pallavas, we find other temples like Tillai or Chidambaram further south and Tirunallūr, Tiruvārūr and Śrīraṅgam to the south-west in the interior acquiring prominence. These were located in the traditional Cōḻa territory.[11] The *raison d'être* of this rapid and smooth extension is brought out by the fact that the Cōḻas were feudatories of the Pallavas.[12] Subsequently, the movement spread further south from the Pallava-Cōḻa territories to that of the Pāṇḍyas during the eighth century where temples in Madurai, Tirunelveli, Kumbakonam, etc. became active centres.[13] It is only during the final phase in the ninth century that the movement took roots in Malaināḍu or Kerala on the west coast and temples like Tiruvañjaikkaḷam, Tirunāvāy, Tirukkāṭkarai, Tirumūḻikkaḷam, etc., became the chief centres of devotion.[14]

The spread of the movement created active cultural links among the various people, cutting across political boundaries of different kingdoms. It promoted a new Tamil consciousness which has significantly contributed to the Tamil heritage. In castewise distribution, we find some Āḻvārs like Toṇḍaraḍippoḍi, Madhurakavi, Nammāḻvār and Periyāḻvār hailing from the brāhmaṇa community while Kulaśekhara was a kṣatriya and other Āḻvārs belonged to kaḷḷar (Tirumaṅgai); and even pāṇa (e.g., Tiruppāṇa Āḻvār) communities of the śūdra caste. A similar composition of different castes may also be found among the Nāyaṉārs.

By the end of the ninth century, the Bhakti Movement had traversed the full range of Tamiḻakam and conquered the three major kingdoms—Cōḻa, Pāṇḍya and Cēra. By this time, the list of the Nāyaṉārs and Āḻvārs was completed and the first edited volumes of the Śaiva and Vaiṣṇava canons were available for use in temples.[15] The movement had already come into fruition by the tenth century, having realized its early social objectives. But as it became part of the established religion and culture, it began losing its original character of dissent, protest and reform.

PARALLEL AND RELATED DEVELOPMENTS

There being a close interrelationship between religious activity and socio-political and economic trends, the Bhakti Movement cannot be understood in isolation. At that time in south India there were several significant, parallel and interrelated developments taking place:

1. The growth and consolidation of new brāhmaṇa-backed feudal monarchies first under the Pallavas, and then under the Pāṇḍyas, Cēras and Cōḻas of the post-Sangam period.
2. The flowering of the early temple movement, especially the rock-cut and structural temples of Śaiva and Vaiṣṇava deities. The temple complex included vast landed property that was administered by brāhmaṇa trustees who lived in settlements organized around the temples, where most of the tenants were non-brāhmaṇas.
3. The emergence of prosperous guilds of traders and artisans in several district headquarters and in the semi-autonomous brāhmaṇa settlements.
4. The eruption of acrimonious Brāhmaṇa-Buddhist-Jain disputes which came to a close with the establishment of the brāhmaṇa supremacy and the triumph of Hindu religion; this relegated the non-Vedic creeds to the background.
5. The establishment of an all-embracing caste system which attracted all the original clans and tribes of south India. These were then placed in a feudal hierarchical order in which the brāhmaṇa was the point of reference for fixing ritual and social status.

The above developments indicate that these three-and-a-half centuries constituted a formative period of society in south India. But an understanding of the processes involved in this formation in which the movement played a crucial role requires the interlinking of diverse phenomena and factors. But not all the data is easily available, especially that of the guilds. However, indirect clues for one field are often revealed from another to provide us with an overall pattern of mutual relationships.

To illustrate, leading personalities of this period played diverse roles in more than one sphere of action; King Mahendravarman I (AD 580–630) of Kanchi, the founder of Pallava greatness, was the patron-disciple of Appar, one of the early saint-preachers of Śaivism.[16] By birth a Jain, he became a severe critic of Jain-Buddhist monasticism in the period of his post-conversion proselytizing zeal as reflected in the Śaiva literature. He was also the author of a Sanskrit burlesque called *Mattavilāsa*.[17] In addition, he was a distinguished pioneer in building temples with large endowments.[18] Although not to the same extent, a multiplicity of roles may also be observed in the case of the Pāṇḍyan king Varaguṇa I (AD 765–815) of Madurai[19] and the Cēra king Kulaśekhara (AD 844–883) of Makotai.[20] Both of them laid the foundations of their great dynasties, and promoted the Bhakti Movement in their respective kingdoms. They also built and endowed a large number of brāhmaṇical temples. That the Cēra king Kulaśekhara took direct interest in fostering the trade guilds, called Anjuvaṇṇam and Maṇigrāmam, is endorsed by inscriptional evidence.[21]

EVOLUTION OF *BHAKTI* IN THE NORTH

Historically, we may suggest that the ideas and institutions which flourished in the more advanced civilizations of the Gangetic valley, as represented in the Gupta Empire, were gradually spreading to the south. It is interesting to note that the emergence of a feudalized monarchy with graded systems of *samantas* or feudatories, chartered brāhmaṇa settlements and trade corporations, temples of Śiva and Viṣṇu, the hierarchical order of caste and a spate of devotional literature centred on personified gods, was a feature not only of the Gupta period of the north, but also of the Cāḷukya period in the Deccan and the Pallava-Pāṇḍya-Cēra Cōḻa period in the Far South. Therefore, it is surprising that a Bhakti Movement was not clearly identified in the Hindu revival of the north under the patronage of the Guptas, variously called 'Hindu Renaissance' or efflorescence, 'Classical Period' of Hindu art and literature, etc. Nevertheless, scanning through the Sanskrit literature of that period, with the redacted Purāṇas dedicated to particular deities like Viṣṇu, Śiva, etc., and the standardized text of the *Mahābhārata* with the *Bhagavad Gītā* as its epitome, one gets the impression that *bhakti* as a distinctive movement had indeed manifested itself there. It must have probably originated in the post-Mauryan period, as exemplified by the famous Heliodorus pillar inscription of Vidisa recently identified as part of a temple complex.[22] The great cultural centres which developed at such centres of pilgrimage places like as Mathura and Varanasi must have given birth to the institution of temple, an institution that was destined to be the carrier and rallying point of the cult of devotion. The *Bhāgavata* movement with its *āgamaic* form of worship appears to have reached a climax in the Gupta period with emperors claiming titles like *parameśvara*, *bhaṭṭāraka*, *paramabhāgavata*, etc., which is suggestive of their attachment to the cult of devotion.[23]

In the north, brāhmaṇa intellectual monopolists had already accepted the path of philosophical awareness (*jñānamārga*) almost exclusively for themselves. This they did while chalking out two alternative paths: one of unquestioning *dharma*-based activity (*karmamārga*), and the other of blind faith and surrender (*bhaktimārga*). The path of *karma*—according to one's *dharma*—was generally ordained for all of the castes. The path of *bhakti* representing a sublimation of the spirit of slavery or *dāsyabhava* was, paradoxically enough, especially meant for the exceptional souls in all groups who sought liberation from social restrictions. It was congenial to the psychology of the lowlier groups in a caste-oriented social structure. This admittedly vulgarized picture of the three paths, justified by providing a philosophical outlook to the caste order with safety valves, has been most succinctly enshrined in the compromise formula contained in the *Bhagavad Gītā*.[24] If the three paths were theoretically equal, the path of *bhakti* was considered natural, simple and comparatively easy to follow. It was thought to be well suited to the thousands of uneducated and undeveloped people who were condemned to take up menial work but also had an aspiration for some form of escape.

The Purāṇic ideology of *bhakti* appears to have percolated to the south through the temple-centred brāhmaṇa settlements where the study of sacred and quasi-sacred literature was taken up as a religious duty by large numbers of priests. This process of study was institutionalized in the post of the *Mahābhārata Bhaṭṭa* created in the temples for the purpose of expounding the *Mahābhārata* and popularizing it among the common people.[25] The development of a Sanskrit theatre in the south fostered the caste of Cākkaiyārs (Cākyārs of later times). They specialized in transmitting the message of Purāṇic literature through a particular form of dance-drama.[26] Again, the Purāṇic myths and legends were portrayed in sculpture and painting; and all the fine arts were employed to make the system of Hindu beliefs palatable to the common people. The way in which brahmanism was transformed into Hinduism through temple-centred *bhakti* in the north seems to have been repeated in the south.

TRANSLATION TO THE TAMIL IDIOM

These processes imply that there was the mutation of Aryan-brāhmaṇa ideology in the course of its translation into the Tamil idiom, and thereby its popularization among the Tamil people. It took roots in the Tamil soil by creating its own mythology and legends. For instance, there are several legends about Tirunāvukkaraśu (literally, Master of the Tongue) better known as Appar (a term of respect signifying literally 'father'). To start with, he was a Jain Veḷḷāḷa from Tiruvāmūr village. A miraculous cure through the intervention of his sister who was a devotee of Śiva converted him to Śaivism. The Jains complained to their patron, King Mahendravarman Pallava, who then persecuted him severely. The punishments included throwing him into a kiln, administering poison, placing him in the path of a murderous elephant and pushing him into the rough sea with a heavy stone tied to his neck. He escaped miraculously, whereupon the king surrendered, embraced Śaivism, pulled down the Jain monastery and built a Śiva temple in its place. Appar is also credited with curing the sick many times and bringing back to life a boy who had died of snake bite. Another story about him says that he sang open the closed doors of the temple of Tirumaṟaikkāḍu (Vedāraṇya) with the magic of his devotion. This may be symbolic of the opening of the Vedic lore by means of the key of *bhakti* and throwing it open to the common people. This is significant because Appar openly proclaimed that caste and class were nothing to him and that he was prepared to worship even an outcaste and a leper because God dwells in them.

Sambandhar, a brāhmaṇa of the Kauṇḍinya gotra from Siyali, is represented as a divine child whose disputation with the Jains converted the Pāṇḍya king to Śaivism. He described Lord Śiva as being both Aryan and Tamil; and is said to have drunk the milk of Parvati at the age of three, received a pair of divine cymbals and all the royal paraphernalia, later, on route to Tiruvaratturai. Then, a divine canopy descended from the heavens to protect him from the sun. He is said to have worked the largest number of miracles.

In the case of Sundarar, who claimed to be a friend of Śiva, the latter himself is said to have mediated his marriage proposal twice. Śiva played the role of a messenger of love at Tiruvārūr, his birthplace. When Kalikkāma Nāyaṉār, another devotee, protested against Sundarar for having dared to employ Śiva in this manner, there was another intervention by Śiva. In the end Sundarar is believed to have disappeared from the temple of Śiva at Tiruvañcaikkaḷam in a mysterious manner. The Śaivas interpret this event as his ascent to Kailāsa on the back of a white elephant sent by Śiva. On hearing this report, his friend and master Cēramān Perumāḷ Nāyaṉār is also stated to have proceeded to Kailāsa on the back of a horse.

Similar stories are woven around the names of the Mudal Āḻvārs or Early Āḻvārs—Poygai, Pudam and Pēy—who are stated to have come out of a flower in a tank, a creeper and a well, respectively. There is also the legend of all the three of them casually getting together in the dark corridor of a house and being joined by Viṣṇu himself as the fourth in the company.[27] Again, Tiruppāṇa Āḻvār, the member of a low caste of wandering minstrels playing on the yāḻ went about singing the praise of Viṣṇu. His devotion was conveyed to the temple priest in a dream by Viṣṇu himself who ordered the priest to carry the *Āḻvār* to the temple on his shoulders.[28] Aṇḍāḷ, the only woman among the Āḻvārs, chose Kṛṣṇa Raṅganātha himself as her bridegroom. Since her love was so intense, Raṅganātha called her into the shrine where she disappeared.[29]

LITERARY STYLE

It is through such myths and legends, charged with emotion and drama, that the personalities and places in Tamiḻakam were sanctified. The cosmic forms of Viṣṇu and Śiva became humanized and localized, playing the roles of companion, child, bridegroom, mother, etc. In this way they endeared themselves to hundreds of devotees around the chief centres of worship. There were new stories of short term *avatāras* of Viṣṇu and Śiva who would help their devotees in times of crises. These deities were endowed with a local habitation and a name in temples. Each important temple was associated with the lives of the saints in some way or other; and temples and saints gained popularity and respectability by this mutual relationship. Stories of local miracles and tales connecting mythical heroes with historical sites were fused into the accounts of temples, thus giving rise to a new genre of literature—the *Sthalapurāṇa*.

The saints, both Nāyaṉārs and Āḻvārs, popularized their creeds not only with the help of miracles, myths and legends but also with that of innovations in literary style. They used new forms of poetry like *antādi* (a poem in which the last word/syllable recurs as the first in the next), *iraṭṭaimaṇimālai* (a poem using two different metres alternatively), *mummaṇikkōvai* (a schematic poem of ten groups of three stanzas, each in a different metre), *ulā* (a song of victory), *pallāṇḍu* (a song in the form of a ritual to remove the evil eye), *tālāṭṭu* (lullaby), etc. They were also responsible for reviving old metres and forms employed in the Sangam literature. Combined with simple and forceful diction, romantic imagery and the music of words, this new literature captured the imagination of the people on a large scale. Incidentally, so much has been written about this literary aspect of the movement that the social content and institutional background have been generally lost sight of.

BHAKTI AND THE NEW MONARCHY

It is significant that the growth of the Bhakti Movement took place at the time of the rise of the new feudal monarchy in south India. In the stories about the early Nāyaṉārs, we find that the royal patronage given to Jainism is now being converted to Hinduism, especially in the Pallava and Pāṇḍya kingdoms. What this suggests is that at the level of the ordinary people, the Hindu movement had to contend with the already established Jainism. But with the growing strength of Śaivism, kings turned away from these heretical creeds. This illustrates the processes whereby popular creeds won over the rulers—a repetition of the history of the Roman Empire and the Mauryan Empire though on a much smaller scale.

Royal patronage seems to have intensified the tempo of the Bhakti Movement. Mahendravarman is alleged to have destroyed a Jain monastery and built a Hindu temple in its place. These seem to have followed a temple-building spree which spread from the Pallava-Cōḻa territory to the Pāṇḍya and finally the Cēra territories. These are the areas where the Bhakti Movement also spread. Hundreds of inscriptions from the seventh to the tenth century bear testimony to this brisk activity of temple construction,[30] which naturally could not have been possible without the active support of kings. Those kings and chieftains who supported the brāhmanical groups in turn became more powerful than those who opposed them.

Consequently, brahmanism with its institutional base in the temple-centred agrarian settlements had emerged as the most dynamic progressive force. For example, forests were cleared and fertile river valleys developed. A communication system linking the courts and marts of south India with other parts of India also came into being. Brāhmaṇa leaders had succeeded in organizing the indigenous people as tenants and temple servants, grading them into castes and sub-castes with infinite variations of economic and ritual status. They were in a position to mobilize the manpower of the vast tenant class for royal military service. The kings and the brāhmaṇas patronized each other.

In time, being a member of the movement of *bhakti* gave a passport for entry into the enchanted world. This was true for kings, merchants or ordinary peoples, on all of whom it could confer a special brāhmaṇas status through proximity to gods and 'gods of the earth'. It served as a popular sacrament of initiation. The status of a person arose in proportion to his readiness to submit to the brāhmaṇa oligarchy. What became the hallmark of greatness in an age of growing brāhmaṇical power was the surrender of pride in the self and the voluntary acceptance of the position of 'the servant of the servant of the servant of the Lord', as Kulaśekhara Āḻvār and Toṇḍaraḍippoḍi had proclaimed. In this way, if kings derived greater socio-political power, brāhmaṇas themselves acquired not only better protection but popularity through this alliance. To give the benefit of doubt, even though this materialist calculation might not have been a conscious one on both the sides, the mechanism of social power worked in promoting simultaneously the power of Hindu kings and the prosperity of brāhmaṇa settlements.

The ideology of *bhakti* served as the cementing force bringing together kings, brāhmaṇa priests and the common people in a harmonious manner. The intoxication of *bhakti* could enable the high to forget their pride and the low, their misery. This provided an illusion of equality while retaining the stubborn walls of inequality in the feudal system of production and distribution. In short, the Bhakti Movement contained all the ingredients of the popular form of Hinduism; the ancient classical brāhmaṇical creed of the Vedas and the śāstras acculturated with the non-brāhmaṇa and non-Aryan population of south India.

Some kings and chieftains like Mahendravarman and other unidentified Pallavas and Cōḻas, like Kaḻarcingam, Ceṅgaṭcōḻa and Anapāya, and even a chieftain of Vēṇāḍu called Vēṇāṭṭaḍigaḷ, are among the patrons of the movement besides the two Cēra kings of Kerala. However, the earliest saints did not come from the ranks of royalty. This may be explained by the fact that when the Bhakti Movement had become popular, the kings appropriated and patronized it both for making use of it and for the sake of enhancing their own prestige and power. Mahendravarman's destruction of a Jain monastery and Nedumāṟan's alleged impalement of several thousand Jains under the influence of the movement indicates clearly that some of the early Nāyaṉārs had at least influenced the rulers in order to use state power for the promotion of their creed even through the use of violence. With the changing order of society this may have helped the rulers to consolidate the power of monarchy as an institution.

PROJECTION OF THE TEMPLE CULT

If the Bhakti Movement is viewed beyond the abstract spiritual ideas of the culture heroes as has been done until recently, and examined at the functional level, we are bound to take a close look at the relation between the saints and the temples. Significantly, because most saints came from the precincts of, or got affiliated to, great brāhmaṇical temples like those at Vēṅkaṭam, Kanchi, Śrīraṅgam, Chidambaram, Kumbakonam, etc.,[31] it is implied that elements of temple propaganda and brāhmaṇical missionary enthusiasm were inseparable components of the movement. *Bhakti* not only started from the temple, but also connected one temple with another through pilgrimages, and this in turn led to the proliferation of temples. Further analysis indicates that these temples, owning large estates as *devasvam* and *brahmasvam* property with brāhmaṇas as their trustees, inspired the movement. In other words, Aryan brāhmaṇa pockets in the midst of the Tamil population were already well established under royal patronage with the temple as the nucleus for the dissemination of culture, which appeared long before the arrival of the Āḻvārs and Nāyaṉārs on the social scene.

It is plausible to assume that the movement originated on the fringes of brāhmaṇa settlements as an unpremeditated by-product of the temple; it was partly the fulfilment of their mission and partly an antithesis in the form of non-brāhmaṇa reaction. In this way there was an interaction between the brāhmaṇas and the non-brāhmaṇas, the latter were generally hereditary temple servants, tenants, guards or soldiers and lay worshippers, all constituting the Aryanized section of society. This represents the second stage in the process of Aryanization, i.e. the socialization or brahmanical ideology.

As noted earlier, the literature of the Bhakti Movement is mostly centred on the temples and many details are available. For example, the chief advocates of the Vaiṣṇava movement were the devotees of the main Viṣṇu temples such as Vēṅkaṭam, Kanchi, Śrīraṅgam, Tiruvittuvakkōḍu, Tirumūḻikkaḷam, etc. Similarly, the chief Śaiva devotees were specially attached to Chidambaram, Tiruvārūr, Tiruvañcaikkaḷam, etc. Moreover, devotees often undertook a tour of all the important centres of pilgrimage in south India by dancing and singing with large groups of followers across fields and forests. This programme must have created a big stir in the countryside. The *Periyapurāṇam* gives accounts of how joint pilgrimages were undertaken by Appar and Sambandhar in the early phase and Cēramān Perumāḷ Nāyaṉār and Sundara in the later phase.[32] Kulaśekhara Āḻvār and Nammāḻvār also undertook such grand pilgrimages in their time.

Besides the processions and pilgrimages, the institution of temple festivals may be cited as a by-product of the Bhakti Movement, as it linked the temple cult with the movement. For instance, the asterism of *Śravaṇa* in the month of Śrāvaṇa was considered to be the birthday of Vāmana, an *avatāra* of Viṣṇu. This day came to be celebrated in Tirupati, Tirukkāṭkarai and Tiruvallavāḻ, three of the *divyadeśams* of the Āḻvārs. A late Sangam work called *Maduraikkāñci* sings praises about this Śravaṇa or Oṇam festival. Among the Āḻvārs, Periyāḻvār has composed two exquisite hymns on this festival. Perhaps it was during the reign of Kulaśekhara Āḻvār in Kerala (ninth century) that the Oṇam festival was introduced. Inscriptions of the tenth century from Tiruvalla and Tirukkāṭkarai demonstrate the popularity of the festival.[33] In course of time this Vaiṣṇava sectarian festival was transformed through royal and brāhmaṇical patronage into the national festival of Kerala. This is an important instance where the interests of the temple cult and the Bhakti Movement coincided in the establishment of a popular festival, and it is reflected in literature. Similar festivals, observed in particular temples or in a general way, had a major share in reforming the sectarian creed of brahmanism and developing it into the popular Hindu religion.

A specific consequence of the movement was the encouragement it gave to *devadāsis* or 'handmaids of gods', *tevaḍiccis* in Tamil. As *bhakti* spread through the media of songs, dance and beauty, *devadāsis* played a significant role in the popular appeal of the temple. Thus, Sundaramūrtti Nāyaṉār was involved with a *devadāsi.* Ceramān Perumāḷ Nāyaṉār notes the reception given to Śiva by *devadāsis* of all ages while he went out in procession around the streets in Kailāsa,[34] and Aṇḍāḷ was herself a *devadāsi* who lived and died in the Śrīraṅgam temple.[35] There is a tradition that Kulaśekhara Āḻvār's daughter, Nīlā, was presented to Śrīraṅgam temple as a *devadāsi.* She is called Cerakula Nācciyār, and a shrine dedicated to her is found in this temple.[36]

The numerous Nāyaṉārs and Āḻvārs, together with their secular and spiritual patrons in the courts and temples, constituted only the elites of the Bhakti Movement. There were a large number of devotees who formed the retinue of each distinguished devotee. All of these people, no longer involved in any form of productive labour, had to be fed, clothed and so on. Therefore, when they moved from temple to temple in a cross-country religious campaign they received food and support all along their route. This would not have been possible but for the sympathy and serviceability of a large class of temple servants and tenants not only in the major centres but even in a network of temples in the countryside. It is these people swelling the ranks of *bhaktas* (because they considered themselves blessed by the opportunity for casual contact and service and still remained anonymous) who provided a strong popular base for the movement. This is an important factor that has to be noted because it explains the force and validity of the cult of *bhakti* and its social relevance.

BHAKTI AND THE GUILDS

In spite of the fact that guilds of traders like Vaḷañjiyar, Nānādeśikaḷ, Añjuvaṇṇam and Maṇigrāmam flourished in Tamiḻakam during this period, merchants and artisans are conspicuous by their absence in playing any prominent role in the movement. Occasionally we come across an oil merchant like Kāḷiya Nāyaṉār of Tiruvoṟṟiyūr who served the Lord with oil for lamps,[37] a fisherman like Adipata Nāyaṉār of Nagapattinam who dedicated all his catch to the Lord and starved himself,[38] a few general merchants like Iyarpakai of Pumpukar,[39] Amaranidhi of Tirunallūr,[40] and Karaikkal Ammaiyār, the daughter of the Dhanadatta of Karaikkal.[41] But these persons have not been considered among the most important of the *bhaktas*. Perhaps one reason for this is that during the period the Bhakti Movement took roots among the rural agrarian settlements, the influence of heretical sects like Jainism and Buddhism continued to be strong in the centres of trade. Prior to the ninth century, this kind of polarization is also apparent from such Jain literary works as *Cilappadikāram, Jivakacintāmaṇi*, etc. The conflict between the heretical sects and the neo-Hindu cult of *bhakti* is clearly discernible in the literature. It is not improbable that, at least partly, this reflects the implicit rivalry between the trading classes and the landowning classes for socio-political dominance. Explicitly, there was no confrontation of religious creeds but one cannot ignore the agrarian-feudal bias of the Bhakti Movement and the trading class bias of Jainism and Buddhism.

RIVALRY WITH JAINISM AND BUDDHISM

In the hands of converted monarchs, the movement fulfilled the historical function of promoting Hindu revivalism with the aim of checking the spread of Jainism and Buddhism. In order to command public support, this neo-Hindu movement had to outdo the Jain-Buddhist rivals both in terms of mass appeal and by providing such incentives which were stronger than any rational codes of conduct. Against this background, it is easier to understand how and why the movement adopted the media of song and dance to invoke popular enthusiasm. It even assumed a relatively egalitarian and democratic approach, unfamiliar to the rigidity of classical brāhmaṇa discipline. Thus, it may be seen that the Jain-Buddhist challenge which had extended to south India, produced this new form of Hindu response.[42]

The success of the Bhakti Movement signified the victory of Hinduism against the non-Vedic creeds of Jainism and Buddhism. The story of Tirunāvukkaraśu or Appar who was a Jain converted to Śaivism and who was instrumental in the conversion of Mahendravarman has been narrated earlier. About Tirujñānasambandhar, it has been stated that he proceeded to Madurai, the Pāṇḍyan capital, on the invitation of the queen Maṅgaiyārkkaraśi in order to undertake the historic mission of saving the city from the clutches of Jainism. He had to undergo a series of trials and performed a number of miracles. With the assistance of the minister, Kulaiciṟai Nāyaṉār, he eventually succeeded in winning over the king Nedumāṟan to the Śaiva fold. The occasion of the king's conversion was celebrated by the impalement of 8,000 Jains, and the story goes that a temple festival at Madurai commemorates this event to this day. Leaving a possible margin for exaggeration, we do have to take into account the grim reality of Jain-Śaiva conflicts which engendered such intolerance on both sides. All the four characters involved—namely, the saint, the queen, the minister and the king—are eulogized as devotees and included in the list of the sixty-three *Nāyaṉārs*. Tirujñānasambandhar dedicates a hymn to the minister in which the whole story is recited. All this evidence suggests that importance was attached to this conflict with Jainism, as seen in the *bhakti* literature.

Parallel stories of such conflicts are found in the case of Vaiṣṇava saints as well. Tirumaṅgai, one of the most celebrated of the *Āḻvārs*, is said to have stolen a golden image of the Buddha from a monastery in Nagapattinam to pay for renovating the temple at Śrīraṅgam. His hymns, full of good poetry, are equally full of venom against Jainism and Buddhism. Periyāḻvār, a brāhmaṇa saint, is stated to have won a religious dispute in the court of Śrīmara Śrīvallabha. The intolerance of Toṇḍaraḍippoḍi Āḻvār, another brāhmaṇa saint from Tañjāvūr, towards Jainism and Buddhism was nearly as strong as that of Tirumaṅgai. However, by the middle of the ninth century, when the movement achieved maturity and stabilized its position, this element of rivalry with Jainism and Buddhism had disappeared from the scene. Evidently, the non-Vedic sects had lost the battle in south India, as they had already lost it elsewhere. The hymns of the Nāyaṉārs and Āḻvārs of the later period are clear streams of devotion unsullied by the muddy waters of controversy.

By now the saints were no longer anxious to win over new sections of people. The earlier spirit of generosity and cosmopolitanism which invited or tolerated *bhaktas* from the lowest ranks like Tiruppāṇa Āḻvār (a pāṇa), Nantanār (a paṟaiya), Viranmīṇḍa Nāyaṉār (veḷḷāḷa), Tirumaṅgai Āḻvār (kaḷḷar), etc., gives way to a new sense of discipline. The whole movement appears to have closed its ranks and consolidated its position after its victory over the non-Vedic sects. There is a new emphasis on the attitude of subservience to brāhmaṇas and temples in the hymns of Kulaśekhara Āḻvār and Nammāḻvār among the Vaiṣṇavas and Ceramān Perumāḷ Nāyaṉār and Sundaramūrtti Nāyaṉār among the Śaivas. To quote one instance, Sundaramūrtti opens his Tiruttoṇḍattogai claiming himself to be the 'slave of the slaves of the brahmanas of Tillai'.[43] Instances may be multiplied by quoting extracts from the devotees of the later period. Thus, the first phase of castelessness, which has sometimes been interpreted by scholars as a protest against the caste system, is followed by a second phase of conformity to caste rules.

Thus, it may be inferred that the tendency towards reform inherent in the neglect of caste rules had been at least partly necessitated by the strength of heretical sects like Jainism and Buddhism which refused to recognize these barriers. In this period of its conflict with the heretical creeds, Brāhmaṇical Hinduism apparently borrowed the tenets of its adversaries. But it was a very short-lived phenomenon, a moment of aberration or lapse from which Hindu society recovered as soon as the point of danger had passed.

REFLECTION AND LEGITIMIZATION OF THE FEUDAL ORDER

This victory of Hinduism in south India, spearheaded by the Bhakti Movement, registered and firmly established the agrarian feudal order supported by a graded system of hierarchy in caste. In many ways the new jargon of *bhakti* literature is suggestive of the new feudal class relationships and the corresponding ideology. For instance, if the deity in the temple, which is the central concept, is equated with the king, then a parallel world of authority is also reconstructed on the spiritual plane. Similar words like *kō* and *perumāḷ* are employed to denote the deity and the king; the term *kōyil* is used to denote both the temple and the palace, and the ritual of worship is conceived on the same pattern as the ritual of service to the king. Ceramān Perumāḷ Nāyaṉār's *Ādiyulā* or *Tirukkayilayajñāna Ulā* brings out in vivid form the daily routine of worship in the temple followed by the deity's procession through the streets around the temple.[44] The same procedure may be traced in the epigraphic records of the age. For example, in the Tiruvalla copper plates,[45] the god is awakened with music and dance (*rājopacara*), bathed (*snapana, nīrāṭṭupaḷḷi*), dressed and fed and taken in procession (*pavani* or *nagarapradakṣiṇa*). While everyday is a festive day in the temple, there are special feasts and celebrations to mark the birth asterism of the deity, or other auspicious occasions. Then, the image of the deity has a *mukuṭa* like the king, and payment to the temple is mentioned as *iṟai* (tax) add *tiṟai* (tribute). Like a palace the temple is also constructed with *maṇḍapas* (halls) and *prāsādas* (mansions) surrounded by *prakaras* (fortress walls) and guarded by *dvārapalas* (gatekeepers). The chief deity of the temple is accompanied by his consort and relatives and served by a whole army of musicians, dancing girls, storytellers, actors, garland makers and priests-in-attendance.

It is this elaborate parallelism between the deity and the king that was to authenticate and legitimize the new monarchy in the different regions of the peninsula. However, although the terms employed pertain to royalty, yet the connotation is not exactly royal but feudal. This happens because the same terminology was used for king and lord in feudal society in spite of the difference in status. The plurality and co-existence of different deities, each deity occupying the position of the lord for his devotee, was as much recognized in the Bhakti Movement as the plurality and co-existence of the lords, each lord singularly commanding loyalty from his immediate vassal.

Society in south India may thus be represented by the typical feudal pyramid, i.e. the king at the apex, great landlords, big tenants, magnates, priests, merchants, princes, etc., forming the middle portion, and the small tenants, serfs and slaves constituting the base. The governing principle in this order was the feudal contract, explicit or implicit in the relationship of castes, and the cementing force was supplied by the spirit of loyalty in service. The complete surrender of individual initiative formed the credo, which had to be followed by the majority of the people. There is an amazing resemblance between the lord-serf relationship at the core of feudal society and the deity-devotee relationship idealized and celebrated in *bhakti* literature. As noted earlier, interestingly, Sanskrit words like *bhakta, bhakti, bhagavān*, etc. have originally been derived from the root *bhaj*—'to share', 'to apportion', etc. Gradually, the term *bhakta* came to denote the servant who shared the wealth of his master in return for his personal service.[46] While this was the case in the North, the terms used in the South are also directly borrowed from the terminology of the feudal social structure. The devotee habitually addresses the deity as *uḍaiyār, tambirān*, etc.—all meaning 'lord' or 'master' and describes his own position as that of *atiyēn,* meaning 'slave'. Thus, a kind of permanent, unquestioning and unconditional obedience towards the master forms the badge of the devotee. A large number of songs composed by the *Nāyaṉārs* and *Āḻvārs* praise this bondage as the highest desirable objective in life, in contrast to wealth, and even deliverance.[47]

It is in this manner that the *bhakti* literature created an aura of sentimental romance around the feudal institutions of the age. Both slavery and serfdom in India were sublimated by this equation with the divine order, not only through the intellectual appeal of *karma* and *punarjanma* theories but also through the emotional appeal of the *bhakti* doctrine. Suffering was sweetened by voluntary acceptance of it and by exalting it to the level of sacrifice. The intoxication of *bhakti* gave the lowliest of the low a chance of escape or at least a chance of pride in the exalted fellow-members of the community. This conferred on the entire community of the paṟaiyas the dignity of Nantanār, and the entire community of pāṇas the dignity of Tiruppāṇa Āḻvār. It was an indirect form of acceptance into the fold of Hinduism for the lower castes and tribes though, strictly speaking, only the brāhmaṇas had the ritualistic right to be religious in the full sense. Sentiment replacing ritual, this extension of membership had a double effect—one, of closing the ranks of Hinduism against the non-Vedic creeds of Jainism and Buddhism and two, to some extent, bringing outsiders within the sphere of an Aryanized society. Nevertheless, the brāhmaṇa remained the brāhmaṇa, and the pāṇa or paṟaiya remained the pāṇa or paṟaiya. The communities never mingled, though exceptional individuals from both the sides crossed the boundary with immunity, as in the well-known stories of Tiruppāṇa Āḻvār, Nantanār, et al. In short, an inclusive outer circle was drawn around the Hindu community, in which every member had a common right to participate in the cult of devotion or *bhakti*.

DISSENT, PROTEST AND REFORM

The Bhakti Movement, though a product of the temple and a causative factor behind its proliferation, had deviated a good deal from the orthodox philosophy of Brāhmaṇical Hinduism. This was an age of vigorous intellectual activity at both secular and spiritual levels. For example, Mahendravarman of Kanchi (early seventh century), who was a patron of the movement, incisively delves in his *Mattavilāsaprahasana* into the decay of the established religions, both Buddhist and Hindu, and, makes fun of the extreme forms of asceticism. The court of Kanchi patronized Daṇḍin, the many-sided genius, and probably in the beginning of the ninth century, the great Śaṅkarācārya who propounded the highly intellectual philosophy of Advaita and, more important for our theme, also synthesized the different intellectual and emotional strands of Hinduism including the cult of devotion. Against this background, the rejection of abstract metaphysics by the *bhaktas* denotes a spirit of strong dissent. Their general indifference to caste regulations carried a mild form of protest against the established social order. But there was no direct attempt at social reform, though the recognition of saints among outcastes amounted to a relaxation of caste rules. Here was a faint approximation to the principle of the potential divinity of man.

In terms of historical evolution, the very concept of the shrine, whether it is considered to be progression or regression, was a deviation from the concept of the abstract and amorphous powers—natural or supernatural—worshipped in Vedic rituals. Vedic ritualism itself came to be replaced by *āgamaic* ritualism by the beginning of third century AD in the north and by the beginning of the sixth century in the south. In fact, there was a ludicrous and syncretic combination of Vedic and *āgamaic* elements.[48] Thus, while Vedic-*āgamaic* ritualism was applicable and relevant for only the brāhmaṇas who followed it inside the temple—non-brāhmaṇa Hindus participated through *bhakti* much as spectators vicariously participate in games.

It may be pointed out at this stage that the *āgamaic* form of worship in temples had its own separate existence apart from the Bhakti Movement. A certain element of devotion or *bhakti* was involved in its routine, too.

However, this element of *bhakti* grew out of all proportions in the movement. It exceeded all limits of rules and regulations, ritualistic or social, and proved its eccentricity by subjugating every aspect of life to this one principle; an intoxication of overdevelopment which claimed its own right of existence. Of course, no qualitative change took place, though they made the temple immensely popular through the promotion of songs, dance and stories. This led to the creation of several temple servants rendering artistic service. Consequently, even after the decline of the movement, though there were isolated cases of individual *bhaktas*, yet in most cases they did not rise beyond the status of local celebrities. Theirs remained essentially an individual pilgrim's progress towards salvation devoid of any social implications, as was the case earlier. Therefore, it was the peculiar social background which transformed *bhakti* from an esoteric creed into a dynamic social force.

The starting point of the *bhakti* cult was the system of offering material objects like land, cattle, utensils and lamps.[49] In place of the material objects, one could offer one's own self in the spirit of service in the same way in which commendation took place. This meant that devotion was offered in return for the assumed guarantee of protection, i.e. just as the small landlord or the free peasant wanted protection from the fluctuation of fortune and encroachments of powerful neighbours, the ordinary devotee wanted protection from death, poverty and disease. A step higher, in the full intoxication of *bhakti*, the ideal devotee was not concerned with wealth and poverty or power and insecurity; and this is the attitude which nurtured the pure flame of devotion. When the movement was at its peak, the most sublime and sophisticated expression of sentiments represented a spirit of equality. This was clearly against the caste system, and the spirit of renunciation was also counter to the gregarious instinct of the brāhmaṇa-kṣatriya power elite.

It is a truism to state that there is often a gap between precept and practice. While the former is confined to literature, nevertheless, the very formulation of these concepts contains a streak of dissent, protest and reform. Even if it did not change society altogether, this deviation from the tenets of orthodox philosophy, accompanied by a sense of liberation from the rigid code of ritual, certainly contributed towards the refinement of society. The shining ideals of liberty, equality, and fraternity—liberty from ritual, equality of caste and fraternity in devotion—were placed before the people. Of course, untouchability for the pa<u>r</u>aiya and the miserable state of poverty of lower classes continued. But all this was made more acceptable, and even more dignified, in the light of the ideal of renunciation. Besides, there was at least some exposure and criticism of the evils of greed, licentiousness and sensuality. Thus, there was some deviation from the unbridled course of vanity and worldliness due to the spontaneous evolution of a code of moral conduct among the community of devotees who propagated a new set of values in life. It was almost a revolutionary idea that Nantanār the paṟaiya could be admitted to a temple even after a series of ordeals and that Tiruppāṇa Āḻvār was counted as a favourite devotee of Viṣṇu and worthy of being carried on the shoulders of the chief priest of the temple. A king's readiness to forget his pride and mix with commoners, apologize to the lord and priest for offences committed and be a humble slave at the feet of the deity was in itself a spectacle that chastened the minds of the people. The freedom which the devotees enjoyed from all rituals, and even rules of society, was a step forward in establishing the individual's inherent right to rebel, provided rebellion was legitimized by devotion. These devotees mixed freely and fearlessly with kings and brāhmaṇas, assuming equality and even superiority at times. In this way they set up a parallel spiritual-social authority, different from royal courts, and brāhmaṇa councils, which derived its power from the conscience of the people. The badge of *bhakti,* in the form of the sacred ashes or the sandal paste on the forehead and chest, gave a certain immunity from punishment in this period, serving the same purpose as the sacred thread through the ages.

The same deviation from social norms may be noted in the case of the status of women. Notwithstanding the injunctions of Manu and other lawgivers, the eligibility of a woman for the highest honour of direct communication with god was admitted in the ease of Maṅgaiyārkkaraśi, Aṇḍāḷ, Karaikkal Ammaiyār, et al. This departure from orthodoxy occurred at a time when brāhmaṇa domination was responsible for suppressing women by keeping them at home and away from education, except in the case of *devadāsis* or courtesans of the temple. The recognition of the equal status of a woman with man before god implied that her spiritual inferiority and inherent wickedness were momentarily set aside. In fact, the *devadāsi* system which raised a number of educated and dedicated women to high status through renunciation was a by-product of the movement. It had a progressive content to begin with, though in later times the *devadāsis* degenerated into common prostitutes. The readiness to dispense with rituals, priests and the restrictions of sex and caste brings out the importance attached to the individual self with its infinite capacity for development. This is what highlights those *bhakti* elements which dissented from the orthodox creed, protested against the *varṇāśrama* code—including restrictions of sex—and reformed the social order. It is partly out of a misunderstanding of its exclusive Tamil context and partly out of a desire to discover modern ideas in early Indian society that some scholars have exaggerated these elements to the extent of identifying the part with the whole.

RETURN TO ORTHODOXY

These deviations were, it has to be remembered, partial, temporary and counterproductive. As the popularity of Jainism and Buddhism waned, and many more kings and landed magnates patronized Hinduism through the Bhakti Movement, the openness and flexibility of the movement gradually disappeared, i.e. it became a part of the establishment. Intellectual dissent—anti-ritualism, anti-caste protest, etc.—came to an end by the beginning of the tenth century. The Āḻvārs and the Nāyaṉārs no longer exist, instead their place is taken up by the *ācāryas*, all of whom were brāhmaṇas and uncompromising ritualists. Naturally, with the threat of heretical creeds disappearing and with the achievement of social harmony, the forward urge of the *bhakti* cult came to an end. There was a return to orthodoxy in all walks of life, especially culture. The temples with enormous landed property and established position in society became the conservative custodians of power and wealth. In the new context, there was no place for the aberrations of the devotee although the exploits of earlier saints continued to be sung and cherished. *Maṭhas*, headed by brāhmaṇa *ācāryas*, increased in number and championed the cause of the *varṇāśramadharma*. Kings depended no more on the prop of *bhakti* for consolidating their political power. Even the Tamil language was increasingly replaced by Sanskrit in the field of religion. The living spirit of the Bhakti Movement which rebelled against many things now gave place to the decorative charm of its myth and literature.

NOTES

1. An earlier wave could be identified in the Vedic Sastraic-Puranic influences in the literature of the Sangam. For details, see M.G.S. Narayanan, 'The Vedic-Sastraic-Puranic Element in Tamil Literature', *Proceedings of the Indian History Congress*, Aligarh, 1975, pp. 76–91.
2. The identity and chronology of individual saints have been subject to much controversy among scholars. We have adopted the dates as given by K.A. Nilakanta Sastri, *A History of South India*, 3rd edn., Madras: Oxford University Press 1976, pp. 368–72.
3. Sundaramūrtti's *Tiruttoṇḍattogai* shows a comprehensive understanding of the Śaiva saints. See K. Subramanya Pillai, ed., *Periyapuranam enru vazhankukinra Tiruttontar Puranam*, Sri Kumarakuruparan Chankam: Srivaikuntham, 1970, pp. 54–7. Nammāḻvār's knowledge of the temples of South India is again an index to this fact. See Tirarammalli K. Gopalacharyar, ed., *Nalayira Prabhandam*, pt. 24, Madras, 1959, p. 1196.

4. For a discussion of the Sanskrit terms *bhakti, bhakta, bhagavān, bhāgavata*, etc., see Suvira Jaiswal, *The Origin* and Development of Vaiṣṇavism, Delhi: Munshiram Manoharlal, 1967, pp. 37–9; 110–11. This point is strengthened by the fact that in the Indonesian language, possessing a large number of Sanskrit words borrowed in the ancient period, the word bakta *(bhakta)* is used in the sense of a servant. See Venugopala Panikkar, 'Bahasa Indonesia', Sarani: Calicut University, 1977, p. 32.
5. A large number of inscriptions from early medieval south India pertain to temples. T.N. Subrahmanyan, *South Indian Temple Inscriptions*, 4 vols., Madras: Government of Madras, 1954–7.
6. There are many temples in which the saints are deified. See No. 400 of 1916 of the *Annual Reports of Epigraphy*, Archaeological Survey of India, which records the consecration of a temple to Kulaśekhara Āḻvār in *Mannarkoyil.* Bronze statues of Cēramān Perumāḷ Nāyaṉār and Sundaramūrtti Nāyaṉār are set up in the temple at Tiruvañcaikkaḷam. Events from the lives of the Śaiva saints are depicted in temple paintings in *Tañjāvūr*. See R. Champakalakshmi, 'New Light on the Chola Frescoes of Tanjore', *Journal of Indian History*, Golden Jubilee Volume, 1973, pp. 349–60. For Śaiva sculptures, see *Annual Report of Epigraphy*, 1908, paras 65 and 66; and ibid., 1920, p. 102 ff.
7. K.A. Nilakanta Sastri, 'Hindu Renaissance of the Pallava Period', *The Hindu*, 25 May 1961.
8. See V. Kanakasabhai, *The Tamils Eighteen Hundred Years Ago*, Madras: Higginbothams, 1996, p. 10.
9. Kallāḍaṉār, *Akanāṉūṟu*, p. 209. There are different theories regarding the origin of the Pallavas but there is no certainty about their early history. This view is put forward by the authors as a possible solution to the riddle.
10. C. Minakshi, *Administration and Social Life under the Pallavas*, Madras: University of Madras, 1938, *passim*. Also see Sastri, *A History of South India*, pp. 146–50.
11. See S.R. Balasubrahmanyan, *Early Chola Temples*, New Delhi: Orient Longman, 1971; and S.R. Balasubrahmanyan, *Middle Chola Temples,* Faridabad: Thomson Press, 1975.
12. Sastri, *A History of South India,* pp. 174–5.
13. K.A. Nilakanta Sastri, *The Pāṇḍyan Kingdom*, London: Luzac, 1929.
14. M.G.S. Narayanan, 'Political and Social Conditions of Kerala under the Kulasekhara Empire', unpublished Ph.D. Dissertation, University of Kerala, 1972. This has since been published: M.G.S. Narayanan, *Perumals of Kerala*, Cosmo Books: Thrissur, 2013.
15. See n.5. See also K.A. Nilakanta Sastri, *The Cōḻas*, Madras: University of Madras, 1955, pp. 635–40. There is the case of Māṇikkavāsgar, one of the greatest names in the history of Tamil Śaivism who belongs to the ninth century but who is not, strangely enough, counted among the *Nāyaṉārs.*

However, his *Tiruvācakam* embodies all the qualities characteristic of the Bhakti Movement including the superb form of ecstasy, opposition to Buddhism, attachment to the temples and complete surrender to the master. For a recent study of the saint, see Glenn E. Yocum, 'Mainkkavacakar's Image of Śiva', *History of Religions,* vol. xvi, no. 1, University of Chicago Press, pp. 20–41.

16. T.V. Mahalingam, *Kanchipuram in Early South Indian History*, Bombay: Asia Publishing, 1969, pp. 64–76.
17. N.P. Unni, ed., *Mattavilāsa*, Delhi: Nag Publishers, 1998.
18. Mahalingam, *Kanchipuram in Early South Indian History*, pp. 71–3.
19. Sastri, *The Pāṇḍyan Kingdom,* pp. 59–66.
20. Narayanan, *Kulasekhara Empire,* pp. 623–36.
21. Ibid. Also see M.G.S. Narayanan, *Cultural Symbiosis in Kerala,* Trivandrum: Kerala Historical Society, 1972, pp. 31–7.
22. For the inscription, see *Select Inscriptions,* l, Calcutta, 1942, pp. 90–1. For the identification of the pillar in a temple complex, see John Irwin, 'The Heliodorus Pillar: A Fresh Appraisal', *Art and Archaeology Research Paper,* no. 6, London, December 1974.
23. *Corpus Inscriptionum Indicarum*, vol. iii.
24. Jaiswal, *The Origin and Development of Vaiṣṇavism*, pp. 112–13; and D.D. Kosambi, *The Culture and Civilization of Ancient India in Historical Outline,* London: Routledge and K. Paul, 1965, pp. 114–15.
25. Minakshi, *Administration and Social Life under the Pallavas*, p. 176; and Narayanan, *Kulasekhara Empire*, pp. 556–9; 568–71. See *Annual Reports of Epigraphy,* no. 250 of 1926; no. 154 to 1895, *South Indian Inscriptions,* vol. iii, no. 202: 20. *Annual Reports of Epigraphy*, 120 of 1925. Narayanan, *Kulasekhara Empire,* pp. 568–71.
26. In fact, Sanskrit theatre survived in south India through these, as performed by the Cākkaiyār or Cākyār in the performances of *kūttu* and *kūṭiyāṭṭam* in the temples, staging dramas drawing heavily on the epics.
27. K.C. Varadachari, *Āḻvārs of South India,* Bombay: Bharatiya Vidya Bhavan, 1966, p. 1.
28. Ibid., p. 105.
29. Ibid., pp. 133–4.
30. Subrahmanyam, *South Indian Temple Inscriptions*.
31. The songs of the saints testify to this. For example, there are only six hymns of eleven or twelve verses each by Sambandhar, thirty-nine by Appar and four by Sundarar which are not dedicated to particular temples. Even many of these eulogize the temple cult. With regard to the Śaiva Nāyaṉār's relation to specific temples, see George W. Spencer, 'The Sacred Geography of the Tamil Śaivite Hymn', *Numen*, vol. 17, December 1970, pp. 232–44. Kamil Zvelebil also points out the importance of the cult of sacred places to both Śaiva and Vaiṣṇava saints. See Kamil Zvelebil, *The*

Smile of Murugan, Leiden: Brill, 1973, pp. 198–9; and Subramanyan, ed., *Periyapurāṇam*, pp. 229–68, 665–73.

32. Travancore Archeological Series, ii, i no. 9 (3), pp. 85–6; no 7 (L), pp. 46–8; 131–297.
33. Narayanan, *Kulasekhara Empire*, chapter on 'Religions and Religious Culture'.
34. Ceramān Perumāḷ, 'Ādiyula', in *Cēravēntar Ceyyuṭkōvai*, ed. M. Raghava Aiyangar, Trivandrum: University of Travancore, 1951, pp. 136–64.
35. For details, T.A. Gopinatha Rao, *The History of Sri Vaiṣṇavas*, Madras: University of Madras, 1923, p. 5.
36. For details, Narayanan, *Kulasekhara Empire*, p. 569.
37. Subramanyan, ed., *Periyapurāṇam*, p. 629.
38. Ibid., p. 625.
39. Ibid., p. 66.
40. Ibid., p. 81.
41. Ibid., p. 271.
42. Nilakanta Sastri has pointed out how Cēkkiḻār's *Periyapurāṇam* is indebted to Camundaraya's *Triṣaṣṭilakṣṇamahāpurāṇa* for its title. So also, even the number 63 for the Nāyaṉārs is an imitation of the 63 Jaina saints of the Mahāpurāṇa. See n.7.
43. Subramanyan, ed., *Periyapurāṇam*, p. 54.
44. Aiyangar, Ceramān Perumāḷ.
45. TAS, ii, iii, pp. 131–207. See also T.N. Subrahmanyan, op. cit.
46. See n. 4.
47. See for example, Perumāḷ Tirumoḻi. IV. 2: *Mukundamālā*, V3. The following hymn of Sundarar, translated by by K.R. Srinivasa Iyengar which offers another typical illustration of this sentiment:

    I'm the slave of all His devotees true.
    The slave of all the laureates of the spirit.
    The slave of those whose minds do rest in God.
    The slave of all the inhabitants of Tiruvarur.
    The slave of the priests who daily conduct the divine service thrice.
    The slave of the ascetics anointed all over.
    The slave of the *bhaktas* beyond Tamilaksam's courses.
    The slave for ever of Tiruvarur's Lord.

    See R.C. Majumdar, ed., The History and Culture of the Indian People, iii, Bombay: Bharatiya Vidya Bhavan, 1954. 1962, pp. 331–2.
48. See Sastri, *The Cōḻas*, pp. 635–6.
49. Subrahmanyan, *South Indian Temple Inscriptions*.

Index